THE LONG DISTANCE EATER:
A Competitive Eater's Diary

By Crazy Legs Conti

This book is dedicated to all the Major League Eaters, the brotherhood and sisterhood of the stomach. To International Federation of Competitive Eating founding fathers - George Shea, Rich Shea, and Dave Baer. To the Major League Eating office heroes and road MCs and all who have worn the boater. And to you starry-eyed stomach dreamers, who will soon learn that a professional eater's long journey starts with a single bite. Make it a big one!

I EAT FOR AMERICA
(May 7th, 2013)

Competitive eating can take one some pretty interesting places — Singapore to eat CP Shrimp wontons, Guantanamo Bay to entertain sailor soldiers eating hot dogs, or the gym of Paul D Schreiber High School (Home of the Vikings!) to eat a pizza in six minutes against two health teachers.

How did I end up on a random Thursday, furiously eating pizza with a reverse fold, while standing in a wrestling ring as 1,000 high school seniors cheered, laughed, and were slightly disgusted? As a kid, one is told to finish their vegetables, but how many kids end up as the three time corn-on-the-cob eating champion (42 ears in 12 minutes!) I have been a Major League Eater for 11 years — yes, there really is a league, check out www.majorleagueeating.com to see when we are coming to your hometown to eat a lot of food in a short amount of time. There is a documentary that charts my journey from casual diner to pro eater immodestly titled, "Crazy Legs Conti: Zen and the Art of Competitive Eating," but I will try to give you some highlights from my career. I've eaten oysters on Letterman, hot sauce on Emeril, and cannolis on the Sopranos. I am even a video game avatar, where folks can try to out eat my corn total on their phones. Many of these achievements were goals I never had for myself, until the opportunity presented itself. And all these opportunities I owe to my stomach.

I played three sports at a Division III college, but was always better at the pre-game meal than the actual athletic endeavor. I measured pasta in pounds before we played Haverford in basketball. In football, against Muhlenberg, I ate nine bagels the morning of the game (full disclosure: I was the third string punter). I was on the high jump team, but only Fosbury flopped enough to be on the jump team. However, at The Rotisserie, an all-you-can-eat joint near Franklin and Marshall that features food in a giant turning wheel, I had the kitchen staff cheering and the head chef crying after I finished all mashed potatoes, single stomachely, in a one-wheel rotation. I am a gourmet and a gourmand; I love good food in large quantities. A great meal doesn't send me belt unbuckled to the couch, but excites me for the next meal or the left side of the dessert menu. I stay in shape by going to gym, jogging the Williamsburg Bridge three times a week, and, in the competitive eating off-season, trying not to each French toast 11 days in a row. I do watch what I eat — every bite, chew, and swallow — so that I can compete between 25 and 45 times a year, eating everything from Ben's Chili (three-quarters of a gallon in six minutes) to Krystal Hamburgers (49 in eight minutes) to cannoli (22 in six minutes). Well, I eat everything but quinoa, which the MLE has yet sanction (although the world record in grits is 21 pounds).

Everything in moderation, including excess. Yes, that was me at the Showboat Casino on Fat Tuesday drinking a beer and smoking a cigar after eating just under four pounds of King Cake, so perhaps I am not the food role model for everyone, but every Fourth of July, 40,000 faithful gather at the intersection of Stillwell and Surf in Coney Island, 2 million more watch on ESPN, and news cameras around the world focus on the maelstrom of meat — the Nathan's International Hot Dog Eating Contest. Granted, I am a table-ender, generally getting my wiener number lapped by Tim "Eater X" Janus or Joey "Jaws" Chestnut, but here the pre-game meal is the main event. The Nathan's contest is the Tour de France, the Masters, and the Super Bowl rolled into a hot dog bun. I've been fortunate to be at the final table for a decade. Where can eating too many hot dogs get you?

In 2009 Navy Entertainment partnered with Major League Eating and we've sent more than 15 gurgitators on seven tours of duty to entertain at military bases across the globe. Besides seeing and eating in places like Guam, South Korea, Diego Garcia, Japan, Italy, Greece, and Gitmo, the experience for most eaters is life-changing. The experience for the military is enjoyment as the pro-am format allows for soldiers to cheer or jeer their fellow men and women. I've toured the USS Ohio, a nuclear sub, and eaten hard-boiled eggs on the USS Fitzgerald. I've talked to thousands of soldiers about their favorite foods, what they miss the most being overseas, and where to get the best (or strangest) chow near base. It is humbling and amazing how hard these men and women work so that I can celebrate patriotism with a stomachache on July 4th. Occasionally, I eat too much, but I do it for America and it feels great. So the next time you sit down to a lunch, perhaps even in the Paul D Schrieber cafeteria (Tuesdays are sloppy joe day,) don't look at it as the same old humdrum food — think of it as training for the Major League Eating circuit and dream as big as your stomach capacity will allow.

IT'S WEENIE WAR
(June 1st, 2013)

A brisk zephyr blows across the Coney Island boardwalk as a man in blue blazer and an Italian boater hat starts screaming into a microphone, "They say that competitive eating is the battleground upon which God and Lucifer wage war for mens' souls, and they are right!" This is not some Evangelical Preacher proselytizing to the gathered masses, this is George Shea, founder of Major League Eating, and he is just getting warmed up to introduce the first qualifier of the Nathan's International Hot Dog Eating Contest. It is not a battle between Heaven and Hell, but hot dog and stomach... it's weenie war.

The Nathan's International Hot Dog Eating Contest has been held at high noon every July 4, with the exception of 1941 to protest the war in Europe and 1971 to protest the reign of free love. This year however, due to Hurricane Sandy, the contest was in serious jeopardy. As winds and water blew in, flooding over the Boardwalk, Dick Zigun, unofficial mayor of Coney Island, watched from the second floor of Coney Island USA's Freakshow Building as Fisherman's Vibraphone and countless other memorabilia was literally washed away. Lola Starr, who operates a souvenir mecca, including shirts that read, "Sodom by the Sea" could do nothing as her entire inventory shrunk three sizes in the surf. At the corner of Stillwell and Surf, the original Nathan's — a hulking building in faded yellow and red neon, with one wall dedicated to the countdown to July 4, listing the mens' and womens' hot dog records (both in 10 minutes, men: 68, women: 45) and the grizzled visage of many competitors (I'm the guy in the hat and gloves) — a building that has been open 365 days a year, serving millions clams, lemonade, waffle cut fries, and tubesteaks by the 40 pack — shuttered it's doors due to damage. The garlicky aroma of a well charred Nathan's dog disappeared from Coney Island for the first time since 1915.

Coney Island has often been the phoenix rising from its ashes and Nathan's was the beacon that highlighted its return. Saturday, Nathan's began doling out dogs on the boardwalk, Lola Starr sold postcards, and Ruby's, the true surviving dive bar and spirit of Coney Island began serving suds in the cold March air (a guy sitting on their crapper once fell through under the boardwalk. He survived and the bar didn't even close.) Sunday, the venerable Cyclone, the Scream Zone, and rides opened. Back to George Shea on the mic, "We will go through a journey, you and I, and we will be changed on the other side...count down with me from 10..."

Nathan's holds 12 to 15 qualifiers around the world, all 10 minutes, all hot dogs and buns, but only the winner of each qualifier makes the final stage, the big show on July 4. We don't like to use the word, "cutthroat" in competitive eating, but qualifying for the finals is fraught with pressure that pushes all 50 ranked Major League Eaters to their satiety and sanity extremes. To win a qualifier, moral compasses have been broken, marriages as well, and the carcasses of great eaters' careers have been left strewn, like bun detritus floating in a dunking cup, across the intestinal highways of the United States. Today's event was going to be fairly straight forward as the Notorious B.O.B, the sixth ranked eater in the world and a vegetarian away from the pro-eating circuit, announced his presence at the table. Most competitors shied away from this early qualifier due to the cold air — as any male who has ever skinny dipped in March in the northeast knows, shrunken wieners are hard to manage with dignity. B.O.B, dipping his buns (the hot dog buns that is) in a fruit punch concoction turning his hands blood-red, as if he were strangling the cows that become the dogs, did amazing well, digesting 36 hot dogs and buns in 10 frigid minutes. Larell Marie, aka "The Real Deal" represented the female form — her purple highlight hair only lightly greased in hot dog run-off — ate 17 dogs to ensure her place at the table on July 4. As the Frankster, the Nathan's mascot boogied on the boardwalk, George Shea proclaimed the qualifier as epic, historic, and over. Like a communal belch, the crowd's exhale, was forceful and poignant.

I did eat on Saturday and in competition — granted it was the kids division's neat eating contest. One hot dog and bun, garnished liberally with ketchup and mustard must be eaten as slowly and cleanly as possible. On my knees, between a pig-tailed girl and a pouty 12-year old I managed to get mustard all over my goatee and even on my nose. I became the first person ever disqualified from the neat eating contest, another blemish to add to my pro-eating resume. I will be out there on the qualifying circuit in 2013 (Moscow, June 1 — me, "George, can American Citizens eat in the Moscow Qualifier?" George, "I'll have to check with our former contacts at the KGB"). I'll be chasing the Coney dream with hope, intestinal fortitude, mind over stomach matter, and Pepto-Bismol. My stomach will see you soon.

I THANK MYSELF FOR CALLING ME A HERO, YOU'RE WELCOME
(Sept 21st, 2017)

Willis Reed's leg, Curt Schilling's ankle, and now Crazy Legs Conti's back right molar (number 31 to be exact)…all destined for Hall of Fame status as the greatest injuries overcome in championship sports. An NBA Championship, A World Series, and the Major League Eating White Hut Cheeseburg Contest…all venerable events awaiting immortal sports greatness. Humbly, I am glad to join the pantheon of elite athletes who pushed through immeasurable pain to perform for fans. No need to call me a hero; I've already done it myself.

Before I reveal the worthwhile origin of the injury, I am not the first Major League Eater to face dental disaster in competition. One of the original gurgitators Ed "Cookie" Jarvis would often complain pre-contest about his latest oral surgery. In retirement, Don "Moses" Lerman sold the teeth that had fallen out due to years of furious chomping bologna and butter. Rich "The Locust" Lefevre, the only pro-eater still competing beyond age seventy, once swallowed a tooth in a rib eating contest. That tooth was never recovered. At the most recent Buffalo Wing Festival, Ronnie "Megabyte" Hartman took a minor bite on a chicken paddle and chipped his lower right central - his "meat stripping" tooth - and was not able to recover.

Major League Eating wanted to put me on the DL list through Trenton Pork Rolls, but I refused. I simply cannot do that to the fans assembled at the Big E, West Springfield's massive fair and the site of the 2nd annual White Hut Cheeseburg Eating Championship. In 1939 White Hut opened a single location that is famed in New England due to the perfectly grilled onions, placed upon melted white cheese, a splendid burger, and a soft (never brioche) spongy bun. In my seventeen years on the circuit only five foods have had such a delicious taste that some eaters forgot they were in a contest - White Hut Cheeseburg, CP foods shrimp wontons, spot shrimp in Alaska, Lobster in Maine, and inexplicably, Freirich corned beef.

As a longwinded way of explaining my career-threatening injury, I need to bring deadpan genius comic Michael Ian Black into the tale. Years ago, fresh off the success of "Wet Hot American Summer" the movie, Michael Ian Black and Michael Showalter were seated outside the joint where I was a short order cook. A fan of their humor, I offered them free cheesesteaks or tofu wraps. Michael Ian Black responded that it was a sweet offer, but I could see his mind working out that he was grateful to make his living in comedy and not in the spatula laden, cook's apron world of the service industry. Years after that, the two creators hired me for a segment of "Michael and Michael have issues." I was to eat Nathan's hot dogs competitively against a Takeru Kobayashi stand-in (when I asked what the actor had just worked on he casually mentioned he was the lead in the Clint Eastwood movie, "Grand Torino." Not quite a lateral move, I wasn't sure what to say to that.) Sadly, despite the show having bunny stomping moments (as the Michaels did funny commentary) the competitive eating scene didn't make the final cut. I never found out why, but I would guess that perhaps at the time high minded comedy didn't want to sink to the intestinal gut level of competitive eating. Perhaps Michael Ian Black was relieved.

Our next meeting took place two weeks ago on the Justin Warner, the knowledgable winner of the eighth season of Food Network Star and author of "The Laws of Cooking: And How to Break Them," hosted "Snack Talk," a new web series from Thrillist. I had prepared some humor about Grandma's ribbon candy and how Oreo's are so factory made that they are vegan, but when Michael Ian Black strode to the bodega created set, I knew I was in trouble. He put his crossword down and said to me, "Nice to meet you again." But really what he meant was, "I will once again prove that there is no room in competitive eating for the sardonic wit and genius funny insight I am about to unload on this three camera shoot." And unload he did - in a solid half hour, Justin and Michael went back and forth on hundreds of movie snacks - as if "My Dinner with Andre" starred Martin and Lewis instead of, well, Andre and his buddy. All that was left was for me was to speed eat a large bucket of popcorn held aloft by Michael Ian Black. I am the pro-eater most familiar with popcorn eating. I was once buried alive under 80 cubic feet of movie popcorn, dubbed, "The Popcorn Sarcophagus," and had to eat my way out to stay alive. I ate 10 buckets at a DVD convention in Vegas, each sadly with a napkin at the bottom which was meant for butter run-off but was consumed in the frenzy of eating. At the only official MLE contest in LA, I was cheered on by amazing actor Ted Lange. I am a popcorn specialist, but it had been a while since I faced my kernel blown nemesis. I started in on the "Snack Talk" bucket. As I gorged myself, unable to reach the gallon jug of water (I really only needed a cup I could hold), I chomped down harder, chewed furiously, and could peripherally see the glint in Michael's eye and his wry smile - all indicating that the upward trajectory of his comedy career was like a rocket, while perhaps viewing my role as an assassin of eating, as a deflating balloon. I soldiered on, biting down harder, taking kernel husks to the gums and as I would discover a week later at 42nd street Dental Associates (just beyond the Sunglass Hut at Port Authority), a horizontally fractured molar. The earliest date for extraction after the White Hut Cheeseburg Contest.

I am not discouraged. I am not deterred. I know that eating in the Cheeseburg contest is just one small step towards Major League Eating getting it's due in the world of entertainment. Sure, we've had documentaries and video games, but one day I look forward to meeting Michael Ian Black on even ground (The Oscars? The Daytime Emmys? The supermarket where I saw Huey Lewis buying a rotisserie chicken at 1 am?) And that day, we'll shake hands as equals - a hero of comedy and a hero of eating. In the meantime, I'll chew on the left side only.

THE EATING AVENGERS: THE AGE OF UVULA
(July 1st, 2017)

George Shea, Chairman of Major League Eating, has said that this year's Nathan's Famous International Hot Dog Eating Contest has more depth than any other in its 101 year history. I, as a sixteen year pro-eater agree, even though that depth will not include myself because I faltered in three qualifiers needing a win to advance to the finals. I blame heartbreak and heartburn, but the fault is mine. I was simply not physically, emotionally, nor mentally prepared to win a qualifier this year - it takes an almost super human effort to arrive at the final table on July 4th at the corner of Stillwell and Surf, Coney Island (or on ESPN for couch potato skin eaters.) This year's superhuman crop includes so many rookies and new eaters improving that Rich Shea, president of Major League Eating, in the broadcast booth will need a faster tongue to keep up with the speedier mouths. Darren Eats, an independent eater turned pro quaffed a stomach-boggling 38 HDBS (hot dogs and buns) in ten minutes to earn his spot. Also for the first time in digestive history, two eaters at two qualifiers ate over fifty. In the role of the Hulk, former power lifter Jeffery "The Digestor" Esper smashed his PB and ate 50 in a Boston qualifier while Carmen "Cutthroat" Cincotti ate 53 1/2 in NYC and stopped eating at the 7 1/2 minute mark as a "playing possum" move to scare the competition. Oddly enough, Sonya "The Black Widow" Thomas would not be cast as the Black Widow from the Eating

Avengers, despite being the greatest female gurgitator of all time. Miki "Oh Miki" Sudo, three time chomp champ is simply too strong for Sonya in the final two minutes of the womens' contest (ESPN 3) which is where dreams are made, and realities are broken. Plus, with Miki's new blond locks, she is looking more ScarJo these days and is bound for a four-peat. Matt Stonie, the #2 eater in the world, held aloft the bejeweled yellow mustard belt two years ago, but sadly in this scenario is cast as the Jeremy Renner character with the arrows who doesn't get enough screen time. Tony Stark, The Iron Man, is Badlands Booker celebrating his 13th straight time at the finals and minus two years of semi-retirement, 20 years on the circuit. Badlands ingestion engine is powered by more than Paladium as his arc reactor is generating the hip-hop food rock album, "Stillwell and Surf 2" available at www.badlandsbooker.com

July 4th, of course, belongs to Captain America - Mr. Joey Chestnut, The soon-to-be decade chomping champ. He has eaten over 80 HDBs in practice, 70 on July 4th, 73.5 in the nations capital for the world record, and vows that anything less than 75 will be a disappointment this upcoming Tuesday. He needs no shield from those steaming weenies and buns and frankly, they don't stand a chance. The dogs won't catch him but you can at the unofficial official afterparty at 7:33 pm at Professor Thom's (219 2nd ave) where if you think pro-eaters drool a lot eating hot dogs, you should see them switch to whiskey.

Rumor has it that 45th president, Donald Trump will tweet out congrats to the Men's and Woman's champs post contest as July 4th is our country's independence and Coney Island will be Red, White, and Mustard Yellow. Politics and condiments aside, everyone agrees that eating too many hot dogs on July 4th is one of the most patriotic victories one can achieve - Happy July 4th and God burp America!

RETURN TO NACHO MOUNTAIN
(November 1st, 2016)

With the Cubs and Donald Trump, both winning in unimaginable fashion, I felt it was time for me to tackle my longtime losing streak and impossible victory…the nachos platter at Professor Thom's. As a fifteen year Major League Eater, I have had one achilles heel - I've never finished an order of the piled high chips, salsa, guacamole, sour cream, melted cheese like lava and jalapeños as large as Sacagaweas. It has been an embarrassment to my stomach and pride.

My nachos focus on the culinary aspect as opposed to the competitive eating one is revealed in the the new Dovetail Press book "¡Buenos Nachos!" where myself, and various celebrities, chefs, and semi-geniuses contributed their personal nacho recipes (Bill Hader, ever the raconteur contributed a queso recipe.) This is a museum quality coffee table book of nachos, where the everything looks like art. Edward Lee's Gochujang chili cheese chips channel the American abstract expressionist movement while Naomi Pomeroy's Ultimate Asian Nachos prism like Victor Moscoso 1970s rock-and-roll posters. By far the ugliest, are my recipe for Swamp Thing inspired nachos with natto, cynar, Natty Boh beer, and artichoke hearts. My fever dream nachos are meant to highlight the intersection of madness and making food mountains; Richard Dreyfuss' Roy Neary in "Close Encounters of the Third Kind" is clearly an early adopter.

To finish an order of the Professor Thom's nachos by myself, I had to put away the high falutin' culinary creations in "!Buenos Nachos!" and focus on a journey to destroy the ragged chip, rocky mountain at the bar. The nacho mountain looked like Mount Doom, deep inside Mordor, so I channeled Hobbit Pippen Took's appetite (Hobbits eat seven large meals a day) and dug in. Bite after bite, was delicious and filling, but my focus was to pair wetter dipping agents like salsa and guacamole with the dryer outside chips. I was concerned with flavor fatigue. Around me sat glorious sudsy beer, but I knew that carbonation would cause a powder keg effect in my belly, alerting the dark forces of urges contrary to swallowing and up-chucking my quest.

Sauron, Saruman, and sour cream be dammed, I was close to the end when my spirit faltered. I asked the Prof Thom's bartender to change the music to Elvish chants, but none was on Spotify, so we settled on Rihanna. I pushed on, folding the chips inside themselves, seeing only nachos fractals, but putting each piece into my mouth knowing that the fate of Middle Earth and whatever Earth we are on was is doubt (actually, The Celtics tip off was approaching and I wanted to catch the game.) At last, hours in, on my plate was one single perfectly ringed jalapeño - one jalapeño ring to rule them all. I cleared my throat, making an odd Gollum like sound, and popped the mighty ring in. Evil was averted and a mountain of Nachos had fallen and I was, as improbably as it seemed, victorious - a better man, a finer Major

League Eater, and someone in need of a napkin. I was poured a beer and then left to my own. Around me, no one noticed the expansive empty tray, the mountain conquered. I learned then that Nachos are meant as a fellowship of consumption - to be eaten with a group and with a lot beer. Nachos, even those as large as the entire Shire, are meant to be eaten in fun with friends. The sour cream dripping from my dreadlocks made me appear like Radegast the Brown, but no wizard was needed to realize, the magic in Nachos is in the communal aspect of the pointy chips and toppings. I belched and then paraphrasing Gandalf said, "All we have to decide is what to do with the dessert that is given to us."

PROFILES IN CHEWAGE: GEOFF "NAMELESS" ESPER
(October 10th, 2016)

With continued apologies to John F. Kennedy and his remarkable volume, "Profiles in Courage," I present another amazing installment of "Profiles in Chewage." While superhero movies clog the theaters and TVs, a real non-cape wearing super powered human eats among us - Jeff (no nickname) Esper. A mild mannered vocational teacher during the week, he morphs into a meta-human masticator on weekends at Major League Eating events. I was fortunate to interview this real life Tony Stark (he does teach electronics and rumor has it that Gywenth wants to consciously couple with him.)

CLC: What eaters do you look up to?

GE: You, Booker, Sonya - Cookie Jarvis - I saw those people on TV. I saw the MTV show with you and Janus. Pat Bertoletti and even beyond MLE, Molly Shulyer.

CLC: You ascended the heights of powerlifting - as did Takeru Kobayashi at one point - do you see a parallel that benefits competitive eating?

GE: I think it actually is hurting me. I had to scale back some, When you lift really heavy weights your midsection gets thick and doesn't stretch well. That was hurting my capacity and would stop. Heavy lifting isn't the best - getting lean is.

CLC: As a teacher, do any of the kids recognize your competitive eating prowess?

GE: Nah, everybody asks me that - they are hard to impress.

CLC: What do you think of the Pork Roll mascot - the large pink disk with pink liver spots and pink tights?

GE: No comment.

CLC: Probably the wisest answer

CLC: What do you think of poutine - it's got to be hard to find cheese curds in Oxford, Ma?

GE: I bought a block of soft mozzarella and I am going to cube it up and give it a go this weekend.

(Note - soft mozz seems to work as Geoff "Still no nickname" Esper did a whopping 18.5 pounds to finish third in the Smoke's Poutine Eating Championship)

CLC: I found Poutine to be delicious - what foods have you found palpable, what foods delicious and what foods, in competition repulsed you?

GE: I haven't eaten anything that repulsed me. As far as the tastiest thing - the cheeseburg contest we just did - I really liked those and the onions were good to the end. I liked Gyros and I don't even like tomatoes and I thought it was delicious.

CLC: Groupie talk - you have your choice - the entire Kardashian Clan but Andy Dick gets to ride on your back leapfrog style through all the interactions or Kate Hudson, but with Colin Firth sitting there with no trousers or underwear on, knitting a sweater?

GE: As long as Firth just keeps knitting....

CLC: What food would you like to see a Major League Eating championship in that you would excel at?

GE: Where I live they have these table top pies. I don't know if you've heard of them. They are little pies in all flavors - they have apple, pumpkin. I think they should have contest with four on a plate, all the different flavors - you eat one and then go the next one. I think that would be a really fun contest.

There you have it, Geoff "He really needs a nickname" Esper is a man who can pound almost twenty pounds of poutine, lift the really big circular weights that I eschew at the gym because the pink handhelds ones seem lonely, and mold the minds of tomorrow's youths, despite their ignorance of his alter superhero ego. How does he not have a nickname yet?

In today's contest based reality TV and social media world (sadly "Eating with the Stars" the competitive eating celeb hybrid show was shot down by the major networks but is still pending at the CW) there is only one way to settle the lack of Geoff Esper's nickname - a contest. Tweet your nickname suggestions to Major League Eating's @eatingcontest and like the Coliseum of yesteryear (the shuttered all-you-can-eat Greek buffet diner), the winner will be chosen by the people. Remember, only fourteen entries per household and the prize - a game worn jersey from Crazy Legs Conti (dry cleaning sold separately.) So take off that dining bib and put on your thinking cap (or earmuffs - it's a bit chilly) and get nicknaming!

WHOSE THE BOSS OF THE UNDERGROUND COMPETITIVE EATING MAFIA? TONY DANZA!
(September 19, 2016)

Omerta, the Italian mafia's code of silence, is easy to keep when your mouth is stuffed with it's twenty-first cannoli in ten seconds away from six minutes. In 2009, I managed one more Major League Eating regulation cannoli stuff at the buzzer to be crowned Cannoli King at the Feast of San Gennaro. The title had eluded me for nine long, ricotta cheese stained years. The contest was created in 2001, as a thank you to downtown New York City after 9/11. No money in fees nor prize money was ever exchanged from the venerable festival to the then International Federation of Competitive Eating (rechristened Major League Eating as less of a mouthful) or to the ranked professional eaters who graced the lunchtime stage and risked sugar overload, cannoli shell teeth chipping, and the dreaded urge-contrary-to-swallowing (its rare occurrence usually known as "Elvis has left the building" but at the feast retooled as, "Pavarotti has left the Opera House.") Nary a complaint was made regarding financial matters as it was understood that this contest stood as a show of immersive pride - America, like the cannoli, with it's industrial tough-guy shell, giving way to a softer sweeter existence once the barrier of empathy and powdered sugar was broken.

The contest existed for fourteen years and disappeared last year - as organizers pointed to one man shutting it down: Tony Danza. That's right, the multi-hyphenate actor, boxer, singer, and cheese shop register jockey is also the Godfather of Underground Competitive Eating. Make no mistake of the fictional abilities of Anthony Morton "Tony" Micelli as a housekeeper and the stone cold gelato-hearted Tony Danza (did no-one find it odd in the TV show that the pro baseball player retired due to a shoulder injury on the same side as his vacuuming arm?). Danza first set out to lay claim to fine cheese by partnering with Alleva Dairy on Grand Street. This provided the perfect front to cover for his nefarious competitive eating strong arming. Alleva has been serving the finest cheeses from old school recipes and techniques for over 100 years. It's reputation, like its daily fresh balls of mozzarella is impeccable. Its slogan, ""Sono Fatte con Puro Latte"" translates to only the purest milk. Like the purest untainted heart of a competitive eating fan who gathered yearly to see Ed "Cookie" Jarvis or Badlands Booker or Tim "Eater X" Janus battle for cannoli supremacy (rumor has it, the Vatican and Dan Brown had separate web cams for previous year's contests) the contest was a nod towards heavenly desserts with digestive purgatory as a way station. With a legitimate cover, Danza began to dismantle MLE's powdered sugar grasp on the confectionary contest. His cause, after a one year hiatus, is to honor his dear friend John 'Cha Cha' Ciarcia, known as the unofficial mayor of Mulberry Street. No ill words will be written here as Cha Cha was beloved by the eating community - his notion of the search for the Holy Grail in Italian pastry - the perfect Tiramisu was well known among the gurgitators. He once, post cannoli contest took Eater X and I into his restaurant to feed us, mind you after we had both a combined forty eight cannolis, his tiramisu. He needed to know what men, broken by cannoli shell, shellshocked by sugar, could find wrong with his tiramisu - we found nothing but ethereal sponginess - as if angel wing dust had mixed with Michelangelo's clouds and fallen, Earth bound, onto Cha Cha's dessert plates.

Danza, in a final attempt to separate himself from being mistaken for John Stamos, decreed that Cha Cha's favorite food, the mighty meatball would be consumed at the inaugural 2016 contest at San Gennaro. If this was the case, no eating contest - not the long standing MLE cannoli one, one which birthed the next generation of historic eaters like Marcos "Monster" Owens and Yasir "The Iron Stomach" Salem, could overshadow the Chi è Capo di Tutti Capi. Danza's emissary sent word through coded zeppole balls that any MLE eater involved in the cannoli contest would, "Sleep with the fishes" - an obvious reference to the former all-you-can-eat sushi restaurant put out of business by "Hungry" Charles Hardy's 7 hour stand-off with it's buffet that left only discarded shrimp tails and trampled pickled ginger. The final message, delivered in person to MLE Madison Avenue headquarters by Danza's Luca Brasi (Joe Piscopo as Joe Pesci had a prior obligation) was that the NJ underground competitive eating mob would issue a one day truce to allow MLE to eat competitively in Trenton. The edict came right from the top - John Bon Jovi (his original song title, "Dining on a Prayer" changed to maintain secrecy about his Consuma Nostra leadership.)

Thus, every Major League Eater, even the lethal food assassin Carmen "Cuthroat" Cincotti, will gather not at the Feast of San Gennaro for meatballs nor cannoli, but at 3pm Eastern, on Saturday, September 24, 2016 at the home of the Trenton Thunder, ARM & HAMMER Park for the World Famous Case's Pork Roll Eating Championship. Pork Roll being the nostalgic meal most often requested at Wiggles, the basis for the Bada Bing club from "The Sopranos."

The delicate balance of the established mainstream Major League Eating juggernaut and the upstart underground speed-eating world will be maintained. No one needs to wake up to a seitan horse shaped head in their bed. Another Italian saying comes to stomach - "tarallucci e vino" which means after all the fighting and drama, we will end with cookies and wine, as it's fine to go to bed with a full stomach but not an angry heart. Of course, as far as Tony Danza and Major League Eating...it will be, "polpette di carne di maiale a rotolo di maiale" or in the words of the immortal Mario Puzo, "Revenge is a dish best served cold." However, meatballs and pork rolls taste better warm.

X MARKS THE SPOT IN THE COMPETITIVE EATING HALL OF FAME
(Sept 16th, 2016)

Saturday, September 17th a new entry into the Major League Eating canon occurs - the White Hut Cheeseburg Eating Championship in West Springfield, MA. Peel back the layers of Americana comfort food and you'll find the grilled to perfection fried onions that this venerable joint has been sizzling since 1939. The Hut could have franchised, gone national, sold frozen burgers on the internet and in vending machines, but they decided to make the more noble choice - eschew doing everything and focus on one thing - perfection. Sometimes the quest to truly understand something you do well takes years to comprehend - Ask any retired professional athlete of a certain caliber and they may know now, having left the game, what exactly it is to achieve at the highest level of sport. Why is this? Nathaniel Hawthorne wrote: "Happiness is a butterfly which, when pursued, is always just beyond your grasp, but which, if you will sit down quietly, may alight upon you."

In 2016 these three very similar professional athletes retired: Peyton Manning, Tim Duncan, and Tim "Eater X" Janus. Scoff if you will at adding a competitive eater to the list but these three workmanlike athletes used their brains to focus their talents smartly to ascend the lofty heights of their respective sports. It wasn't flash nor trash talking nor hubris that allowed them to become the greatest in their sports - it was the quest to always be better - to study more, watch more, learn more, and when victory occurred to not revel in the moment, but to look ahead to what could be improved upon. All three are first ballot unanimous entrants into their respective hall of fames, except in Eater X's case, for the entire 12 years of his professional eating career, the Eaters Hall of Fame, linked here: http://www.majorleagueeating.com/halloffame.php is simply coming soon.

I have tried to talk to Tim about his quiet retirement, but he has rebuffed me at each conversation - he will talk about his future of new opportunities - acting on "Billions" or traveling to Australia to interact with crocodiles and dangerous snakes, but not his place in competitive eating. I'm not trying to interview him - I see him every day as we've lived as roommates since the 2006 cannoli eating championship (the trophy is on his side of the apartment.) As Eater X, warrior facepaint covering his visage, he is a mystery behind the mask. In real life, Tim Janus, the actual human hiding behind the persona, is more of an enigma. His accomplishments in competitive eating guarantee him as a top five greatest eater of all time - you can find those elsewhere online and from the stories of gurgitators he has bested through the years - stats like 55 Hdbs on July 4th, single handedly creating the alternative beverage movement (pairing sweet dunking drink with salty food to avoid flavor fatigue), or his pro-am victory at Guantanamo Bay as part of the first MLE/Navy Entertainment tour. I want to talk about his dedication over the years that went unseen - he was a pioneer of speed eating - the last guy who came from the Trophy era when there was no money, no TV time, simply the food competition that fired up early International Federation of Competitive Eating participants. At Belmont race track in a Nathan's qualifier in the early 2000s, Tim was a rookie who tried to eat all the dogs first and left 16 uneaten buns on the table. He was disgusted with himself and his performance but instead of quitting he dedicated himself to the science of competitive eating. He would wander four supermarkets a night, looking at foodstuffs - trying to understand how they would break down - he was a Terminator of digestion, scanning shapes to see how he could fit them into his stomach like a game of intestinal Tetris. Takeru Kobayashi, the greatest eater of all time, once confided in me that Tim had found a food for technique training that they both were the only humans to discover and Takeru was astonished that Tim unearthed it. Tim's nightly food studies had paid off. I won't reveal the food stuff here, but it's barely available in the US and is considered the holy grail of low calorie, high volume esophagus stretching, but with my less capable abilities it proved to be worthless. One needed a Jungian self-actualized focus to unlock it's benefits. Tim spent countless hours on the internet, seeking knowledge not only of competitive eating, but everything that might improve his life. This came in handy when we were on Cash Cab and won the most money in the show's history (Tim knew all the answers. I only knew the ones that were needed to impress chicks.) For years in the apartment I would enter and every light in every room would be on, but not the one in the room where Tim was hunched over his laptop - researching, studying, learning - only laptop light illuminated his seeking face, like a reflection of fire in Plato's cave. I always thought this odd until on another Navy Entertainment trip with a different group of eaters. We toured the USS Ohio - a massive nuclear sub. A sub can go underwater for three months if needed, limited by only by coffee, laundry detergent, food, and toilet paper. Go even further into the submerged environment and one finds the sonar room - men and women in complete dark studying an Atari 2600 like screen that lights up their faces in the pitch black. A coffee cup holder sits in front of each console - 8 hour shifts to simply see what may be out there in the future path of the sub - you have no torpedo buttons, nothing to play the hero - simply quiet never-ending study as one's focus. After pleasantries with the somber group were exchanged and chit chat had ended, one sailor solider asked, "Do you know Eater X? Here in Sonar we are big Eater X fans." I had to laugh because, as I explained, he was miles away in NYC in our apt doing the exact same thing these folks were - sitting in the dark, illuminated by only a screen, and searching for future knowledge. At once, every sonar specialist became giddy high school cheerleaders lauding their pride and respect for Eater X.

Perhaps the existence of those who appreciated Eater X's mastery of the nebulous dedication to competitive eating don't fully honor his legacy in the way that stats and trophies and championship do, but truth be told, none of those mattered to Tim. He gave away almost all of the trophies, he can't remember his own impressive consumption numbers, and he shrugs off any notion of recognition of his career. I've spent countless hours in Tim's company in cities that competitive eating was the sole reason for our arrival. Cities like Davenport (catfish), Knoxville (sliders), and Bettendorf (Loose meat sandwiches.) I've spent years in New York City with him - we've been a duo on every morning show, most late night ones, once graced the cover of the Village Voice together and I, with over a decade of proximity and reflection, cannot understand what drove him internally. Externally, it's easy to see why he is a fan favorite - he looks like a Ken doll by way of the WWE. His dedication rests not in his stomach (he often tells reporters he doesn't like to feel full) but in his mind. It is unknown to us and perhaps to himself as well. My career is more Don Quixote, I'm often daydreaming of victory in a haze of created chaos, while Tim's was firmly rooted in reality. Tim and Eater X may not be the same person but both aligned with Galileo Galilei's studies and knowledge seeking. Galileo opined, "You cannot teach a man anything; you can only help him find it within himself." When the face paint washed off for the final time, I wonder what was found?

Down the road from White Hut, in Springfield, MA is the NBA Hall of Fame - busts, plaques, and statues herald the greatest in roundball history. In the round stomach history of Major League Eating, for now, Eater X's legacy has not been digested. Why followed

X, but the answers elude even those who know him best. For the next generation of pro-eaters, Tim "Eater X" Janus has created a map, but if one dedicates years to the pursuit of self-improving knowledge, what one will find on the marked spot is known only by one face painted food warrior, forearms crossed above his head, standing proudly, gazing forward.

THE HEALTHIEST HUMAN ON THE PLANET (July 7th, 2016)

At the Kale Yeah! World's Healthiest Eating Championship (sponsored by Healthy Options) on Saturday, at 2 pm in Buffalo, NY the person who eats the most poundage of kale in 8 minutes will undoubtably be crowned the healthiest human on planet Earth. Kale, once relegated to garnish on free-fixing bars of fast food joints is now the uber-food - lauded for it's nutrient rich benefits to the body that include everything except perhaps the ability to levitate. It's got vitamins, antioxidants, flavonoids, bile acid sequestrates, sulforaphane, indole-3-carbinol, fiber, lutein and zeaxanthin. I, however, will not be chomping as much kale as I can in eight minutes for any health benefits. My competitive eating glory will be focused on the $4000 grand in prize money which I will spend on chicken wings and beer as Buffalo is the greatest bar food city in America. I will also be expecting kudos and support from the irresponsible protest group Direct Action. After all, a lot of plants will be killed in this eating contest, but surely they will be on hand to promote their misguided message that vegetarianism must be the choice of everyone on the planet. If you are not familiar with this grass-roots outfit, they have charged the stage at Ribfest in Chicago and this week, assaulted competitors, spectators, and a two-year old boy with fake blood at the Nathan's Famous International Hot Dog Eating Contest. They claim to be for animal liberation, but terrorize humans to spread their flimsy message. I enjoyed celebrating the birthright of our country and it's freedoms on July 4th on stage at the hot dog contest and believe in our civil liberties but found the illegal actions of the protest group to be violent and dangerous to all. I will always welcome responsible protesting and differing opinions, but in today's America, using violence to spread your message is poor public relations. I can only assume that since this Major League Eating contest features a vegan option, the mighty kale, that perhaps Direct Action will simply show up with some ranch dressing to happily hand-out. I think it's always important to stand up for what one believes in, but exhibiting barbaric behavior to force feed people your opinion...well, that is hard to digest.

As for digesting the kale in competition, it will be finely chopped and lightly dressed with oil, vinegar, salt and pepper. Major League Eating will require a fork and early reports have Carmen "The Mutiny" Cincotti claiming he will use two forks to shovel the kale like a punk drummer covering a "Ramones" song. Six-foot nine inch Gideon "The Truth" Oji will have some difficulty as he has a much longer way to bend to get to the bowls of kale. The favorite will be Badlands Booker - a man mountain who has used cabbage to stretch out his stomach - in an effort to lose weight several years ago, Badlands retired his spray can cheese for leafy greens and has become very familiar with the hearty kale discipline. Badlands also eats to his own signature rap beats which allows quicker manual-to-oral dexterity. Personally, I feel good about my chances at becoming King of Kale - I like a technique food that requires strategy and have been studying videos of hummingbirds eating.

Regardless, whomever emerges as the green giant of the veggie world this Saturday, will be able to find dessert at The Taste of Buffalo event. With 450,000 patrons, and 150 of Buffalo's finest food selections there will be something for everyone to eat. After all, choice in America is one of our greatest freedoms - perhaps Direct Action will one day learn this because no matter how much Kale is consumed, moral fiber is what keeps humans healthy .

PROFILES IN CHEWAGE: CARMEN "CUTTHROAT" CINCOTTI
(October 10, 2016)

With apologies to John F. Kennedy and his remarkable volume, "Profiles in Courage," I present a magnificent masticator in this installment of "Profiles in Chewage." Instead of a Pulitzer Prize perhaps consideration for a James Beard award is in order.

Carmen Cincotti is called by Major League Eating, "The Mutiny" for his ability to tear down order and cause chaos - going from a plebeian thirteen HDBs in 2015 to an astronomical 42 at both his qualifier and at Coney Island in 2016. The gurgitators on the circuit know him by another name - "Cutthroat." He has slashed the elite competition and given Joey "Jaws" Chestnut and Matt "Megatoad" Stonie heartburn at cheeseburger championships from Charlotte to West Springfield. This weekend his stomach does double duty - Poutine in Canada and Pumpkin Pie in Elk Grove, California. It's as if he wants to wipe out cheese curds from history and cancel Thanksgiving dessert, causing most of North America to flee to Mexico (unless he sets his hunger on Flan - oh the humanity!)

Here is my in depth discussion with Cutthroat where I used interview techniques ranging from "Law and Order" to wartime torture to a pamphlet about manners co-written by Geraldo Rivera's cousin.

CLC: Who if any, are you eating heroes?

CCC: That is a really good one. I really look up to the veterans - Joey Chestnut, Tim Janus absolutely, Pat Bertoletti - also the showmen - like you. I try to entertain the crowd but I don't. Badlands - he knows how to hype a crowd. I also look up to the new generation - Jeff Esper and Gideon Oji especially.

CLC: You debuted at Coney with ten more hdbs than Joey Chestnut.- 42, fifty is only eight away. I know you're going to duck this question but how did you get so good so fast?

CCC: It's consistency. That is all it is. I had ambition and I had a drive to get to Nathan's. Maybe I overshot it a little bit - worked too hard - got too good, too quick. That is all it is. Consistency. With anything you do - you have to be consistent. I Made it habit to be good.

CLC: Let's talk groupies - you have your choice - Bai Ling and Maggie Gyllenhaal or Gigi Hadid, but Adrien Brody is naked in the corner making eye contact with you. Which way do you go?

CCC: God? Naked making eye contact with me? (uncomfortable laugh) That's a good question. For fun, I'll go right.

CLC: Adrian Brody. Locked in. Got it. He says it's for role research but you don't believe him.

CCC: (More uncomfortable laughing)

CLC: Let's talk chili - do you think the 2 gallon barrier can be broken and if so how?

CCC: I hope so. I have never done a "liquidy" type of food. I don't know what I am capable of with this kind of stuff - do I think it can be broken? I think if you are ambitious and willing to put your body on the line, then absolutely. I think it's going to be really tough. I think it takes a certain kind of maniac to do it and I hope to be that maniac.

CLC: Last question. What food does Major League Eating currently not have a contest in that you know you would excel at?

CCC: That's easy, Mac and Cheese. There is no question about it. I would love some Macaroni and Cheese and if it's good Mac and Cheese, I could do more than ten pounds in ten minutes.

And that was Carmen "Cutthroat" Cincotti whose svelte 150 pound frame tweets bon mots at his twitter handle. Also, his contest results from this weekend's double digester will be at their twitter handle.

EXCUSE ME WHILE I EAT THE SKY - I EAT HOT DOGS ON TOP OF THE WONDER WHEEL (June 23rd, 2016)

Coney Island is a magical historic place that is close to my heart, my soul, and especially my stomach. I am celebrating my fifteenth year as a Major League Eater July 4th on stage at the Nathan's Famous International Hot Dog Eating Contest as Nathan's celebrates its 100th year. How often in life does one's stomach not only be a part of the collective digestive history of our country, but also eat something a century in the making? I honestly don't know what I will feel, either in my enteric or cranium bound brain, but I predict a sense of being one with everything. Ida and Nathan Handwerker opened their Nathan's hot dog stand on the corner of Stillwell and Surf Ave as their belief of "making it" in America — they undercut the competitor's wiener prices and charged 5 cents a dog for their secret spiced frankfurter. Today, Nathan's Famous is a behemoth corporation eternally linked to July 4th because of Major League Eating. I get to quaff one of their natural casing wieners a century later on the day of our country's independence. There are no words to describe what it will be like to literally eat the American Dream but there will probably be a burp or three.

Because of the intersection of history, encased meats, and the eternal ballyhoo of Coney Island, I've decided to risk death and celebrate the carnival spirit of Coney Island by eating Nathan's Hot Dogs atop the 96 year old Wonder Wheel...while it is in motion. Friday, July 24th at 11 am, wearing a patriotic Sky Suit, I will ascend 150 feet in the air, frankfurters going down my esophagus while my stomach rises 15 stories in the sky. Any butterflies in my stomach not crushed by the incoming hot dogs are free to flutter away in the clouds. Why risk vertigo, getting knocked out by a moving car, or falling to my demise? The fabric that makes Coney Island the tapestry of the human condition is a sideshow banner that can sum up the place in one word: "Thrills!" Becoming Icarus on a fast lunch break may not be the wisest life choice I've made, but it's the daring spirit of Coney Island that I hope will thrill you, thrill me, and make for the meal of a century.

As a food stuntman, I've earned the monikers, "The Evil Knievel of the Alimentary Canal," "The Houdini of Cusini" and the slightly less regal title the "David Blaine of the Bowel." — I've eaten my way out of a popcorn sarcophagus, struggling to breath below an avalanche of buttered airy kernels. This has earned me many accolades and occasional groupies, but as for my hot dog and bun numbers they are a personal best of 25 1/4 in ten minutes. On July 4th the focus will be on the eaters at the center of the table, the maelstrom of meat, while I will likely be on the outside. These gustatory gurgitators include Joey "Jaws" Chestnut, Sonya "The Black Widow" Thomas, Matt "MegaToad" Stonie and "Oh" Miki Sudo whose hot dog and bun totals will be astronomical. By comparison over the year, my totals are paltry — the Major League Eating circuit does have contests each weekend that a wily outside-the-top 10 ranking veteran can excel at due to food technique (I've already started getting hungry for the Hell Yeah Kale contest sponsored by Healthy Choices in Buffalo on Saturday, July 9th — If I eat the most Kale in eight minutes that makes me the healthiest human on the planet correct?) For the 100th running of the dogs and future July 4th contests, Nathan's Famous is offering prize money to every finisher, male and female which acknowledges the juggernaut event the ESPN 1-3 broadcast contest has become and creates a fiercer man/woman eat dog-eat-dog competition. Eaters like Yasir "The Iron Stomach" Salem, Gideon "The Truth" Oji, and Geoff "The Digester" Esper have increased their 10 minute chowdown HDBs numbers from the 20s to the 30s. Michelle "Lescimo" Lesco — nicknamed because like the complex many-meanings-for-the-same-word Eskimo language, her stomach has 13 different ways of digesting hot dogs and buns - will be pushing her totals to cause a bun buzzer beater against the two previous female chomping champions. I can admit that at the end of the 10 minutes of marathon eating, I won't be hoisting the bejeweled yellow mustard belt but I can earn other monikers — "The Liberace of Lunch" (My Julz Kroboth created SkySuit is going to cause Anna Wintour to lose her lunch), "The Salvador Dali of the Deli" (can one get more surreal than eating hot dogs in the clouds plus I have a killer mustache) and lastly, "The David Bowie of the Bun." I feel the loss of David Bowie because of his chameleon ability to take us somewhere else through his storytelling. It is not just his music, but was his ability to encapsulate all forms of the human condition even while becoming someone from another planet. At the top of the Wonder Wheel, I'll be closer to those other planets and I'll have my story to tell, however it will have to be with my mouth full.

Should I not survive the death-defying Wonder Wheel hot dog stunt, in lieu of flowers send apple pie dessert to his fellow competitors on July 4th.

A JULY 4TH PRODUCT PLACEMENT AMERICA
(July 10th, 2016)

Bill Murray as Franklin Delano Roosevelt in "Hyde Park on the Hudson" solves world peace by encouraging The King of England to eat a hot dog. At first the King is reticent, expressing to The Queen, "...But, to answer your question, Elizabeth, I am going to eat a hot dog - five hot dogs - Ten!...I am going to shove them in my mouth, stick two up my nostrils, two more in my ears and walk around so that people can take pictures of the King of England with hot dogs hanging out of his orifices!" - But then the King eats one, albeit picnic style, and America goes wild! It's basically the story of Joey "Jaws" Chestnut's entry into Major League Eating and the July 4th Nathan's Hot Dog International Hot Dog Eating Contest, except Joey knows to separate the dog and the bun and that nostril stuffing and ear chomping don't count towards one's total. The mouth is the only orifice that counts and Joey is King of the Wieners. If FDR had vacationed elsewhere "Hyde Park on the Hudson," could have been titled, "Stillwell and Surf on the Coney," but Bill Murray is masterful as the former president, adopting the difficult speech pattern and look of the great FDR. I thought the hot dog stuff was stellar and it made me overlook the genesis of the film which seems to be FDR getting an over-the-pants-handjob from his cousin in a swanky car parked in a flower strewn field. It is Bill Murray's 2nd most iconic foray into frankfurt cinema, but more on that later.

July 4th has been digested and what better way to celebrate our country's great birth than to casually dine on too many hot dogs at a BBQ while watching the gustatory gladiators of Major League Eating professionally chomp too many Nathan's hot dogs on ESPN at high noon. I have been fortunate to travel with Navy Entertainment on six tours to entertain the armed forces by eating pro-am style at bases all over the world. It is simply the best thing I have done not as a competitive eater, but as a human. To witness the daily and yearly sacrifices that the men and women of the military make to allow the freedom for me to stuff my self back home July 4th is awe inspiring, humbling, and life-changing. You can never be satiated on Patriotism. Still, a call from President Obama to the women's hot dog champ and the first lady to the men's champ would be nice. I know that First Lady Michelle is big on physical fitness and vegetables - not to worry, I am the four time corn-on-the-cob eating champ (46 ears in 12 minutes) and in November will be running the New York Marathon (5 hours and 33 minutes, predicted.) There is no better public relations than believing in America.

Shea Communications is the PR company that represents the Nathan's brand and facilitates the contest. Love of country and cased meats is in play, but also altruism as 100,000 Nathan's hot dogs are donated to the Food Bank for New York City each July 4th. To be an MLE eater at the finals on the 4th one must win one of the fourteen or so hot dog qualifiers all over the US. The champ, and for eight consecutive years it was Joey, gets a worthwhile bye to the finals, and one wild card is awarded to the highest HDBs non-winning total. Since 2011, Title 9 was demolished in pro-eating and the women have their own division, prize money, and yellow mustard belt in a smaller waist size. Each eater must pay his or her way to the qualifiers and is allowed to eat in three. Winning a qualifier gets each eater a spot at the finals (described as The Masters of Mastication, The Super Bowl of the Bowel, and The Tour de Feed), flight and accommodations, a per diem, and of course, free lunch on July 4th. If you live in NYC like myself, the flight is replaced by a $2.25 Metrocard but we do get to escape our tiny apartments for a hotel room for a couple nights and I'll use my per diem to get my after-party suit tailored to shorts and buy a yellow mustard premiere carpet for the entrance (the eaters pay for their own unofficial official afterparty but MLE kindly picked up the food tab - it was at Professor Thoms at 7:33 pm and the password was, "Swordfish.")

The prize money offered at the finals pays only to the 5th place for both men and women. That means ten eaters are taking a substantial loss to appear in the biggest event for our sport. Granted all of this is by choice, but one would ponder that for the most important lucrative day in competitive eating this seems odd. In 2009 Forbes Magazine wrote the following,"...But the clear winner was Nathan's. For what Eric Gatoff, chief executive, describes as a "high-six-figure" investment for the sponsorship (including the regional qualifying circuit competitions), the return was astronomical. Last year, the event generated more than $125 million in media value worldwide." That was seven years ago and since the price of eggs, milk, and gas has gone up; I'm guessing PR contracts and worldwide media value has too. Should every eater on stage deserve a pay day after shelling out their own coin to get there? I say, "Oh Yeah," but to prevent any dyspeptic displeasure from the primary sponsor, I have solved the problem. If Nathan's or John Morrell (the making of the hot dogs) can't pony up to pay out the table-enders (top ranked eaters who are not in the maelstrom of meat at the center of the table) I am willing to bet my lunch that some other sponsor will. After all - it's America, it's food, it's patriotic, and it's commercial. In a time where hallowed sporting events like the biggest boxing fight of all time or the triple crown producing Belmont Stakes are besieged by the appearance of fast food and energy drink product placement, it is time that competitive eating collect it's due.

At Major League Eating headquarters, each year preceding July 4th, they approach the major paper towel companies for sponsorship and each year, Bounty, Viva, Scott, Brawny, etc turn them down. Shame on you paper towel conglomerates...don't you see the value in being the one paper towel that can wipe the chin of someone who eats 20 - 60 hot dogs and then also clean up the mess that 30 people eating close to a combined 800 hdbs make. If you've seen the frankfurter and bun flotsam and jetsam on the table post-contest you'll realize that epic mess needs a durable amazing paper product. You, corporate

American company, could be the detritus savior…if you also pay prize money to the rest of the field.

Why stop at cleaning products and paper towels. We've had additional sponsors in year's past from condiments to digestive aids but those were not specific to any eater and in a time where pro-eating only fully supports the top dog (the #1 eater makes over $200,000 a year in appearance fees, prize money, and sponsorship, the #2 makes about $35,000 - I am ranked #19 so you can do the math) it is time for each eater to make some funds via advertising, like NASCAR drivers, for his or her distinct brands.

I am an easy brand - a dreadlocked hippy hipster (often wearing Goorin Brothers or Pork Pie Hatters hats to keep the hair out of the food and Warby Parker sunglasses to protect from the glare of food fame) plus I have been sampling all the top mustache wax brands to see which (Firehouse, Fisticuffs, or Mountaineer) can hold up during a 100 wing outing at the Hooters World Wing Eating Championship. As an every day all-year-round shorts wearer, I was going to transition into culottes with either a mustard pair of golf knickers from www.kingscrossgolfknickers.com or a pink pinstriped pair from www.golfknickers.com but I was informed that all eaters' must wear official sponsor uniforms. At least I wore my Retromarine bathing suit under the contest shorts for a dip at Coney post contest. That allowed me to throw my game worn shorts to the crowd so they can sell them on Ebay (I am predicting the lucky recipient got well under $3 dollars). I also need strong sneakers for a suitable eating stance and debuted some Nike's in denim and day-glo baby blue with my name on the back. I am hoping those Nike reps saw the prototypes for aerobic eaters everywhere and sign me as their first stomach-centric athlete. "Just Eat It," could be my motto. Also, if you saw my ESPN entrance, I was wearing pink feather epaulettes, LED american flag dreads, and a Vivienne Westwood knock-off Buffalo Gal hat - I could have been an ad for the upcoming Columbia Pictures "Pixels" movie.

I am not alone, prospective sponsors - take a look at this commercially viable field of eaters. Joey does pretty well in his soccer Mom high-waisted jeans, but the #2 ranked male, Matt "Megatoad" Stonie wears skinny jeans exclusively. Hello H&M - talk about stomach styling and foodie fashion. Some say the skinny jeans and his tight top center his belly like a magnet to the mastication. Megatoad is playing Tetris in his esophagus and could do so in your signature pants. And what did Megatoad do on July 4th but hoist the yellow mustard belt, stealing it from Chestnut's gaping maw. Heavy is the head that wears the crown, but heavier still is the belly that bears the belt and now Matt Stonie could be bearing it in a signature H&M accessories line (plus his haircut, done by his aspiring stylist brother Morgan, is the new "Rachel" ala Aniston from Friends - One side is long, one side is shaved - it's like Natalie Dormer in an Anti-"Hunger Games" side bob! So cool. So cooling.)

Eater X, the #3 ranked MLE member, wears face-paint a la the Ultimate Warrior or a rodeo clown, but have you seen his model looks sans the make-up? Hello L'Oreal or Mac - you know you want into the unheralded masculine demographic. This is it- if your make-up can hold up to Eater X's third place finish, it can hold up to mascara running from all those screaming groupies (non-gender specific) when Eater X accepts the trophy . Wait, there is more...

(Cue Beyonce) "All the stomach ladies, all the stomach ladies..." Put your scrunchy sponsorship on now two-time female chomping champ Miki Sudo's pony tail (her style of digesting is known as, "the angry pony" as she shakes her head to aid swallowing.) Or maybe Miki should have shampoo or conditioner endorsements - her stunning locks, shining in the Coney Island sun thanks to Neutrogena or Dove. Former female champ Sonya "The Black Widow" Thomas works at Burger King on Andrews Air Force Base, so perhaps just have that creepy plastic King as her counter (does his have plastic hands? Can he flip counting cards with them?)

Other top-ranked females include Michelle Lesco, a schoolteacher ("Buffalo Jim Reeves on the men's side is also a school teacher) and I think any textbook company would love to bring a little education to a lot of eating - or maybe Lesco and Reeves can be sponsored by a #2 pencil maker. Their eating is sharp and on point. Meredith "Deep Fried Diva" Boxberger has the best smile in competitive eating - while heading past twenty hdbs she still has time to flash the pearly whites (Hello Crest or Aim or even Tom's of Maine in the fennel flavor.) Really, any mouthwash company would be wise to get on board because if you are going to make out with some pro-eating groupies, minty hot dog breath is a must.

Rookie eater and Maxim model, New Zealand's Nela Zisser was flown in making the contest international as it says in the title. Perhaps Zales would like to sponsor her for a "One ring to rule them all" promotion or simply because she shattered all records for unwanted marriage proposals. There is an eater for every sponsor and a sponsor for every eater...a symbiotic relationship between the stomach and the stock prices.

Let's get back to Bill Murray, not as FDR, but as Tripper Harrison at Camp North Star, coaching the underdog Fink to hot dog glory in the movie, "Meatballs." It is the most iconic competitive eating scene in cinematic history - the one that all other's are judged by (it even inspired a podcast titled, "Fink beats the Stomach" on the heavy hitters network.) The engrossing film scene is inspirational and was my mantra when I took the stage at high noon this past and every July 4th.

Tripper: Mmmmm. Look at all those steaming wieners. Do you know what they're saying? They're saying, "This is the year that Fink beats 'The Stomach'."

[Fink picks up a hot dog and holds it to his ear]

Tripper: No, it's a couple of them over here... but they're saying it.

And Corporate America should start saying Major League Eating is where the action is regarding sponsorship, product placement, and endorsements. The possibilities are endless (I once wore an adult diaper to a bratwurst final due to an almost accident in a qualifying round. I ate 27 brats with confidence and comfort and lucky didn't have to use the diaper). Representatives at MLE headquarters are standing by, awaiting calls, emails, and offers. All I ask is that the sponsor pick up the slack and pay the prize money to the last place finisher - the eater without the trophies and novelty checks. The eater who ignored by The Foodarazzi, but chowdowns for the camaraderie - the brotherhood and sisterhood of the stomach. The eater who chews for the love of the gaminess, whose heart is clear and stomach pure...those who truly eat for America. I hope in the future that everyone one can have a happy product-placed consumer-driven commercially viable July 4th and God Bless the American Stomach!

I know I should have stopped at that patriotic high note, but Harrison Tripper also said, "more important than the score of this game is to score at the big social at our place tonight," so I thought you should have all the details on the unofficial official hot dog after party at Professor Thom's on July 4th. There was an actual yellow mustard carpet for everyone's entrance and The Foodarazzi was snapping photos the way that

6'9" Gideon Oji snapped dogs at Coney. Everyone looked hungry, fierce, and focused as the dress code was John Hughes prom semi-formal. Who was I be wearing? My shiny sharkskin suit (I didn't eat the shark myself) was paired with feather epaulettes from Danyell Gollwitzer's Axentz Easy shop and a Katy Perry tie from Staisha Grosch's DawgMutha Ties (she made me a wonderful plaid Britney Spears tie when I was going through my plaid Britney phase and I wore it in all it's white trash glory to a NJ Pork Roll contest.) If you think competitive eaters drool a lot at the competition table, you should have seen us at the after-party. Professor Thom's generously supplied mammoth trays of nachos and wings for the non-pro eaters and this year, superstar baker and chef, Sam Mason made us a custom ice cream from his Oddfellows Ice Cream stores - the flavor - "Whiskey Cigar Lobster" - which combined many of my favorite July 4th activities in one sweet final bite. I served it at midnight, wearing a plastic lobster bib, and the taste was a seafood rich lobster milk that gave way to an Islay peated whiskey followed by a carcinogenic throat closing. It was the perfect midnight snack.

PORK ROLL HAM(LET), I DOTH QUOTE!
(Sept 25th, 2017)

Crazy Legs Claudius Here - heading into my third year battling my greatest adversary - Pork Roll Ham(Let) at the Trenton Thunder World Famous Case's Pork Roll Eating Championship. Why compare this Major League Eating event with a most difficult food and myself to Ole Billy Shakespeare's two fiercest rivals? Well, Cliff Notes is now available online (where most of the literary info has been gleaned for this post) and my battle with Pork Roll goes far beyond the Hatfields and the McCoys or Trump vs America.

As Claudius, (according the professor of Cliff Notes), I am socially adept, with great charm and can turn mourning into celebration (you should attend an afterparty to see this magic happen.) Pork Roll Ham(Let), recognizes that his "offense is rank" and "smells to heaven," [Cliff Notes, internet page...well, cliff notes]. He is fine with his actions and will live with his consequences (a lot of disturbing burps.) Pork Ham(Let) kills in the light of day and suffers the pangs of his conscience (Pork Roll as a sentient being - I shutter.) As Claudius, I subvert my conscience and refuse to ask for divine forgiveness (or Alka-Seltzer.) The final quote from Cliff Notes on the subject (really like a George Shea intro, but George never buries the lead:)

"Hamlet seeks contrition and absolves himself of guilt before he dies; Claudius receives no absolution and seeks none. Hamlet will spend eternity in Heaven; Claudius will burn in Hell."

So there you have it. This epic battle will take place at 3.30pm Eastern, on Saturday, September 30, 2017 at the home of the Trenton Thunder, ARM & HAMMER Park, 1 Thunder Rd, Trenton, NJ 08611. While "Cutthroat" Carmen Cincotti attempts to obliterate Joey "Jaws" Chestnut's Pork Roll record of 43 sandwiches in ten minutes, I, Crazy Legs Claudius, will attempt to simply get to double digits. I have separated the hardened bologna slices from the rigid roll, I've ripped and dunked the sandwich, it's immunity to softening liquid like Gortex in rain. I've squashed, mashed, mooshed, and manhandled the so called NJ delicacy - and the Pork Roll(Hamlet) has simply killed me. It's smiling mascot, less like a pork product, and more like a red angry pulsating zit, dances joyfully on my grave amidst spilled Gatorade, breadcrumbs, and the rubber strands of uneaten pork roll rinds.

KING OF CORN
(June 28th, 2016)

My Uniqlo white linen long-sleeved shirt was splattered with blood. My cigar bag also and bits of bright red speckle dotted my Sol Moscot clear frame glasses (Gary Oldman has a pair, so I had to have one.) The back of the boat was drenched in blood as if it was a scene from "Dexter." All the beer had been consumed before 1 p.m. I was sunburned as red as the blood and later a scalding cafe con leche would do the same to the inside of my mouth. Some would say that this was no way to prepare for the Sweet Corn Fiesta in South Florida and attempt to become the five time world corn-on-the-cob eating champion, but I would argue that was exactly the way to prepare for the twelve-minute, all-you-can-eat, hand-cramping, jaw-locking, and kernel-discomfort scenario. I was beer soaked, blood drenched, burnt outside and in, and battle ready. Bring on the sweet corn!

I should mention that the blood was dolphin blood or more accurately mahi mahi blood, but that in this hidden enclave near the Florida Keys, they call this wondrous green iridescent fish, "dolphin." I was in a place that no Google map can find, a community where the fish-crazy folks are drunk by 9 a.m., asleep by 9 p.m., but up at 5 a.m. to seek out the water's bounty. My host, Ryan (Think a youthful Ian Ziering from "Sharknado 2") has an awesomely named boat, "The Danny Glover," but Buck (Think Christian Bale in 20 years - but good Bale, like Batman Bale with "The Machinist" and "American Psycho" thrown in) has a larger boat, "Blue Diamond," and with a competitive eater joining the crew we were going to need a bigger boat. Also on board was the sublime Wendy (Think Cersei Lannister but much nicer), who brought fried chicken, cucumbers, and ginger snaps to complement the 2 cases of beer for 4 people. As they say, "The fishing was good, the catching not so much." At least for the morning, but when the beer was gone and we had to head in to restock, our luck changed. Indeed as Ernest Hemingway writes so aptly in The Old Man and the Sea, "Luck is a thing that comes in many forms and who can recognize her?" It is easy to recognize when the beer is gone though.

I received a "D" for my senior high school thesis titled, "The Sea in Literature," a daunting task that included a whale named, "Moby," an Albatross that had a Rime (not the Black Sabbath version sadly), and of course, an Old Man and the fish that was trying to kill him. Or was it the other way around? I deserved that "D" but out on the "Blue Diamond" I finally understood Hemingway's masterpiece - or at least understood his life lesson that everything is more intense and better when one is drinking. Indeed, the only rule on Buck's boat was that he, The Captain, would never ask for a beer, but if he didn't have one in his hand, it was implied he wanted one. Let's compare these two masters of the sea:

"Why do old men wake so early? Is it to have one longer day?"
– Ernest Hemingway, The Old Man and the Sea

"You can't drink all day, if you don't start in the morning."
– Buck of the "Blue Diamond"

And this:
"Fish," he said, "I love you and respect you very much. But I will kill you dead before this day ends."
– Ernest Hemingway, The Old Man and the Sea

"Fish," he said, "I love you and respect you very much. But I will kill you dead before this day ends."
– Buck of the "Blue Diamond"

Right? They have the sea and fish world figured out. Which is why as Wendy insisted that a landlubber like me, hold the supple fish that Ryan just caught for a photo, it was implied that if the fish jumped overboard, so would I have to. Buck took a look at the flopping fish and the floppier competitive eater and said, "You should get that in the ice box before it starts hemorrhaging..." And on cue, the fish exploded as if shot by a sniper. The blood spurting and splatter (Think Herschell Gordon Lewis' The Gore Gore Girls) was so impressive that it took a scrub brush and ten buckets of sea water to clean the backside of the boat. The front side of the competitive eater would not be cleaned. That white linen shirt was polka dot now and I felt fine about it. I had taken on South Florida by land and sea and both had entranced me.

The day on the water was preceded by a day driving through Big Cypress National Preserve - I was feet away from alligators, vultures, giant grasshoppers, and small newts. It was awesome. If one enters into a YouTube search "Sam Barclay's Outstanding FLA tour" there is a 16 video playlist of my stellar day. Sam Barclay is a Major League Eating MC (Think Ryan Gosling's dad) and was working in Las Vegas at a Nathan's Hot Dog Qualifier, but recommended all the stops of both nature and food (I cannot recommend more El Palacio De Los Jugos for open air Cuban delicacies and Robert is Here for the weirdest most delicious fruit and fruit-only milkshakes.) Sam and Ryan are Miami residents who gather at the infamous Mac's Club Deuce bar in Miami Beach and plot swamp land buying, fishing trips, and at the afterparty for the corn contest, coordinated with an AIDS Walk Dance Troupe whose synchronized moves are better than anything on reality TV show competitions. Ryan, for his generous hosting, received my 2nd place, but still quite tall, corn on the cob eating trophy.

That is right, 2nd place. This four-time champ with a 50% success rate at winning since 2007 (Now a Scalabrine 44%) lost by two ears to Erik "The Red" Denmark (Think Matthew Lillard in "SLC Punk".) I blame the corn - it was the sweetest haul ever and as such was not as starchy. For causal diners this corn was perfect, but in competitive eating, one needs the ears to fight back a little, making them easier to clean as opposed to the kernels popping prematurely in a burst of sugared goodness. The deductions were heavier this year due to the corn state, but retired eater turned corn judge, Sean "Wrecking Ball" Brockert (think who Miley Cyrus was thinking of), did a stellar job, with the unenviable task of shifting through corn detritus and giblet mess. In the end, I had hoped to become the five-time champ and King of Corn, but due to my financial difficulties, I needed anything in prize money to pay my bills so 2nd place with the Sweet Corn Fiesta's substantial prize structure is more than enough to please my credit card company, Obamacare bill, gas, electric, and land-line phone bill. If you are fiscally irresponsible, always be harvest savvy - and this year's crop of Florida sweet corn is pure gold - literally and figuratively. No butter or salt needed, but go butter your body with suntan lotion and hang around salty folks like Ryan, Wendy, Sam, and Captain Buck because they are the best people in the world and I am not being corny.

FEAR AND DIGESTING IN LAS VEGAS
(June 20th, 2015)

I just canceled my flight to Las Vegas, which is bittersweet. Perhaps more sweet than bitter as the song goes, as I canceled because I have already qualified to compete at Nathan's Famous on July 4th in Coney Island. Major League Eaters get three shots at qualifying, and while I fell short in Plant City, Fla. in March, I did win the Atlanta Qualifier on April 12. Had I not, I'd be flying to Vegas this Friday. So canceling my flight was a tad bitter because, if the July 4th Nathan's Famous Hot Dog Contest is the patriotic destination, the Las Vegas qualifier at the New York-New York Hotel & Casino in Las Vegas (this year on April 25th) is the American Dream journey. After all, what could be more patriotic than celebrating the birth of our great nation on its founding day at high noon by overeating frankfurters. To become a competitor there, one must win one of the dozen U.S. qualifiers around the nation. Perhaps no other location is as hotly contested, as an important harbinger of future champions then the Las Vegas qualifier. It makes sense that to make it to the Boardwalk of Coney Island, one starts at the mini-boardwalk of the mini-Brooklyn Bridge in Vegas. A journey of a thousand chomps starts with a single bite and usually the Nathan's Famous circuit kicks off in the hot Las Vegas sun. The sun beats the dogs until they glisten, uneven seams pushing to break free. The buns toast until they are dipped in hot water, following the weenies into the maw of Major

League Eaters, creating a whooshing swallowing system not dissimilar from the barrel roll and 144 foot drop rollercoaster that circles the casino. When the going get tough, the tough turn pro-eating.

The NY NY Hotel and Casino is one of the only places you can casually snack on a Nathan's hot dog and then stroll to the sports book to bet on how many a competitor will eat at the July 4th finals. Most of the bets are under/overs (always bet the over) and some are one-on-one matchups (The easy money is betting for the guy facing this author as I often eat in the low 20s). Joey Chestnut is the eight-time champion with his best at 69 hot dogs and buns in 10 minutes. My qualifying total this year was 21 in the same time, so to become a champion against Joey, I would have to eat three times as fast, three times the food, and then add an extra plate of five at the buzzer simply to tie "Jaws" Chestnut. Heavy is the head that wears the crown, but heavier still is the belly that bears the belt.

For most of Major League Eating's years, 50 hot dogs was the 4-minute mile so Joey, within one of 70 would be running/eating the equivalent of a two minute mile. He is that fast. He is that good. In previous years, he has made over $200,000 opening his mouth every weekend in different cities for Native Grill and Wings chicken wings, Denver Outlaw World's burritos, and St Elmo's Steakhouse shrimp cocktail. By comparison the 2nd ranked eater makes about thirty grand a year, usually attending more contests. The top dog is the only dog whose makes the bread. How did this happen? It happened in the city of glitz created out of the desert, the city of greed and gamble. It happened in 2006 when Joey ate 50 hot dogs and became a challenger to reigning dominant champ Takeru Kobayashi. In a PR highjacking Joey remained media silent for three days until Nathan's Famous ponied up prize money for the top five finishers at the finals. If only Joey had held out for an extra day, maybe we could have gotten prize money for the whole field as it is MLE's signature event, a media juggernaut, and an ESPN ratings winner, but Nathan's pays flight, accommodations, and a per diem so I'll should probably stop bellyaching. The eaters do host their own unofficial official after party (post contest at Ruby's on the boardwalk, and that night in NYC at Professor Thoms where the password is, "swordfish." If you think Joey drools a lot at the contest, you should see him at the afterparty)

In 2011 Major League Eating reversed their stance on Title 9 in athletics and made a female only division of the Nathan's contest. For many years, the greatest female eater of all time, Sonya "The Black Widow" Thomas was the champ, but what people eat in Vegas, doesn't usually stay in Vegas, and after a ten pound bowl of "Phozilla" Miki Sudo won $1500 and a billboard of her likeness and entered the ranks of Major League Eating. She is currently ranked #4 overall and last July 4th she ate 34 hot dogs to ascend to Hot Dog Queen supremacy. Rumor has it she has broken 50 hot dogs in practice and because she doesn't have to qualify, she will likely be spectator on April 25th in her Vegas hometown. Since she doesn't have hot dog skin in the men's game, it will be interesting to see if she cheers on the skinny jeans-clad man who will undoubtably break Joey Chestnut's Vegas record of 50.

There are few certainties in competitive eating, but Matt "Megatoad" Stonie will win the Las Vegas qualifier by a large margin. He has broken the 50 hot dogs barrier several times and finished behind Joey on July 4th by five with 56 hot dogs. But why is the Megatoad headed to Vegas so early in the hot dog circuit unless he wants to make a statement, draw a line in the frankfurt detritus that says, "You shall not pass!" Usually, he will wait until the last East Coast qualifier to get one more run in before the big day. Perhaps the NY NY casino has beckoned him, tempted him, with the interesting circumstances of this year's contest. Joey "Jaws" Chestnut had said he would break Kobayashi's 6-time consecutive champion record and then retire, but now Joey is heading towards number 9. On July 4th, no one beats Joey — no one. He knows his yearly income is based on those digestive 10 minutes, but more than that — he is unstoppable when it comes to Nathan's Famous hot dogs. He is like Lance Armstrong on a bike (drug testing has yet to come to Major League Eating) or Mike Tyson in the ring. There is something primal about the way Joey eats, his body shakes and bobs like a New Orleans jazz trombone player, but his hot dogs input is almost robotic. He is a jazz-playing Cro-Magnon robot who has no time for mustard, ketchup, or losing. Where other eaters (myself included) rely on gimmicks like costumes or pyrotechnics, Joey has said his sole gimmick, "Is winning." He wins, even wearing high-waisted Mom jeans. The Megatoad, in his painted on skinny jeans, stands as Joey's nearest competition. The Megatoad has bested Chestnut in gyoza (384 in 10 minutes), slug burgers, (43 in 10 minutes), and pumpkin pie (20 pounds 13 ounces in eight minutes), and perhaps he sees an opening this year. Both competitors are from and live in San Jose, California, but Joey has gone suburban. He owns a house, a dog, and last year, pre-contest proposed to his girlfriend, Nestle on stage at Coney Island. I asked him if MLE or ESPN wanted him to propose after the contest and they did, but Joey felt that after 60-plus hot dogs, he couldn't bend on one knee and didn't want to throw up or crap himself, thus ruining the heart-sweeping gesture. This man knows romance. Nestle said yes. Joey won the contest.

Joey and Nestle's wedding is in early May — prime hot dog training season. If their honeymoon will it be somewhere tropical and if so where will be the nearest Nathan's stand? This could be a problem for Joey's dogmatic and bun approach to Coney Island. Is the Megatoad counting on Joey being out-of-shape come July? Vegas is a town made for guys like me who like whiskey, cigars, buffets, and strippers available 24 hours a day. The Megatoad is a near teetotaler, a nutritionalist, and eschews peeler joints the way I avoid vegans. He would rather stay home and make Youtube videos eating obscene amounts of food in 60 seconds (37 mozzarella sticks, 8 filet-o-fish, and 32 peanut butter cups.) The NY NY Hotel & Casino is not a place for the weak-willed, the hesitant, the unsure. It is where hot dog eaters, like Joey Chestnut and Miki Sudo go, "All in," before the July 4th final. The Megatoad is poised to join those champions on April 25th. Will he hit 60 hot dogs? More? There is nothing in Las Vegas for him, except for those ten minutes of hot dogs and buns and in the gambling mecca that is the NY NY Hotel & Casino, always bet on the man with nothing to lose.

A BIG TRIBUTE TO THE LITTLE MAN
(June 17, 2015)

I have been feeding my ears a steady stream of early AC/DC thanks to my American-by-way-of-Australian friend, Sam, who hooked me up with all the early releases, both American and Australian. I have been reading books about the Young brothers (George the older is a producer/manager type, while Malcolm and Angus play in the band.) It seems almost impossible that two diminutive fellows could produce such extravagant wonderful noise from their instruments. Indeed, AC/DC does in rock stadiums and stages, while the two members of shorter statue are elevated to giants of entertainment, music and devilish fun. I was thinking about a closer-to-home shorter friend, who also exceeded his stature in dance, entertainment and patriotic or leprechaun duties. My close friend, James Mastrangelo, "Little Jimmy" to all, passed away very close to his 69th birthday.

His visage as Little Uncle Sam on July 4th still exists at the Nathan's Coney Island Hot Dog Contest countdown wall. His professional salsa dance moves, over 1,000 shows with Tito Puente, are captured in photos and video. His love of Grand Central Station, of trains and driving cars, is evident in the locomotion of a modern New York City. His favorite organization, The Little People of America, continues to support and celebrate little people everywhere — in fact, their slogan, "Think Big!" was adopted by Little Jimmy for his autobiography, "Little Man, Thinking Big."

His other, less-known slogan: "What you do on your knees, Little Jimmy does standing up," was even referenced by the priest at his funeral. He mentioned it bringing snickering from the pews, and acknowledged the carnal attachment to the saying, but then brought it around where Little Jimmy was benefited from receiving the Lord standing up, while all others must kneel in prayer.

In short, Little Jimmy was closer to God, but still, how often does a cunnilingus joke get cracked in church? Little Jimmy was a God-loving man, but also a lover of people and good times. He loved Coney Island and the July 4th contest where he and I could celebrate America, and then stroll post-contest to Ruby's on the boardwalk.

History is in those wooden planks from Little Jimmy's time disco dancing at Club Atlantis (until it fell through the boardwalk returning to the mythical status of its namesake), from Coney Island U.S.A. where Little Jimmy, despite ignoring the "freak" designation, found a home as a special guest in Dick Zigun's Sideshow, as MC of the Motorcycle and Tattoo Convention and as a performer in Todd Robbin's amazing "Carnival Knowledge" off-Broadway play.

Randy Watts and Nathan's Famous sent a beautiful flower bouquet to Little Jimmy's wake, George Shea of Major League Eating showered the often curmudgeonly Little Jimmy, with flowery quotes that made the "Daily News" (The story was buried with Little Jimmy along with a little bible.) Little Jimmy, despite his hardships and brutal honest manner, was loved. He was always kind to children, explaining about dwarfism and how other folks were, "average" versus "normal," as is often mistaken. He pointed out that the "M Word" is not acceptable, and he loved the LPA who provided him with driving pedals (he was, to this day, the safest driver I have ever ridden with) and conventions where he could cut lose and enjoy the company of little people from all over the country. His pride of Brooklyn was evident when the national convention came to Brooklyn in 2009.

A return to Brooklyn, notably Coney Island on July 4th was on my mind and stomach as I took the stage at the Atlanta Dogwood Festival on Sunday, April 12th. One must win a qualifier for the right to compete at the final table, and I have missed by one fourth of a hot dog two years in a row. My NY Post horoscope said to ignore revenge, despite the fact my main competition had trash talked me in defeat the previous year.

My Chinese fortune cookie said, "Be full," The two days before a contest I ingest only protein shakes, Icelandic skyr — Siggi's vanilla is my favorite — and Mee Noodle soup — foods that stretch the stomach, but digest easily. I have never worn ear buds while eating, but for this contest, I took to the stage as AC/DC's "Highway to Hell" blared in my head — indeed, my friends were there too — SuperPaul Bonebreaker Barlow, a Carfax rep who is a star extra (sometimes with lines) in all the Hollywood-made Atlanta shot movies, and Damien Boykin, the smartest pallet broker in history, whose competitive eating takes a back seat to his love of Star Wars (his first child's name is going to be "Skywalker.")

My first bite of the Nathan's dog, bite being more of a woodchipper-esque load in of the grilled frankfurts, was accompanied in my ears by the ominous clanging gong of "Hell's Bells." And then, I heard no more — neither the rest of the AC/DC song, nor the Irene Cara "Flashdance" theme, nor the Katy Perry song, nor the Phish jam.

For that, I had to wait until I was airborne flying home an hour later. I ate with no revenge in my heart, with only the thought that Little Jimmy would insist I be on stage July 4th. I ate with purpose, and for a change, supreme cleanliness (my judge was a bomb squad expert with two glocks on his person — he was very serious about counting the hot dogs and buns detritus.) I ate with joy. I ate 21 hot dog buns, and despite a rookie Nigerian college hoops star eating 20, I ate to victory.

The basketball standout, Gideon Oji, announced for the draft just after the contest — not the pedestrian NBA draft, the more exclusive Major League Eating draft. My 1st place trophy went to Professor Thoms bar later that night, the Nathan's dogs to my lower intestine soon after, but the moment of victory belonged to a 15-year career competitive eater and his missing little person friend.

If you are lucky on Delta airlines, you'll be seated just right as the plane flies at sunset and you can see the fire-red Parachute Jump of Coney Island, low and below. You can squint and see the Wonder Wheel and Cyclone, but you'll not be able to see the Nathan's on Stillwell and Surf Avenues. You can sense it though as you stare at Coney Island from miles above ("Mmmm look at all those steaming weenies," — Tripper Harrison.)

It helps if you crank Ace Frehley's "New York Groove" as you peer below, digesting dogs, thinking of whiskey and a victory cigar. You stare into the future, but realize all you really should count on (like Little Jimmy always did) is the present. As Ace sings, "Feels so good tonight, who cares about tomorrow. I'm back, back in the N.Y. groove." See you July 4th at Coney Island to celebrate Little Jimmy's, Nathan's, Major League Eating and America's N.Y. groove!

WHY READING THE NEW YORKER WILL GET YOU PUNCHED IN THE HEAD
(May 18th, 2015)

I saw a blinding white light — or rather felt it — as the sucker punch hit the left side of my temple. Later, staggering on The Bowery, I would be amazed that my Goorin Brothers newsboy hat stayed on my head and that my library book ("Duff" by Kody Keplingeri) would remain in my back pocket. I had taken two shots to the noggin and the next day my shoulder would feel pulled out of the socket (had the guy grabbed my arm or had it happened as I pushed towards him before the second white light punch?) The day after that, my left tricep would be sore, perhaps where the two girls were banging on me. All in all, I was fine, nothing a day of ice packs and Netflix (American Horror Story season one) couldn't fix. I was sorry to miss the rest of The Dwarves punk show at the Bowery Electric, but glad not to be blindsided by punches. It was a good show, but I won't be attending anymore punk concerts and I blame the New Yorker magazine.

The New Yorker has had a lot of punk history stories — the Cro-Magnum's singer has a new autobiography and the old NYC scene of CBGB's, modern street urchins, skinheads, straight edge suburban kids and the angry celebrated. My favorite band is The Tubes, which is straight-up rock-and-roll via performance art, so the punk/hardcore movement passed me by. I never minded the bollocks and was happy hearing The Tubes live over 40 times in 30 years. The first naked female breast I saw was at The Tubes show in Worcester, Massachusetts as an eighth grader. I procured a fake ID my senior year of high school so I could see The Tubes at The Channel in Boston. The Tubes have been all the music I need and the soundtrack to my life (fine, I like me some Katy Perry too.) The closest to punk was hearing stories about the DC punk scene from fellow window cleaner Ivor Hansen, who later wrote those stories down in the excellent book, "Life on the Ledge." Ivor is the son of an Admiral and rebelled by drumming his path to a punk pioneer in the '80s with luminaries like Ian MacKaye (Minor Threat/Fugazi) and Henry Rollins (Black Flag and large biceps). Ivor and his wife and family now travel the globe for the United Nations, drumming a better world for all of us. That was my punk experience until I attended a Dropkick Murphy's show last week and wrote lovingly about it for The Huffington Post.

With the New Yorker making it seem like punk was safe for everyone, I attended The Dwarves show. I had seen the flyer — a curvy topless woman with panties — and checked out their shirts online (prior to the beatdown I bought the hot woman drumming in XL.) I realize that this is not the best way to judge a band's music, but the New Yorker led me to believe that it's not about the music, but the scene. I took in the scene at The Bowery Electric and it got the better of me. My friend Sam told me that The Dwarves have an entire album of 12 songs that lasts 13 minutes total and indeed the band plays fast, loud, and the songs are over quickly. I had pregamed at Coyote Ugly's happy hour (two for one Bud Light as I have consumed my lifetime quota of PBR, and prefer some shots of Bushmills Black Bush Whiskey). I wasn't drunk, but ready for the punk, or so I thought. Midshow on the balcony (I don't do the mosh pit for the same reasons I don't do certain yoga poses — my body just doesn't bend in that way), a girl who looked like the actress Lake Bell but with Warby Parker glasses was motioning to her blond friend (think Busy Phillips) that she wanted to go upstairs to smoke. She did this by jostling me, knocking into me as if it was the last subway train at rush hour. I pointed this out to her and she responded with a flurry of expletives not printable in a family-friendly blog. I verbally responded as well with some not-so-nice words and adjectives (like the wash-your-mouth-out-with-soap ones) and the girls went upstairs. The guy next to me on his Blackberry said to me, "What's up with her?" I didn't know.

She returned and with her back to the stage started slam-dancing into me violently. My Bud Lite went flying and as I tried to put my hands up in defense, I was sucker-punched from behind. White lights twice and I was up the stairs and out (knocking down almost Busy Phillips I believe, but she might have been the one attempting to give me Tommy John shoulder surgery.) I was out on The Bowery not far from the former CBGB's (perhaps the new punk esthetic is $600 sweaters) and wondering what happened and what to do next. I thought of going back but didn't know what my male attacker looked like (perhaps shaved head, goatee, black leather jacket

— but I might be punk profiling.) I thought of calling the police, but with what reason; it's only in Williamsburg that beating on a hipster is a hate crime. I thought of posting a nasty Yelp review but really, who has time for that asinine negativity? So I went to Croxley's Ale House and bought some chicken wings to go, which I ate with a sore jaw while watching Netflix (switching from American Horror Story to Unbreakable Kimmy Schmidt for some levity and laughs.)

It was only the next morning, with a sore head and a ringing pain, that I wondered if my jaw would recover in time for Brisket King NYC. That was my main concern as I prefer punk-rock chefs over, well, punk rockers. My jaw did recover and I attended Brisket King NYC (in a yellow ascot — good thing I wasn't wearing that at The Dwarves show.) It was stellar. The highlights include brisket innovation from kimchee to brisket tacos, but no one did it better than Red Hook's Hometown BBQ — it was thick, moist, and both mouth- and eye-watering due to perfect peppered spices. I asked one of the faithful who follow Pitmaster Billy Durney, the smoked meat master said that they just put in the time and if it's not right, they won't serve it. It sounds a lot like the philosophy of pizza genius Dom DeMarco and it worked at Brisket King NYC. I also ate an excellent potato bun-clad sandwich from Dinosaur BBQ, and the guys from Pig NYC made some fine goods but were a write-in ballot entry for the judging, which is always tough in the grease-stained world of sliced meat-ranking. I rubbed shoulders with luminaries like the guy who owns the Waterfront Ale House and the fifth generation of Katz's Deli (who is charged with not changing a thing to do his job.) Joey Deckle was there as was Jimmy Potsandpans, so it was a swell gathering.

Of course, no NYC BBQ event would be complete if it didn't resemble The Walking Dead and the crowds ate most of the brisket in an hour, mumbling for more, more, more. I took dessert in the form of Sheepdip Whiskey, which like the meat around it, was smokey with a nice mouthfeel. Oh, and no one punched me in the head, which I now consider essential to a pleasant night out.

Brisket digesting, scotch evaporating, I guess the lesson is to stick to one's own brand of punk — or simply don't believe everything you read in the New Yorker. Finally, I want to apologize for my unkind words to fake Lake Bell and almost Busy Phillips, but I think they owe me a Bud Light and I don't want to get hit in the head anymore... just in the gut with some hardcore brisket.

ARE YOU A TRUE BOSTONIAN OR DO YOU LIKE NYC BRISKET (MUTUALLY EXCLUSIVE MUCH?)
(May 12th 2015)

I am a big Jay McInerney fan and I heard him speak years ago at the St. Luke's Church on Hudson street. He told a harrowing tale about almost dropping his coffee cup onto the heads of St. Luke's students when he lived above the school across the street. He also told a much more personal harrowing tale about his mother who was publicly shamed in their hometown due to rumor. It made him leave and subsequently dislike his hometown. Post reading I approached the table and told him that I also disliked my hometown and his piercing cobalt eyes locked in one me and he said, "That is a sign of intelligence."

I am from Boston, or more specifically the suburb of Belmont which borders Cambridge which is hip, while Belmont in my time was a dry town (no booze) with no cable TV nor fast food restaurants (no teenage angst outlets.) As an adult I have lived in New York City for twenty odd years but I retain a certain love (and some dislike) for "Bahstan," as my friend Margie from Dorchester says. It is true that Beantown bars are too brightly lit, close to early, and overall the city could use a little more diversity (and another Celtics championship - Kelly Olynyk this will only happen if you start wearing hightop sneakers.) My favorite sporting event is the Boston Marathon which as a small child, I would watch and cheer for the costumed runners, especially the guy with the afro and horns. I would see Dick Beardsley lose to Alberto Salazar by two seconds battling police motorcycles and potholes. I would watch a massive guy 1/2 mile from the finish line, on the course, berating the five hour runners to finish, that the finish was just ahead. I would watch him massage cramped hamstrings and wheel his arms towards the end goal. I ran the Boston Marathon in 2007 and my girlfriend ran along side me for 100 yards which was so joyous that I felt all the energy of the finish line guy transferred to her and then to me, propelling me like the runaway train that Dick Beardsley became even in his heartbreaking loss. I feel heartbreak currently, following the Boston Marathon bombing court case, for those who lost their lives, limbs, and joy at such a special event. I grew up thinking that Patriots Day. the Monday day off for the April marathon, was a holiday everywhere. That everywhere one would spill out of an afternoon Fenway game and watch the tired runners push their bodies and minds to their limits, while crowds drank warm beer and cheered. I ran in a T-shirt that I silkscreened that read, "I ♡ Dirty Water," a song

originally sung by The Standells about the polluted Boston Harbor and Charles River. It was a 60s mock tribute to Boston as the producer of the song had been mugged and also felt the girls' college curfews too strict. The chorus is, "Well I love that dirty water. Oh, Boston you're my home." I ran with the song blazed upon my chest before it became the Boston Sports anthem it is today. Young kids asked why I liked dirty water while older folks began humming or singing the song which was nice.

The cover of "Dirty Water" by Quincy's (and the world's) Dropkick Murphys is one of their two songs that I knew prior to Monday night's awesome kicksass show at Irving Plaza. The other song, "Shipping up to Boston" was featured in a bunch of Boston movies, but I primary know it as it is played after each Beantown sports victory at Professor Thom's at 219 2nd ave ("Behind enemy lines since 2005.")

I now will posit that one is not a true Bostonian until he or she attends a Dropkick Murphys show. If one ever thought that the banjo or accordion were instruments of pansies, I dare them to take that view to the punk Celtic chaos that is a Dropkick event. Granted the place smelled of stale beer, halitosis, and newsboy cap fop sweat, but the music transported some to the rafters and others into the firm loving embrace of the stage bouncers as they crowd surfed while the band yell-sung anthems, swore, and sweated. The show was pure Boston and I don't mean because it was whiter than an albino in a wedding dress - it was the energy, the fight (not always on the right side - see busing in Boston in the 70s), and the might of a crowd that would lose itself in delirium as if the finish line was only 1/2 mile away. The show reminded me of the 1919 Boston Molasses Flood (OK, fine I just Googled it - don't harsh my metaphor, man) and how before the 30 foot tall, 35 miles an hour molasses tsunami killed 21 people and destroyed an elevated train, all that was heard was a, "dull muffled roar." Perhaps that is why only the

Amish like shoo-fly pie and Boston Creme Pie is the most popular creme pie flavor (suck it Bavarians!) The Dropkick Murphys provide a dull muffled roar every show, every city, every time the bagpipes kick in and they play their love ballad, "Kiss me, I'm Shitfaced."

Where was I going with this post? I am glad you asked, because it reminded me that this is the segue where I introduce further controversy by pointing out that the lyrics from the above mentioned love song, "I'm soaked, I'm soiled and brown," can also apply to New York City brisket. Is NYC barbecue an oxymoron? Can the finest cuts of brisket be produced by the city that never sleeps (which helps if you are up all night tending a smoker.) I use to run with the meatcogcenti - a carnivore group that included Mr. Cutlets (nee Josh Ozersky) and Joey Deckle (Deckle being the fattest moistest part on the brisket - on Joey, I would guess it was that loose skin at the elbow.) Robbie Richter, BBQ master use to greet me by name and preferred side dish ("Crazy Legs, German Potato Salad.") I was someone in the meat community based on my years as a competitive eater and buffet food champion (5.5 pounds in ten minutes including brisket, baked beans, cole slaw, and mystery side.) I filmed rib eating commercials for Daisy Mae's BBQ and superstar chef Adam Perry Lang but I was respectfully playing it safe, eating Hooters wings with John Popper and accepting free snout from Mt Wilson Farm leftovers during the Madison Square Park BBQ Festival. Monday night at Brisket King NYC, I put my comped admission where my mouth is, as a judge of the 20 plus establishments and chefs who will prove, once and for all, that brisket belong in New York City, because if it didn't...we'd mug you to get it. Join me, Monday, March 16th to prove that you can take the Dropkick Murphys out of Boston, but not the Bahstan out of the Dropkick Murphys the same way you can eat brisket out of NYC, but you can't take that soaked, soiled, brown out of NYC brisket where Monday night, Brisket will be king. And as for Tuesday, St Patrick's Day, as a Masshole and New Yawker, I'll be quaffing green beer and chomping leftover brisket and I'm not even Irish. And as for the day after that, well, there won't be enough wet naps in the five boroughs to clean me up.

OVER THE TOP. UNDER THE BUN
(May 3rd, 2015)

In preparation for my Nathan's hot dog qualifier at the Plant City, Florida strawberry festival, I have been listening to a lot of Frank Stallone music. Not just the hits from the 1980s films "Staying Alive" and "Over the Top" but his new stuff like "Carry On" from the film "Reach Me." With lyrics like, "It's got to have feelings. It's got to have meaning. Because I need a reason to carry on," Frank could just as well be singing about eating hot dogs competitively for 10 minutes.

I am a film junkie, but "Saturday Night Fever" is so much better than, "Staying Alive" and in the arm pressing 80s genre I much prefer "PK and the Kid" over "Over the Top." Granted, I was one of the few individuals who thought that the world needed two competitive arm-wrestling movies and time has not dampened my opinion. My sport, Major League Eating, is known for strength in the dunking forearm versus the bulging biceps from professional arm-wrestling. In subculture sports — beer pong, cup-stacking, and the rock-paper-scissors championships — strong forearms are highly valued. This is also true of chronic masturbaters, but it's more difficult to turn pro in pornography so I stick with competitive eating.

I have written about past Nathan's qualifiers for the Huffington Post — all losing efforts as I have been absent from the final table on July 4th the previous two years. The reason for hot dog prelims is because one must win one of the Nathan's qualifiers to gain a spot at the final table - paying their travel and accommodations to various US cities, race tracks, or fruit festivals. Besides earning that table spot, one gets an expensed trip to Coney Island, a per diem, and some free shirts and frisbees. The top five get prize money, but for the table enders like myself, we settle for some ESPN exposure, cheap drinks at Ruby's on the Boardwalk, and the occasional groupie. I'm not in for the money nor the free hot dogs (although I think that Nathan's garlicky snap is the best wiener around or to quote Frank Stallone, "I do believe in you after all we have been through.")

I am a Major League Eater for the journey. To compete in the Nathan's International Hot Dog Championship is a vision quest (minus Mathew Modine - although he is invited to the after party at Professor Thom's - Modine the password is, "swordfish." and you are a plus three). For me, it's the warrior's journey in "Il Topo" or something out of a Hunter S. Thompson story - when the going gets weird, the weird turn pro-eater. It's Rutger Hauer's Roy Batty's soliloquy if he was full at an all-you-can-eat buffet - "I've eaten things you people wouldn't believe... shrimp toasts on fire behind the sneeze guard of Orion Diner. I've quaffed soup dumpling c-beams in the dark near the Tannhäuser Gate Restaurant. All those... food items... will be digested in time, like snow-cones... in... rain. Time... to diet..." Anyway, it is not exactly clear why one becomes a competitive eater, but there is one Last Supper each summer at the corner of Stillwell and Surf at high noon (or three o'clock if we get bumped by Wimbledon coverage.)

Perhaps Frank Stallone has been singing for his supper all along. Is his "Bad Nite" about a poor hot dog outing? ("I see the clock ticking time. What I want I can't find. I've been waiting for so long...") Perhaps his "Fly Together" is sung from the viewpoint of the frankfurt - "Hold me close, it's cold in here...I need you so much," and something about not touching the ground which is a disqualification or a sizable deduction so Frank's musical hot dog is correct on that account. It is possible that every Frank Stallone song has been about competitive eating and he is waiting for his brother Sly to star in a competitive eating movie to reveal this elusive truth (Hollywood pitch - It's "Rocky 3" meets "Rocky 4" but with more cheesesteaks) I will let you decide as here are the lyrics verbatim (except for the part where I replaced, "Darlin'" with "some hot dog and buns") to Frank Stallone's greatest anthem, "Far from Over."

"This is the end
You made your choice and now my chance is over
I thought I was in
You put me down and say I'm goin' nowhere
Save me [some hot dog and buns]
I am down but I am far from over
Give me somethin'
I need it all 'cause I am runnin' over
Back in the race, I'm movin' in 'cause I am getting closer
I'm diggin' in

I want it more than anything I've wanted
I am down but I am far from over"

It's Nathan's Hot Dog Qualifying season and it time to cue up that walkman and crank that cassette. Hang the banner, set the table, and start the clock. It's ten minutes of gurgitating glory and digestive defeat. Plant City is going to be a bun buzzer beater, a maelstrom of meat, all out wiener war...that's right sports and music fans - I may be down. I may have been out, but like Frank Stallone, I am far from over.

KATY PERRY, FORMERLY GUILTY PLEASURE, NOW JUST PLEASURE
(March 30th 2015)

I have been listening to some of the Katy Perry deeper cuts, like "Waking up in Vegas" ("Get up and shake the glitter off your clothes") and the accusatory "Mannequin" ("You're not a man, you're a mannequin.") and beginning to think that her first album may be her best (not including her contemporary Christian music release with her name spelled wrong.) Don't get me wrong, her star pop power ballads ring across her entire oeuvre and my favorite still remains, "Firework." According to her movie, "Katy Perry: Part of Me" which I saw opening day, "Firework" is also her favorite to perform. Once in Bangkok to prevent offered sexual shenanigans, I commissioned four strippers to dance to "Firework." It wasn't Bob Fosse, but it was pretty good choreography short notice and my libido, ears, and boner's spirits remained raised.

I own every Katy Perry song, three T-shirts, and have seen her twice in concert. I also received in the mail recently three of her costumed outfits, including one that has whipped crème canisters as a bra. I contend these outfits are for a potential fund raising competitive eating stunt, but let's be honest, if I make it back to Bangkok, I know a lady boy bar with the talent to pull off the dance moves to "Peacock" ("Are you brave enough to let me see your peacock. What you waiting it's time to show it off. Don't be a shy kind of guy, I bet it's beautiful").

At Madison Square Garden, Katy and I shared a moment near the end of her expertly choreographed musical production. She was flying overhead on a balloon contraption and I looked up, locked eyes, and tilted my Goorin Brothers newsboy hat towards her. She looked down, spotted me among the mothers and 12-year old girls and nodding back with a tilt of her invisible hat. It was a real moment, man. Of course, a couple nights later at the Barclay Center I was in the cheap seats among Jason Kidd's retired number banner so Katy couldn't possibly see me up there. I could barely see her (although her double smiley face brassiere did help.)

Katy, is of course, performing at the Super Bowl this Sunday. My hometown Patriots are also playing (I was born in Beantown but have lived in NYC for twenty years making me the conundrum that is both a Masshole and a New Yawker.) It's going to be a banner day and I intend to wear my newly minted "Crazy Legs - number 33" Patriots jersey (note: if you are ordering from the NFL shop you really have to spend 3 bills for a quality jersey, the buck fifty ones are pretty chintzy, while for the same price at the NHL store you can get a near game ready Bruins jersey). Halftime will be Katy Perry time and it will be hard to focus on the food, even as a competitive eater, but here are some tips from a pro on how a casual diner can eat into the fourth quarter without slowing or suffering from "a reversal of fortune."

1. There is no deflategate when it comes to passed hors d'oeuvres. Feel free to squeeze the extra juice out of jalepeno poppers or the unwanted cheese run-off from mozzarella sticks.

2. I am serious about the 7 layer dip, only eat the first 3 layers.

3. The end of the first quarter is a great time to cut back on the carbonated beer and switch to whiskey or diet whiskey, if you are on weight watchers.

4. Proper chicken wing technique is essential. Please refer to previous posts regarding the Magna Carta of Meat, the Meat Umbrella, and The Drexel Hill Reverse Smokeshifter.

5. Celebrate Patriots touchdowns by spiking a geoduck into a bowl of baked beans.

6. New England Clam Chowder is the only kind of chowder there is. Don't serve any of that mouth breathing Eli Manning Manhattan crap. Potatoes, Clams, Elmer's Glue - that is all you need for a good chowder or chouwda as it is correctly pronounced.

7. Don't even think of changing the channel at halftime. Katy Perry is way cuter than any puppies and turn the volume up when she sings, "Firework." What are you un-American?

Katy may be my favorite 1/2 time performer, but my second favorite band (behind The Tubes) is not performing at half time of the Super Bowl. Indeed, The Knobs - a three piece punk band with a tuba as one of the pieces, was not even asked to audition to join Katy (they gave the spot to Lenny Kravitz and I hear he didn't even have to audition.) I asked The Knobs if they would take some time away from their upcoming album "Denim on Denim" to record something for the Super Bowl - something Katy Perry would notice and be proud of - Something she would notice and perhaps ask me on a date to the Corner Bistro, where she would flip her multicolored hair and say things like, "That Knobs song has some great guitar riffs - is the same guy as on their first album, "Live in Siberia"? Oh Katy. Anyway, The Knobs recording under the moniker "Elvis Helmet" put out this epic anthem, "Pat Riot 2015" Katy - the video is here.

What is that? You remember the first Elvis Helmet song "Pat Riot" and the video from 7 years ago as the Patriots were heading into the Super Bowl against New York with an undefeated season on the line. You mean this one?

...well, I mean, there was some slight hubris there. Yeah, some Icarus wax wing stuff, but isn't better to crash to Earth on melted dreams than to never try to fly to the highest height. I mean truly if I am going to fly into the Sun, I would want to do it with you, Katy Perry.

THE TRUE FOOD OUTLAWS ARE IN CHICAGO (March 1st, 2015)

More than any other human on the planet, I would like to have a beer with Bill Murray. You know Bill Murray's walk. It's more of a strut or stutter step filled not with hubris, but with a smirk and some effervescence. You can see it in his John Winger character from Stripes, as he pays for his shoe shine and exits with, "My philosophy: a hundred dollar shine on a three dollar pair of shoes." Bill Murray is from Chicago and I wish I could get a copy of the Cubs game where he sat in for Harry Caray and called everyone on the other team bums, derided the Canadian National Anthem, insulted the umpires' fashion sense and pointed out that the Cubs shouldn't have to play day games because they like to party all night. He also supports cutting off beer after the eighth inning because, "anybody who can't get drunk before the 8th inning doesn't belong here." Bill Murray is an outlaw.

I know some other outlaws in Chicago, the true food outlaws of America — Glutton Force Five. It would be wrong to call Glutton Force Five simply a food truck (Glutton Force Five) and a brick-and-mortar place in a mall (Taco in a Bag.) Glutton Force Five is a food lifestyle brand. Run by Pat "Deepdish" Bertoletti, who handles the food creation part, and Tim "Gravy" Brown, who handles the magical marketing and promotion, Glutton Force Five is as kick-ass as food gets.

As I stared at the graffiti art stained side of the food truck (besides the likeness of Gravy and Deepdish in space suits, other mascots include PartyBot, a drunk robot, a pink Unicorn whose name I don't know and Mr. Snugglesworth, Gravy's porky bulldog), I asked Gravy why he started the distinctive food lifestyle brand and he said he always wanted a real life "R" rated version of a Johns Hughes movie to become his existence. I can ascertain from many late nights spend with Gravy that he has achieved his dream. He once tried to cash in his mortgage check at a strip club in Indianapolis asking for all singles, he played drugs roulette with a baggie of pharmaceuticals the middle of a tiki bar, and after a blueberry pie eating contest to commemorate the 25th anniversary of Stand by Me, he jumped into a creek naked inviting the entire crowd with him. Some would call those nights epic, eccentric or historic, but Gravy called them Friday, Wednesday and Sunday, respectively. As Gravy launched Glutton Force Five, he held down a day job doing marketing for HVac while at night marketing The Admiral strip club (his "Comic Strip Live" at the peeler joint during Chicago's Comicon was a monster hit due to enlisting Harmony, Dakota, and Bambi as a topless Darth Vader being flanked by two topless Stormtroopers. The ensuing concurrent combination of high SAT scores and premature ejaculation has never been topped.

Deepdish went to culinary school at Kendall University and while his classmates were setting up mis-en-place on the line at fine restaurants in Chicago and New York, Deepdish was working as a fish monger, at a giant catering place, and traveling the intestinal byways of America on weekends as Major League Eating's #2 eater. At the catering job while cooking hundreds of duck breast, he removed all the cooked skin and made duck skin tacos with homemade salsa verde and tortillas. It was one of the most delicious and decadent foods I've tasted. He quit all those jobs to focus on the food creations his palette dreams of — flavors that on paper would be diametrically opposed but together form a harmony of outrageous deliciousness. A lifetime fan of biscuits and gravy, but living in a Mexican neighborhood, he created a chorizo breakfast gravy that is generously layered upon his homemade chips, garnished with tomatillo sour cream, pepper jack and green onion. It is vicious, spicy, and addictive. Also, like the Glutton Force Five brand itself, unapologetic.

There are no appetizers in the Glutton Force Five universe — just mains and dessert. After selling out of queso cheesesteak Shepherd's Pie, the food truck would offer Elvis bread pudding with a banana peanut butter frosting. Taco in a Bag makes fresh donuts to order with three dipping sauces to follow a meal that might include, The Norberto (spicy braised chicken thigh, sautéed pepper and onion, pepper jack, avocado jalapeño sauce, dried cranberry, Sriracha drizzle), The Sudo (black bean and corn salsa, citrus marinated shrimp, romaine, cilantro and lime) or cheeseburger nachos (ground beef cooked in old style beer, cheddar sauce, poppy seed and crumbled potato chips, special sauce) or all three.

Chicago is an anti-food truck town (food trucks can only operate on private property limiting them to festivals and private parties) and Taco in a Bag is 45 minutes from downtown Chicago in the Spring Hill Mall because Gravy and Deepdish received a year's free lease by winning the Food Network's Food Court Wars. Rumor has it that Taco in a Bag will open a Chicago proper location soon, undoubtedly becoming a foodie haven for those who miss Hot Doug's Hot Dogs. Gravy and Deepish's vision for Glutton Force Five's future may be more esoteric than the staid Chicago restaurant community is willing to commit to — it's an unabashed bacchanalia of food, a culinary "Caligula," an orgy of '80s movies, tamarind spice, punk rock, and two shirtless men riding a pink unicorn. Simply put, Glutton Force Five are America's True Food Outlaws and one day I expect to be in line behind Bill Murray at Taco in a Bag and we can finally have that beer.

THE CREAM PUFF INSIDE THE OCTAGON-SHAPED CANNOLI SHELL
(November 24th, 2014)

Marcos "The Monster" Owen's hands, strangled his opponent barehanded. His opponent's insides came gushing and squishing out in a spray as the hard exterior crumbled into broken bits. And then, before his sweet opponent could tap out, "The Monster" raised what was left of his defeated, dying opponent and bit into it, ala Mike Tyson. I don't know if what Marcos did is legal in MMA fighting, but it is in MLE cannoli-eating. Marcos is on his Derek Jeter-esque retirement tour from Major League Eating, but the only gifts the talented gurgitator receives on his swan song are free food. (Note: No swans were eaten on his "closing mouth" farewell tour).

Will Marcos, a mild-mannered TSA employee, take what he has learned — every bite, chew, and swallow — from his years on the competitive eating circuit and apply it to his burgeoning mixed martial arts career? I know he has the manual-to-oral dexterity in cannoli-eating (breaking the world record with 34 Ferrara's cannolis in six minutes at this year's Feast of San Gennaro contest), but inside the octagon, eating your opponent is probably frowned upon. If Dana White, the man who reinvented MMA fighting, could have worked in cannibalism along with the arm bars, chokeholds, and rabbit punches of his sport he would have (Note: No rabbits were wrested during the cannoli-eating contest).

I won this very contest in 2009 with 20 cannolis in six minutes and improved five years later to 21 cannolis in the same six minutes. In Major League Eating this is known as "Cannoli Drift", the glacial movement of ricotta cheese and sugar when surrounded by tectonic pastry shell. However, my consolation, bestowed upon me by festival producer Mort Berkowitz and PR maverick Les Schecter, was to be invited to Ferrara's attempt to break the Guinness Book of World Records for largest cannoli. Post contest I spoke with Ferrara's head baker Ernest Lepore about what it takes to make the world's largest Italian pastry. Ernest said he was baking the shell in three parts and making six extra parts in case of breakage. The filling would be 300 pounds. I, of course, asked about the leftovers. Perhaps it was OSHA requirements or that pesky NYC department of health, but he said, a fresher non-record-breaking cannoli stuff would be handed out in cups (ala Steve Martin's pizza-in-a-cup). I often extol that the greatest sports memorabilia is the leftovers from a competitive eaters plate and having consumed both Hungry Charles Hardy's rookie hot dog detritus in the late 90s and 15 years later, his son Fast Eddie Hardy's remaining half dog, I asked Ernest if I could, with a signed waiver, taste a little of victory. With his silver hair and sparkling eyes, he just winked at me and made off in cloud of confectionary sugar. Ernest and Ferrara's unveiled a record-setting 305-pound cannoli. This author can neither confirm nor disconfirm that in the victorious moment, while Grand Street celebrated, the giant cannoli was reduced to 304 pounds.

In 2001, as a thank you to the city of New York, Major League Eating held the first cannoli-eating contest to kick off the Feast of San Gennaro and encourage New Yorkers to gather together after the horrible September day that had occurred. No money, either in fees or prize, was taken or awarded and Major League Eating has kept that tradition for 13 years. One year, there was $95,000 total prize purse offered at other contests on the weekend but eaters like Tim "Eater X" Janus and Badlands Booker decided instead to partake in the cannoli freebie. The only prize is a Luciano Pavoratti box set, which is actually just a box with Pavarotti's picture on it and no music inside (Note: The victory box was hurt or at least stolen. No word yet from Elizabeth's Street's 5th precinct if there are any leads, but clearly this was a crime that violated the moral code or the mascarpone code or something.) On the positive side as a protest against the instant access social media of today like live tweeting an event, a drawing-on-location art class from New York's School of Visual Arts live sketched the cannoli contest. Post contest, I saw the drawings and they all captured the best side of my stomach.

As the only competitor who has eaten in all 13 annual cannoli-eating contests people always ask how I prepare for the Sisyphean contest. It is a punishing discipline as the shell will cut up the roof of one's mouth and the filling will inflate someone like the Stay Puff Marshmallow Man (for older cinema viewers the contest is a version of, "Leave the gums, take the cannoli.") You can't just cram for this contest

— it takes a year-round dedication to eating Italian pastries. I actually warm up with French pastries in the morning, like crew rowers rising early to get the softer waves, before tackling the rougher shells of Italian pastries at night. I could say I train on "Osso Di Morte" from DiRoberta's (a chalking wonderful caramelized dense cookie) or the petrified bagel-like (in a good way) taralli from Rocco's, but the truth is I do one thing before the contest. I go to DiPalo's on the corner of Grand and Mott and I open my nostrils. That is right, I step into the venerable Italian delicatessen and like a Pavlovian response to soppresata and fresh mozzarella I eat an olfactory meal and am ready for dessert (at the contest, outside DiPalo's door.) It is similar to the scene in Roald Dahl's Charlie and the Chocolate Factory where precocious Violet Beauregarde eats the three-meal chewing gum and swells up like a blueberry, Willy Wonka sighs, "It always goes wrong when we come to the dessert." (Note: Gene Wilder added another, "always" — take that Johnny Depp).

Wonka saying, "It always goes wrong when we come to the dessert," could be predicting my cannoli contest outcome, but since I have been eating competitively I don't enjoy the Feast of San Gennaro the same way. So I have a tradition. Just as the cannoli contest kicks off the 11-day festival, I arrive on the last night and buy a sausage and peppers sandwich (usually from Johnny Fasullo on Grand and Mullberry) and one cannoli. This year I sampled the Alleva cheese-filled cannoli and found it light and airy. I also added some Umberto's Clam House fried shrimp — Umberto's has moved locations a bunch, but historically is known for their clams on the half shell and a good place for a mob assassination. At $17 dollars for a soda and fried shrimp, my wallet was massacred, but the medium tomato sauce on top made it all good. Besides on the closing night of the Feast, the workers at Umberto's were more concerned about collecting free goldfish from the fish vendor, who was giving away bags of live fish. One Umberto's worker scored a tank too, but when I asked how much for breaded deep-fried goldfish, he paused, as if contemplating a price (no goldfish were... you get the idea.)

Monday morning, my tradition continues as I walk through the decimated streets of Little Italy, refuse- and puddle-filled, like Bourbon Street on the Wednesday morning after Tuesday Mardi Gras. I pop into Piedmonte Ravoli where I decimate their buccatini stock (a hard-to-find dry pasta in the shape of a tight tube) and then I wander into DiPalo's where all three of the next generation of the family is behind the counter. I pick up Lou Di Palo's just released book, Di Palo's Guide to the Essential Foods of Italy and talk with Lou (Lou is the brother who looks like Chaz Paliminterri, while brother Sal looks like Matt Lauer and sister Marie just looks beautiful.) He is proud of the book and doesn't cite the Martin Scorsese forward or Pete Hamill or the celeb chef endorsements — he says he wanted to write the book with storytelling, the way he learned to love Italian food. I have a story of my own love of Italian food, as I get two books — one for my father whose aunts moved to America and didn't speak to each other due to some long forgotten feud, but made great ravioli; and one book for my unofficial uncle, Paul Camarto, who as a kid I called, "Tomato." Uncle Tomato learned his pizza craft from Joe Timpone of Boston's Santarpio's fame. Joe worked for 44 years at Santarpio's and I still order a "Timpone" — extra cheese, garlic, and sausage in his honor. Uncle Tomato with Amy Bucci would relocate to the West Coast and open a pizza place in the East Bay that turned into a disco at 10 p.m. Finally, near the abandoned Heinz ketchup factory in Emeryville, California, Paul "Uncle Tomato" Camarto, Amy Bucci and another partner, Les Julian (now retired) opened Bucci's, an Italian restaurant in a 1900s industrial building. Uncle Tomato refused for years to put his carbonara pizza on the menu, but would make it for me, pulling the half-cooked pie out to throw on egg, cheese, and pancetta. It is my favorite food place in the world and even when Pixar moved to Emeryville, Uncle Tomato kept the carbonara pizza off the menu. I believe the off-the-menu carbonara pizza may be the reason for Pixar's long delay regarding The Incredibles 2, but no one will confirm that for me.

Back in the olfactory heaven of DiPalo's, Lou offers to take the books in the back to sign them so he doesn't get grease on them. I say that without the grease, how will anyone know that the signatures are real and I share my story, passed down to me from Uncle Tomato. Uncle Tomato and his gang were raised in Syracuse and the local sausage of note was Squadrito Foods. It was said that the daughter of the purveyor, although not a cheerleader, was the most sought after prom date of high school girls. Since she worked most afternoons in the shop, it was thought that the smell of dried Italian sausage and fresh cheese clung to her like perfume, making her, in a Pavlovan/Freudian way to be irresistible to the hungry opposite sex. I had a sausage eating contest in Syracuse at the New York State Fair and even after five pounds of the sponsor's sausage I drove to Squadrito, where the daughter had taken over the shop. I bought and later that night cooked the sausage, which I and my then girlfriend, agreed was the finest sausage on the planet (and perhaps a fennel-laden aphrodisiac.)

Last year, after 64 years, Squadrito Foods closed as that high school girl was about to turn 70. DiPalo's is still open after 100 years and if you want to know where the best Italian food is in NYC, ask Lou, Sal, or Marie where their products end up before being put on the plate. Thirteen years of cannoli contest eating is a drop in the tomato sauce compared to Squadrito's or DiPalo's or Bucci's, but I am still hungry for more. Rumor has it that Bensonhurst's Italian festival may hold their first MLE cannoli contest… if they say, "Mangia!" I'll say get me a bib!

When Major League Eating goes "Top Gun" with the Shadow Hawks Squadron at Atsugi Naval Base, Japan.
(October 19th, 2014)

"I'm Maverick, you're Goose," says Major League Eating MC Diamond Dave Keating to me as we bake in the sun on the flight line at Atsugi Naval Base, Japan. We are on our last stop of our Navy Entertainment tour and one of the few civilians allowed on the flight path. The argument is moot as soon as an FA-18G from the Shadow Hawks Squadron lands and pulls up 100 feet from us. As someone approaches the cockpit with a black brick on a long pole and begins to rub it across the glass, I assume that the New York City squeegee guys have commuted to Japan. However, it turns out that the device removes static that accumulates in flight. How much static? Enough to eject the pilot from the cockpit, and not from the ejector seat. LTJG Nortz and LT Kinghorn answer our many questions about the awesome plane in front of us. LT Kinghorn explains that the Shadow Hawks are considered nebbish compared to the other squadrons (we can see the fiercesome logos of the Warlords and the Royal Mace on other nearby planes) because their planes carry only one bomb and they are tech geeks. However, no plane goes out without a Shadow Hawk escort because what they do have is the finest radar jamming receiver in history. I even notice any bad thoughts that I have were quickly scrambled (OK that might be the jetlag instead). I asked about picking up radio transmissions and they said they created "Growler Radio" where more often than not, "Sweet Caroline" is played while flying at mach speed. The DJs that have been performing with us, perk up and offer their remix of Miley Cyrus and "Ride of the Valkyries."

We then head inside the hangar to meet LCDR "Mongo" Mattson. The military has the finest radar, tracking, and surveillance equipment in the world. When a piece of detection equipment becomes obsolete, Major League Eating requisitions its use to keep tabs on buffets and all-you-can-eat restaurants around the globe. Mongo Mattson was already known to Major League Eating because to win the first pick in the Shadow Hawks fantasy baseball league he ate a spicy pickle and five and half hot dogs in five minutes (a cross disciplined athlete). MLE eaters Adrian Morgan, Michelle Lesco, and I asked if Mongo would like to join us in a rib and chicken wing sprint. He did, while still in his flight suit. It was an amazing 90 second victory for Michelle Lesco, but Mongo hung tough cleaning his ribs like Joey "Jaws" Chestnut and using the meat umbrella technique for the wings (Mongo is an eating prodigy).

We meet CDR Ernie "Bert" Winston who graciously judges the contest. Winston is from Metairie, LA so he and Adrian (from Baton Rouge) talk beignets, crawfish, and how hard it is to get good grits in Japan. I corner Mongo to ask what he does. He is a EA-18G pilot and I ask what it feels like to fly one of the "Speed Racer" like jets. He said take-offs are just pure adrenalin, especially off a carrier when the

60,000 pound plane goes 160 miles in 2.5 seconds. Mongo added that sometimes high in the air, the rainbows are amazing and he feels an inner calm and serenity usually seen only in bubble bath commercials. However, landing on a carrier deck at night is a much different feeling. Mongo describes it as, "crapping your pants and orgasming at the same while feeling really happy that you did." I hope publishing Mongo's thoughts doesn't get him into trouble with the squadron, but hey, I can now imagine what it's like to land a war plane in the pitch black dark on a carrier deck, although I won't be attempting to duplicate the feeling in casual company. I promised Mongo that when he is done serving his country, Major League Eating would be happy to serve him some free food.

The next day was the Bon Odori open base festival, where 10,000 Japanese civilians are allowed on base to see the Navy Entertainment acts and interact with the American service men and women. The most popular place was MH-60R, a swanky super fancy helicopter. The tail is painted with cherry blossoms and Koi fish, but don't let that fool you into thinking that this helicopter isn't badass. AFCM Greg Behrends of the Warlords Squadron takes great care of every inch of this supreme flying machine. Each eater sat in the cockpit and learned what controls did what. Since this was after our eating pro-am and I was digesting 21 hot dogs and buns I found the MH-60R (or "Romeo" for short) to be very very comfortable.

The eating contest preceded the rain and our pro-am partners ranged from Yoshihiro Kono, a Japanese Corpsman, to Romalic Buggage from Kenner, LA whose job it is to work on the ejector seats (at the five minute mark of the contest, Romalic looked like he wanted to eject his stomach so he just ate the buns and I took over with the franks). HN Taeson Park was paired with Michelle Lesco who, showing off, did twenty HDBs in three minutes and then coasted the rest of the way. That gave Adrian "The Rabbit" Morgan time to catch up and his team went onto victory. Lesco was gracious in defeat, but I saw the competitive glint in her eye and I wonder if an ice cream shortage was about to commence on base.

This Navy Entertainment tour had the most synergy between the performing acts as DJs Baby Electronica played the Major League Eating intro music like Survivor's "Eye of the Tiger," as Adrian Morgan entered the eating ring with a towel around his neck and his hands on the voluminous shoulders of headliner Kelly Bell - The Troops, all big American movie fans, got to see a real life enactment of Rocky Balboa on the shoulders of Clubber Lang, pumping up the crowd. The Kelly Bell Band would rock through rain and the DJs found their dance floor audience as late as 1 am in an on base bar above the Officer's Club. It was true Navy Entertainment synchronicity.

I have been a competitive eater for thirteen years and despite my dwindling skills and shrinking stomach, I would eat for The Troops anywhere, anytime in the world, any holiday, and any food. Why? Because that is the hours that they keep. While America celebrates, rests, and vacations, the military does not. Navy Entertainment and the Morale, Welfare, and Recreation divisions on all the bases and ships work tirelessly. One of our MWR folks at Atsugi is Jay Mozila, who not only made sure all the entertainers had everything they needed to perform, but also called in favors to get us into aircrafts and onto flight lines. His MWR counterpoint Lena Childs invited the gang over to her house for ribs (no easy invitation, when Ribfest champ Michelle Lesco is hungry). The Atsugi MWR head honcho is Paul Perry and he always tells me I won't see him next time because he is going to retire after twenty-eight years, but guess what, I always see him. His wife and daughter have taken to military base life and Paul has even sacrificed his comic book addiction while spending almost thirty years of military and MWR service. It is people like Paul Perry who make America run, even if they do it from Japan. It is teams like the Shadow Hawks and Warlords, who put America and its ideals, values, hopes, and dreams before themselves, their families, and their lives. My twenty one or so hot dogs and buns may give me an upset stomach, but the rumble of complaint is quickly drown out by the beating of my heart, filled with pride, awe, and respect for our armed forces and the men and women who serve. Upon my return to the States, the next time I see a flag, or hear the National Anthem, I will think of those at Atsugi Naval Base and truly know that my freedom (and stomach) is in safe hands.

Navy Entertainment and Major League Eating Continued: Okinawa Is Filled with Marines and One Amazing Female Competitive Eater
(October 18th, 2014)

Have you seen Demi Moore in GI Jane? Movies would lead us to believe that formerly demure Demi, buffed up and head shaved, could best Viggo Mortensen. As if "One Crazy Summer"'s Cassandra Eldgridge could take Aragorn from "Lord of the Rings." That is just Hollywood hoohah and doesn't happen in real life. Except I saw it happen in Okinawa, Japan on the military base from a 110-pound female competitive eater who beat all the Marines, Navy, and Air Force soldiers, and couple male pro-eaters to boot.

The history of the female gurgitator is a short one. From Japan, Takako Akasaka once ate 90 ostrich egg omelets. Known as "The Sweet Queen," in 2000 she decimated New York city pastry shops and ate a then-record 22 Nathan's hot dogs in 12 minutes at the 4th of July frankfest chowdown. Like female powerlifters giving way to fitness instructors, these days Japan is dominated by eaters like Gal Sone, who is known for her nail polish as much as her curry consumption. In America, where there is no title nine in competitive eating, Carlene LaFevre, a former aerobics instructor, would compete with the men, and even beat her husband to win the posole eating crown. Sonya "The Black Widow" Thomas, a Burger King manager at Andrews Airforce Base, would become the first female phenom — eating 47 dozen oysters in eight minutes, 49 soft tacos in nine, 65 hardboiled eggs in six minutes forty seconds (take that Cool Hand Luke), and consumed 10 percent of her body weight with 11 pounds of cheesecake in six minutes. When asked how she did it, Sonya would reply, "I just beat the men." She is still active and holds over 30 major league eating records.

However, 2014 has become year of the "I am Woman, Hear my Stomach Roar." Miki Sudo, who entered competitive eating after having a 12-pound bowl of Pho soup for lunch, defeated Sonya at the Nathan's contest this year to win her first pink Pepto Belt. In Chicago, I ate next to Miki in Kimchi and felt great about my 4.5 pounds, until I noticed that Miki had lapped me and quaffed nine pounds in the eight-minute contest. Also entering the fray is Michelle "Cardboard Shell" Lesco — her nickname perhaps due to the fact she often accidentally consumes the take-out containers that her voluminous food orders are packaged in. Michelle is a debris food specialist and won the Chicago Ribfest, stripping meat from bone in a show of manual-to-oral dexterity usually not seen in mammals. Michelle was in Okinawa for Navy Entertainment, eating in a pro-am with Navy sailor soldier Wommack. She was eating against pros Adrian "A Drain" Morgan and myself as well as our Marine and Air Force representatives. Her plate of 20 regulation Nathan's hot dogs sat cooling on the stage. Diamond Dave Keating, the MC became a human megaphone, screaming, "We've got the go-no go from Langley, I'll see ya when I see ya, see ya on the otherside, smoke 'em if you've got them, it's time to drink from the volcano, ride the dragon, light this candle, count down from ten..." and at one, like Cookie Monster's wife, Michelle Lesco inhaled 20 hot dogs and buns in five minutes. That is right, while the men were heading towards double digits, Michelle had finished everything on her plate and was putting mustard on one of Wommack's dogs and cheering him on. She evaporated those dogs as if the Okinawa base had provided one of its top secret enzyme ray guns (I cannot confirm nor disconfirm the existence of the Digester 2000). Afterwards I conducted an exclusive interview with Michelle Lesco and to her credit, she did not belch once while answering.

1. How is the Navy Entertainment Tour going?

It's amazing, we've had a lot of fun eating with the troops and giving them some pointers on being the best competitive eaters they can be and using the strategies with varying success. We've seen what normal civilians never see and talking to the servicemen and women is the best part of the trip — and I jumped into a waterfall at Senryuu Falls and that was pretty great.

2. Have you been overseas much? What is your impression of Japan?

This is my first trip overseas and I want to see everything because it is all brand new to me — I love local sights and we have gone off base and toured temples, hiked, and ate a lot of food — all weird stuff I bought at a grocery store and shared it at a community meal trying to figure out what it was. I had one piece of food that looked like a skin sample on a slide that did not taste good.

3. Between Sonya Thomas, Miki Sudo, and you there is a pro-eating female phenomenon going on in 2014. How did this happen?

A big part of it was when Nathan's made a separate womens division and it gave Sudo and I a big opportunity to join MLE. We are a competitive group of girls, it's not that we feel disadvantaged or handicapped by our gender, we know we can beat the guys, and can go balls to the wall or I guess, ovaries to the wall, for lack of a better saying.

4. You are known as an altruistic eater and promote charities for folks to donate to at each event, with the reward of meeting you and talking pro-eating. You've raised thousands of dollars. How do you choose the charities and how do people donate in relation to your contests?

I choose charities that raise funds for issues I care about and try to tie it into the contest. We did a wing contest and donated to Wings of Karen, a fellow competitive eater's breast cancer charity started for his mother. It also has to be easy to donate online so I can track their contributions and personally thank them. Perhaps when I get back to the U.S. I can figure out a charity that benefits children of military members. I am a high school math teacher so anytime I can provide for tomorrow's youth, I do. I don't consider myself a role model, but try to make good choices because kids are impressible.

Last Labor Day, the kids and adults were mighty impressed when Miki, Michelle, and Sonya sweep the Buffalo Wing Festival chicken wing eating contest, beating all the men and causing a ripple in the poultry market worldwide.

Michelle Lesco would like to thank everyone involved in the Navy Entertainment Tour, the Morale, Welfare, and Recreation staff on base, and most of all the men and women of the US Military.

Sasebo Naval Base, Japan : Home of the Fastest BBQ Pork Sliders in Competitive Eating
(October 15th 2014)

When you think of great BBQ pork, stripped sauce-soaked goodness, you probably think of Clarksdale, or Walterboro, or some tiny town in Texas. What if I told you the best I've had was in Sasebo, Japan on the Navy Base? It was so good; I ate fifteen sandwiches in ten minutes. Granted, I am a Major League Eater and on a Navy Entertainment tour, bringing competitive eating to the troops in pro-am events but that pork...

I wrote about this tour's first stop at Yokosuka in my previous Huffington Post piece, but you are probably wondering how does someone become the Bob Hope of the hot dog, traveling the world, entertaining the armed forces. Since, 2009 I have been on six tours to bases like Sigonella in Sicily, Souda Bay in Crete, Chinhae in Busan, Yongsan Garrison in Seoul, Bases in Guam and Diego Garcia and even Guantanamo Bay in Cuba (Gitmo became Eatmo for a Labor Day Jazz Fest). In Japan, I have entertained at Camp Fuji (donuts), Yokosuka (ramen), Atsugi (burritos), and Okinawa (hot dogs). I have been fortunate to do eating exhibitions, contest, or meet-and-greets on warships like the USS Fitzgerald, nuclear subs like the US Ohio, and on this tour in Sasebo, the very cool carrier, USS Bonhommie Richard (great ice cream!) The best part is meeting the enlisted men and women of all divisions of the armed forces and talking food and life with them. It is simply, the most important thing I have done as a competitive eater and an American.

How did it happen? In addition to Major League Eating's support, I owe my good fortune to two people in particular. Ari Nisman of Degy Entertainment is one of the biggest music bookers in the business. He specializes in college tours and bookings and the military relies on folks like Ari to send bands overseas to entertain the troops. He saw me on the Emeril Show and thought that competitive eating is like rock-and-roll with food, plus the demographic of young military men and women might dig the gustatory gladiators of Major League Eating. He then contacted Karen Fritz, who runs Navy Entertainment worldwide, bringing everything from bands to chefs to athlete's around the world. Karen is on the road more than she is home, making sure that even the most remote installations get American entertainers and some fun. Every division of the armed forces has a Morale, Welfare, and Recreation Division (MWR) that works on bases and ships to provide entertainment — popcorn machines on ships, movie nights on base, snorkeling trips and a million other events from 40,000 person open base festivals to a lounge where a sailor can Skype home (or play video games). This is not an easy job.

Karen and Ari agreed that the spectacle of MLE's eaters devouring food fast would be a great opener for some of the bands that they send on tour. In Saebo, we had the help of two great acts to entertain the Naval Base. Kareem and Vito, two world class DJs from Providence, RI form "Baby Electronica" by donning LED light up helmets and glasses (think of them as Daft Punker) and spinning, scratching, and dropping beats with all the bells and whistles. They remixed the eaters' intros so that Adrian "The Rabbit" Morgan could pump the crowd up with "Eye of the Tiger," and Michelle "No Leftovers" Lesco could chomp to the beat of Flogging Molly. Sadly, a forty minute Phish jam, doesn't quite work for my intro, but Baby Electronica got the crowd on their feet and ready for a pro-am chowdown. Each pro-eater lead their team of two service men or women for a cumulative total of BBQ pork sliders in ten minutes. I was joined by two E5 ranked sailors, Walker and Mattson, to tackle the delicious BBQ pork sliders (provided by Brodie's, a stellar on base restaurant). Our judges were members from the Kelly Bell Band, who were kind enough to sit in the spray zone before their gig and total the consumption. It was a BBQ bun buzzer beater, as Team Lesco ate 30, Team Rabbit 28, and Team Crazy Legs 27 $\frac{3}{4}$. Walker, Mattson, and I were a mere three sandwich stuff at the end away from victory. We should have chipmunked.

If Blues Funk Bands were competitive eaters then the Kelly Bell Band would be the top fifty ranked eaters all chomping in harmony. Traveling from Charm City, Baltimore this party band has gone all over the world for Navy Entertainment. They spent July 4th in Bahrain during Ramadan and made it the party place to be in the Middle East. At every Navy Entertainment gig, they give away their new album on a downloadable card (the military travels light). They spent a week on the USS Stennis from Pearl Harbor to San Diego performing six different shows, never repeating songs, making a military maneuver into a dance floor dance-off (like "Footloose" on the water, sailor soldiers are not allowed to dance in uniform, but rumor has it the band was so good, demerits were issued for illegal boogying.) Lead man and headliner, Kelly Bell was a pro wrestler for thirteen years in the Mid Atlantic region and wrestled greats like Jerry Lawler and "Superfly" Jimmy Snuka, almost always as a heel (wrestling bad guy). The insults he would hurl at Dundalk's working class folks would earn him state trooper escorts out of the arena at the end of the night. It's odd, because in the phat blues setting of the band, his smile is as wide as the Chesapeake Bay. He is without a doubt one of the nicest guys in the music business. The rest of the band is more than equal to the task - Drummer John Buell is a Berklee trained master who keeps the beat like Adrian Morgan eats Twinkies. Derrick Dorsey plays base and has fingers that would serve him well on the pro-eating circuit; his manual dexterity would be useful at the Rouse's Crawfish Eating Championship. Ryan Fowler is a guitarists' guitarist. He knows every guitar, every cool case to carry it in, and can (jokingly) rip anything from Rick Springfield's "Jessie's Girl" to Black Sabbath. Word Eldridge backs up Kelly on vocals and congas and exudes such strength and power on stage that his lyrics rain down in the spray zone, like chicken wing bones from Michelle Lesco's plate. The guy I always keep my eyes (and ears) on is Ira Mayfield JR. Known as "Black Steel" Ira's steely gaze reminds me of Scatman Crothers' "Dick Halloran" from "The Shining," but instead of offering Doc some ice cream, he plays his guitar telepathically, thus entering and blowing the audience's mind. As a year round shorts wearing guy, I also noticed that Ira always keeps his shorts neatly creased which I respect. If they would record their soundcheck on CD, I would buy it. To be the opener for them is heaven (even if the competitive eaters leave the stage slick with hot dog juice or pulled pork detritus the band is still nice to us.)

The Sasebo crowd came out on a Tuesday night when the military starts Wednesday morning around 4 am and after the MLE pro-am, the blazing set by The Kelly Bell Band, Baby Electronica - DJs Kariim Hafez and Vito DeLuca JR, rocked the crowd at the Galaxy Club on base. I know little about dance music, hip hop, scratching or LED helmets, but these Providence, RI guys put on a master class. Granted, they didn't play any Katy Perry, but despite the difficulty of digesting fifteen pulled pork sliders I still was able to hit the dance floor and shake my bad stuff because of the way these guys create the vibe.

For the performers, it was a magical night and we hope for The Troops that some of our heartfelt thanks, respect, and awe carried over to them and provided them with a night of joy. My favorite band, The Tubes sings a song titled, "Proud to be an American." The Kelly Bell Band doesn't cover it and Baby Electronica knows you can't dance to it, but

Tuesday night in Sasebo, it was the soundtrack to the evening.

Eating for the Troops: Navy Entertainment in Yokosuka, Japan
(October 14th, 2014)

Have you ever passed a member of the armed forces in an airport and thanked him or her for their service? Or been at a major sporting event when an enlisted member of the Army, Air Force, Navy, Coast Guard, or Marine Corp was recognized by the announcer and the crowd stood and cheered? The sacrifices the American men and women make to serve our country are so steep, difficult, and challenging that when we acknowledge them in person, we feel good about ourselves and our country.

Now imagine performing for the troops, especially overseas where men and women are stationed far from their families and friends, often doing difficult jobs for long periods of time. In 2009 Navy Entertainment partnered with Major League Eating and has sent 15 competitive eaters on seven tours to bases in Italy, Greece, Guam, Diego Garcia, South Korea, Japan, and Gitmo.

I have been fortunate to be on six of those tours and as MLE often opens for a band with a Pro-Am, we not only eat for the troops, but with the troops — each MLE eater is paired with one or two military members and eats as a team.

We've also done ship shows, where we tour carriers, destroyers, and submarines. The feeling of performing for and with the troops is almost indescribable. The stories they have of their day-to-day lives and how they bring America with them everywhere they go fill one with a sense of history, pride, awe, and respect. After every contest we do a meet-and-greet and shake hands, sign autograph cards, talk about home and the future. At Guantanmo Bay, "Pretty Boy" Pete Davekos, the father of two young kids, had never spent more than two days away from his son and daughter. We met a female sailor soldier on her regulation one year commitment, who also had a young kid and she mentioned casually that her young son had just taken his first steps back home. Her service to our country meant that she had missed a huge milestone in her son's life. All of the sudden, Pete understood that commitment. Her calm demeanor describing her son's first steps was amazing as even today, simply thinking about her telling that story makes me tear up. Missing birthdays and graduations, first words and steps, are a party of military service so when Navy Entertainment can send a band, celebrities, or even competitive eaters to far away bases, we try to bring a little bit of home to the troops. The Navy Entertainment tours have been the most important part of my competitive eating career.

I am not allowed to divulge when I am performing for the troops until after I leave a base and travel elsewhere. I can reveal exclusively in this Huffington Post that three Navy Sailor Soldiers (Moore, Kehn, and Babb) are likely still digesting their Nathan's hot dogs from the Yokosuka, Japan Pro-Am the other day. Kehn and I tried to keep up with Babb and

Adrian "The Rabbit" Morgan (who on a previous Navy Entertainment tour ate twenty hard boiled eggs in 84 seconds against the CO and other members of the USS Fitzgerald Destroyer). Even Team Rabbit couldn't catch the awesome eating power of 120 pound Moore and 110 pound MLE ranked #9 in the world Michelle Lesco. Eating a major percentage of their body weight, Team Lesco went on to hot dog victory at the Liberty Center on Yokosuka's base. It was not a bun buzzer beater, but the troops enjoyed the show.

Adrian, Michelle, myself, and MLE MC Diamond Dave Keating then headed to the main stage where we contributed to the evening's pop, funk, and scratching (the complete Navy Entertainment tour includes bands A Great Big World, The Kelly Bell Band, and DJs Baby Electronica) with a Twinkie Off. The Rabbit got his revenge as he quaffed ten Twinkies in 24 seconds, a world record pace (Joey "Jaws" Chestnut ate 121 in six minutes at the Tunica Casino last year.) We then hung out and chatted with other members of the military as A Great Big World belted out, "Say Something", The Kelly Bell Band blew the roof off the theater with their unique funkadelic party tunes, and Baby Electronica turned the place upside down, Diana Ross remix style.

The Yokosuka Naval Base is an amazing place and strives to make everyone feel connected to those back home in America, but it is not easy. For one night though it felt like Coney Island on July 4th and Madison Square Garden on New Year's Eve. The members of Major League Eating on this tour could not have felt more honored, humbled, and proud to do our small part...we love to perform for the The Troops with every bite, chew, and swallow. For the Navy's Kehn, Moore, and Babb, I think they are doing a few extra sit ups today to work off some calories.

They Shoot Wild Harness Race Horses, Don't They?
(October 4th, 2014)

"Trotters or Flats in race four?" I asked a rail side spectator at the Tioga Downs Casino and Racetrack, as if I was a grizzled harness race veteran, looking for an inside tip. The truth was I was three races into my harness race knowledge and despite learning some of the terminology (trotters and flats has to do with how the horse gait, but don't hold me to it), I was losing badly. Riders, not jockeys, propel the horses around the turns as they sit, not Ben Hur chariot style, but leaning back in a sling and I noticed, unlike their jockey counterparts, there didn't seem to be a weight restriction. I kept losing money on a rider who looked a lot like Billy Joel, but I probably should have been focusing on the upcoming Chicken Spiedies eating contest sponsored by Lupo's. That, not the ponies, was my reason for taking in the mountain air at Tioga Downs, a scenic near live gaming casino in upstate New York. What exactly is a Spiedies and for the purposes of competitive eating, is it speedy?

The Lupo Spiedies (pronounced "speedees") are marinated cubes of meat — lamb originally, but now spun off to veal, venison, beef, pork and chicken — that are skewer cooked and placed in a special soft sesame seed top-split roll. Originally from Italy, "spiedo" means "spit" as in the grilling instrument, and Sam Lupo brought the sandwich (not the actual sandwich, but the idea of the sandwich) to Broome County in upstate NY and in 1951 started the Lupo's empire. Now onto its third generation with four stores and seven marinades (including the just released "buffalo flavor"), the chicken Spiedie entered the gustatory gladiator arena of competitive eating. Is it speedy? Well, chicken cubes can be dense and although these were moist and the buns, like fluffy tempurpedic pillows, each sandwich was an overstuffed $\frac{3}{4}$ of a pound. Since the contest was no dunking, this would be a battle of jaw strength and who should be the dominate eater in that regard — Joey "Jaws" Chestnut. Chestnut, channeling the Billy Joel harness rider, would do my potential prize purse in, while chomping his way to thirteen sandwiches — just barely, lapping my six. I was out of the prize money in harness racing and in competitive eating. Still, the Spiedies were delicious to the last bite and the distant mountains reflected in the setting sun making for a pleasant summer evening. I noticed Stephen Lupo handing out trays and foil to the eaters and that more than half the field was taking home their leftover Spiedies. I have only seen Michael "Per Diem" Parrish haul off leftover corn and hot dogs, never the rest of the field. As a Major League Eater, I feel if I have leftovers, I really haven't done my best in the contest. However, Badlands Booker and Marcos "The Monster" Owens seemed very pleased by their leftover sandwich collections.

I rode back with Badlands and The Monster and though it took only 4 hours to arrive, it took 6 hours to return. Competitive eaters, post-contest are known to get the munchies. Not from any illegal substances, but after a sweets contest, meat is desired (I once saw Badlands eat twenty-one cannolis and then line up for a sausage and peppers hero.) After a protein heavy contest, one's sweet tooth kicks in. Badlands and The Monster needed to stop every half hour on the ride home for sweet beverages, donuts and at one point some sort of loaded Doritos, which I could barely identify as human food (it seemed to be leaking neon lava). Their gas station consumption was the opening topic on a podcast I cohost titled, "Eating Disorder" on Sunday night at the Heritage Radio Network. Heritage Radio broadcasts out of a repurposed dumpster behind Roberta's Pizza in Brooklyn and all its podcasts are food related. My cohosts, Chef Paul Gerard and the bon vivant Reverend Spyro, were amazed at the array of "stoner food" that was consumed post eating contest. The topic of that night's podcast was cooking with marijuana and pot edibles, so the alien Doritos were fascinating.

Shameless plug here: http://www.heritageradionetwork.com/programs/122-Eating-Disorder

This week we tackle cannibalism in movies. I have no stories of Badlands nor The Monster craving long pig, but I did once eat "HuFu" — Human Tofu, a vegetarian option for cannibals. How did it taste? Like chicken.

TWAS THE NIGHT BEFORE THE HOT DOG CONTEST...
(July 3rd, 2014)

'Twas the night before the hot dog contest,
And in Coney Island, not a gurgitator was sleepin'
But dreaming of the morrow's Herculean eatin'
The hot dogs were all grilling, near the Wonder Wheel,
Focused on elasticity, snap, and mouth feel.
The buns were all nestled near the roller coaster,
With nightmares of being dunked, as if in a reverse toaster.

The condiments were all safe, hanging with Dick Zigun,
A freakshow needs no relish, you can guess the reason.
The championship belts, one pink, one mustard yellow
Arrived backstage at Nathan's, under guard of a large fellow.
The women all dreamed of more than forty-five,
Sonya the great, Miki the new will have a bun buzzer beater live.
When what to my wondrous stomach should appear?
But Joey "Jaws" Chestnut, the man most meat should fear.
George Shea trumpets, Rich Shea ESPNs
The Nathan's International Hot Dog Contest is about to begin

The Irish oyster champ, a cross disciplined athlete, chomps,
The Stillwell and Surf crowd, all forty thousand, stomps.

Eater X, with smudged makeup, easily hits fifty,
His Adonis looks and personality are really quite nifty.
But this is a battle; Weenie war has come to Coney,
With Sir Chestnut and YouTube sensation Matt Stonie.
Which of these gustatory gladiators will emerge draped in glory?
Find me at Ruby's, buy me a beer, and I'll tell you the true story.
I am the unqualified defeated eater, sipping with a sigh,
Dreaming of next year, but wishing you a happy 4th of July!

THE LAST MAN ON EARTH (or Just the Loneliest Man in Charlotte After a Hot Dog Eating Contest)
(June 28th, 2014)

Have you read, I am Legend, or seen the Charlton Heston movie, "The Omega Man?" Heston is the last man on Earth, minus a few mutants in dark robes. Now imagine me, walking along some desolate Charlotte roads, noticing that there are no cars, no humans, barely any lights and no sounds from the nearby woods.

Sadly, Saturday night I was no legend as I had lost the Charlotte Nathan's Hot Dog Qualifier by half a hot dog and not earned the right to advance to the finals in Brooklyn, on July 4th. Not worse, but somewhat frustrating, I was stuck in Charlotte for the night with no hotel room due to the fact that if I wanted to leave on an empty U.S. Airways flight, it would cost me $822. Way to go U.S. Airways — wouldn't you rather have my early morning seat on the full flight and have me pay the exorbitant $200 change fee to get me back to NYC on Saturday night? It made as much sense as me losing a hot dog contest where the numbers were in the low 20s — a paltry total that most Major League Eaters could eat in their sleep. World Champ Joey Chestnut was on hand, as he will be for the Nascar tie-in qualifiers due to a new Nathan's hot dog maker (John Morell — same recipe, wonderful taste) and he almost ate 20 dogs casually before the contest. Joey had the lavish yellow mustard belt in tow and many fans wanted photos of him and the belt. Heavy is the head that wears the crown, but light is the belly that bears the belt, as Joey seems to be living a charmed life as the first competitive eater with over a million dollars in earnings. By contrast, a table ender like me, pays for his travel and accommodations. Nathans only pays prize money to the top five, so I won't recoup any hot dog funds, but I eat third of what Joey does. I guess I do it for the love of game... or maybe the free food.

During the contest Joey was yelling at me to swallow, perhaps channeling his ability to eat 69 HDBS in 10 minutes, but it seemed more like Chuck Traynor screaming at Linda Lovelace. The winner, Ronnie "The Real American" Hartman is an Army Specialist with dreams of becoming a pro-wrestler. He has posted a video on YouTube of the contest in its entirety, which in the closing seconds you can see the $\frac{1}{4}$ hot dog nub that slips out of my mouth at the buzzer and cost me the victory or at least a chance for overtime. Granted as we took the stage for the trophy presentation, Ronnie's red, white, and blue t-shirt was spotless, as mine has what can only be described as HDB dander. In horse racing, I would be known as a mudder, a messy eater, but I now eat as cleanly as possible, using three cups of hot water and a flavor changing beverage from a bottle. I wanted to avoid any questions of impropriety as Ronnie was very vocal about another eater's propensity to ball up masses of tubesteaks and bread into slurry of mess, making the head judge's job like shifting through a meteor crash site. Why did I lose? Although my mental prep seemed poised for victory, I wasn't prepared physically. Ronnie sports giant biceps and his Army training has kept him in peak shape. My NYC diet of all-you-can-eat half-priced sushi and French toast has kept me in a shape, probably best described as a sagging water-balloon.

Not a religious man, I had also relied on wishing victory on a flying ladybug, a Buddhist statue that had survived Hiroshima and a best actress Oscar statue (as a NYC window cleaning we have some heady clients). Note to all believers — Hollywood, Buddhists, nor ladybugs will help you win an all you can eat hot dog contest. I missed a prime opportunity and will have to seek a win elsewhere on the circuit, while Charlotte will likely have the lowest total to advance to the finals.

My evening (after leaving the airport in frustration) started at the Hiest Brewery in NoDa where I had two Coca Colas (a big Nascar sponsor — so there's the plug), three beer cocktails, a sour and two pitchers of seltzer. After a hot dog contest, one craves either ice cream or all the beverages in the world. I couldn't manage any solids, but Tyler my server encouraged me to keep drinking, and I smoked a cigar (I assume Red Auerbach smoked a few second-place cigars, but I wouldn't bet on it.) Hiest was wonderful, but I craved a dive bar and the hostess gave me directions. It was roughly four miles to The Thirsty Beaver, a bar of reputation as the finest dive in Charlotte. With time to kill I walked the highway off-shoot roads, the woods and found myself in complete desolation by a closed business called, Junk Rescue. I paused, realizing that, "Junk Rescue" described my hot dog abilities. I have made the finals 10 out of 12 years, but did not make it last year and gone are the days when 20 dogs would be enough. Thirty is the new twenty in competitive eating. I plan on refocusing my efforts. Wing Kong of the Drexel Hill chicken wing circuit sent me some work-out tapes which sit unopened in my apartment next to Jillian Michaels' Ripped in 30 DVD. It is about 30 days before my next Nathan's qualifier so I would be wise to lessening my waistline and removing the subcutaneous fat that impedes stomach expansion. I could also get a few ribs removed, but jogging would be less painful.

At the Charlotte moment though I needed beer and whiskey to enlarge my liver and dull my frustrated mind. The Thirsty Beaver looks like a small prison made out of Legos. The High Life Mat is stained and worn; In fact the logo can only be made out by admirers of the champagne of bottled beers. The Thirsty Beaver sign is carved in heavy wood with one of the "Ts" about to fall. Inside though, is pure heaven. The back room has a pool table with spectators lounging on couches and is filled with black light portraits not only of Elvis but of Kenny Rodgers, Wayland Jennings, and a nude woman (indicating the ladies bathroom). The front room also has a 10-foot ceiling, a juke box, and beer ads from the '70s. The clientele hanging outside (you can drink outside!) is a combination of bikers, cowboys and tall girls with tattoos. It was a non-ironic Williamsburg and a beer and shot was $7. The Thirsty Beaver is a place where hipsters and rummies mingle and the piped out music is a lot of Seeger. Plus the bartender was genuinely polite. Let's just say this bar does not exist in New York City.

I had planned to fill in the rest of this post with my next two stops, strip clubs that were open until 4 a.m. and 5 a.m., both which served food — a 3 a.m. breakfast buffet and $9 chicken wings in 10 different sauces respectively — but I ate neither. I thought of the hot dog nub left on the contest table, and the uneaten one that would have given me victory, but I never seem to do anything easily. Some say the journey is more important than the destination — for the hot dogs or me? My journey to Stillwell and Surf on July 4th will take me all over the country, while the hot dogs only have to go from the plate to my mouth and down into my distended belly. As if on cue, my paltry total, gurgles, telling me that close only counts in horseshoes and hand grenades... in Major League Eating, the thrill of victory replaces the agony of digestion, but as the loneliest man in Charlotte at 5:33 am, the only sound heard was my angry belly.

Mediations on Cronuts, Chicken Wings, Pastries, Beer Puzzles and Unfilled Dreams
(July 12th 2014)

The New York Post dubbed 2013 "The Year of the Cronut," celebrating the heavily hyped, often bootlegged, first pastry to be scalped like concert tickets, hybrid of a croissant and a donut. The Ansel Dominique bakery in Soho has lines for over three hours for the Prius of pastry. I jogged there and had one for my birthday breakfast in December and although rich in taste, I liked the other signature item — the DMK — much better and there was no waiting for this popover/cruller combo. Since then the mad bakers have invented a shot glass made of cookie dough (filled with milk) and are soon releasing some sort of Frankenstein waffle-cone float with espresso and ice cream as if an angry barista and a carnival concession worker collided mid-order. I personally have noticed an uptick in my pastry consumption (and its resulting waistline increase). Even for a competitive eater such as myself, I have travelled NYC re-tasting cannolis, sampling tiramisu, and quaffing sfogliatelli (my favorite). I have pushed beyond the basic Italian pastries and searched Bruno's on LaGuardia Place for a tall donut like pastry that had layers like onion-skin made of sugar. I went to the bakery beyond at DiRoberta's and tried to chew their Ossa di Mortu (bones of the dead), a chalky rectangle of sugar that when cooked oozes out caramelized brown liquid that petrifies. It is rough on the jaw and teeth, but nothing compared to the hard bread, split bagel shaped taralli that require old

Italian men with no teeth to dip it in their coffee, and "gum it down." The taralli is a placeholder for the saying, "Finire a tarallucci e vino;" A reminder that all disagreements or unpleasantries end with biscuits and wine.

As I looked beyond the table at the Pork in the Park Eastern Shore Wing War, as I looked beyond my bowl of ten pounds of Mountaire Farms chicken wings, I saw my biscuits and wine, or rather a cigar stand next to a beer stand, and wished that my argument with the chicken wings would end sooner than the allotted twelve minutes. I had worked my way through all my flats (the two boned paddle) and was treating the drumsticks with some disdain as I stripped the meat with my hands and stuffed it into my mouth, chewing more thoughtfully than with the recklessness that competitive eating requires. Chicken wings in record numbers were the dreams of others like Joey "Jaws" Chestnut who would win the event with 220, or Adrian "The Rabbit" Morgan who would place second with a courageous 186. My thoughts were still on dessert and unfinished plans, unrecognized dreams. I would find my solace in a dive bar later with my favorite beverage in the world, National Bohemian Beer, or "Natty Boh." I would buy plenty of the cheap beers with the puzzles on the cap for my fellow competitor eaters at the after party for the event. Eaters had flown in from California, Vegas, New Orleans, and up and down the East Coast and I always insist on an after-party. We gathered at Roadie Joe's, a dive bar in a mini-mall that features a bridal store and a grand piano in the lobby.

Wicomico County was pleased to have pseudo-celeb Joey Chestnut drinking in their bars (Joey was promised a frat party in the woods later with a 30-foot bonfire). I was pleased to have Natty Boh beer even without the answers to the beer cap puzzles. I cornered Adrian Morgan and discussed the idea I had for a New Orleans bakery called, "Dat Bakery" which would sell our invention, The Croneignet (pronounced "Cro-yeah"), a combination of the New Orleans beignet and a croissant. The subtitle of the bakery would be, "NOLA pastries with a little NYC grease." And I imagined a place in the French Quarter that would turn out lighter fried goodness than the nearby belly bomb beignets and over-cooked café-au-lait. The suds in my Natty Boh beer bottle slide down the inside of the glass, like the dreams of the bakery, settling to evaporate, recycle and disappear. Our bakery is likely not to happen or at least not by us, as many of my goals of late have disappeared into the ether. I can't say what it's been - heartbreak, financial limitations, or a complacently where my beard grows as long as Grizzly Adams, and I don't recognize the face in the mirror or the voice in the thought balloons above the dreadlocked head. I still have the goal to live off my creative endeavors in writing, film, and TV, but without a show in the food space, or a sold screenplay, my goals are easily drown in Natty Boh (I brought back to NYC a thirty pack and a tall-boy six pack of the Mr. Boh dressed as a Baltimore Oriole - the beer is only sold in Maryland) I spend a lot of time at Coyote Ugly with some very decrepit regulars, losing myself in beer and the jukebox, playing old Billy Joel, The Tubes, or Ace Frehley's "NY Groove."

I imagine myself hearing Ace's chorus of being back in the NY Groove, if I can qualify for the July 4th frankfest at Coney Island (one must win a Nathan's qualifier to earn a spot at the final table). It is another goal of this year that will hard to accomplish. Despite excelling at debris foods like corn and crawfish, hot dogs and buns are my personal hell, and I have yet to break the 30 hdbs in ten minute barrier that would help me win a qualifier.

I am happy to delay my NYC return in Salisbury, MD where the Natty Boh is cheap and plentiful, the women tattooed and tight-shirted, and the promise of a bon fire to burn away the boredom is enough to look forward to. After twenty years, I find NYC to be as tough as ever - a harsh city for dreamers as snow, concrete, and the rush of technology seems to weigh heavily on one's soul. Perhaps I would be better in NOLA, taste testing Adrian Morgan's confectionary recipes, writing during the day with open windows and drinking Abita beer. Perhaps I should hole up in the woods of Maine, writing as much as the hours will fill and eating lobster and drinking Geary's Pale Ale. Perhaps I should set out to LA, as I almost did post-college, but instead pointed a beat up pick-up truck toward the New York film world rather than the LA Television one. I found it harder to make art in NYC and the fake laughter of my time in LA made me crave the authenticity of NYC. What beer do they drink in LA anyway?

I've digested those wonderful Mountaire Farms chicken wings (a paltry 68 in the contest) and started a diet of Siggi's yogurt and peanut butter sandwiches. I want to crave Nathan's hot dogs and meat by the time my first qualifier takes place. I want to hunger, literally and figuratively, for the July 4th goal. Will I hear Ace Frehley's strain? Will I sip a victory beer at the Professor Thom's July 4th afterparty? Or will it all be bittersweet - like an imaginary bakery, an unsold screenplay, or an aging competitive eater. I don't know anything about Emily Dickenson's dietary habits, but she wrote,

"Success is counted sweetest
By those who ne'er succeed.
To comprehend a nectar
Requires sorest need.
Not one of all the purple Host
Who took the Flag today
Can tell the definition
So clear of Victory
As he defeated—dying—
On whose forbidden ear
The distant strains of triumph
Burst agonized and clear!"

Who knew that an all-you-can-eat hot dog contest could be so poetic?

UNICORN POOP TASTE DELICIOUS!
(June 24th 2016)

Before I get to the magical unicorn poop sold exclusively at Taco in a Bag in downtown Chicago - the wondrous rainbow patty shaped, rainbow sprinkled meringue-like dessert - that is the perfect compliment to an entire appropriately priced taco-in-a-bag like the Norberto (Spicy Braised Chicken Thigh, Sautéed Pepper and Onion, Pepper Jack, Avocado Jalapeño Sauce, Dried Cranberry, Cilantro) I have a public service announcement to all pro-eating protest-minded folks. If you are going to protest a competitive eating contest, please do so respectfully. Yes, we are the stomach 1% , an elite exclusive club of signed Major League Eating gurgitators. And yes we enjoy the birthdate of our proud country on July 4th celebrating better than anyone by eating too many Nathan's hot dogs. And yes, the founding fathers (rumor has it Ben Franklin could put away four or five cheesesteaks in a sitting) put a lot into the constitution (a much better placemat than the Magna Carta) providing for freedom of speech (and condiments.) But still...if you are a group, covered in fake blood, and you charge the stage at Ribfest trying to disrupt eight minutes of Uncle Bub's rib eating, holding your signs and blocking the amazing manual-to-oral dexterity in the BBQ discipline, at least put a website on your signs so we know what the hell you are protesting for (and blocking Juan "More Bite" Rodriguez's view of the crowd.)

As a Major League Eater, I have been protested before. A polite young couple protesting for world hunger greeting me with frowns at a Nathan's qualifier at the Mall of America in Minnesota. I was protested again regarding Larry the Lobster, a caught 25 pounder, when I aligned myself with the group PETA - not the one you are thinking of - but the "People Eating Tasty Animals" and insisted that Larry be served to me with single-origin drawn artisanal butter on the side. That got me some flak from another lesser known group with the same initials. Even the Shea Brothers who ran the non-televised Nathan's International Hot Dog Eating Contest in the mid 1990's (now fortunately, you can tune in live on ESPN 2 at high noon) hired a woman in a pea suit to protest their own event on behalf of vegetarians. They had someone protest against themselves to stir up media attention. It is true that Nathan's Famous hot dogs does not have a vegetarian option, and when I asked high ranking Nathan's executive Randy Watts why this was the case he replied that they had worked on a veggie option for years, but they all tasted disgusting. I think that is a fair reason to pass on tofu or seitan or soy-laden wieners, but perhaps the plant eaters will still go ahead and demand crappy food in tubular shapes to be put on gluten free whole-wheat non-GMO buns (they might be right about the buns, but still...)

I was mid rack rip at Chicago's Ribfest, tearing the top meat off the mouth-watering ribs when the protester appeared in front of me. A large man, dripping fake blood (it wasn't ketchup because who would put that on ribs), stood on stage yelling something about violence. To me, it felt he was on stage, disrupting the action for minutes, but as this Youtube video shows from the 1:31 mark to 1:49, it was closer to a scant 18 seconds of embarrassing stage disruption. Major League Eating fans don't do pay-for-view (although a Mayweather - Pacquiao gazpacho eating contest is rumored) and they don't pay exorbitant ticket prices a la most major league sports so when MLE representative Sam Barclay says that each fan is choosing to watch pro-eating in their leisure time, we should give them the best show possible, every bite, chew, and swallow. Of the three protestors, two waifish ladies were gently escorted off stage by MLE ref Matt Raible. The guy in front of me was big, maybe 225 lbs and 6 feet. I grabbed the back of his shirt and started to push him forward, until I noticed he would likely fall on Juan "More Bite" Rodriguez's sister ("Nikki Mouth") and their Aunt (no nickname). I pulled the protester back and he hit the table, knocking into debris trays and my clearing liquid (cucumber lime Gatorade, only available in bodegas in Chicago and LA and the most wonderful Gatorade flavor ever.) Later, MC Sam Barclay would compliment myself and the eater to my left for eating one handed while pushing the protestor off the stage. I didn't recall that until I watched the Youtube video and saw that indeed, I must have some stomach-body muscle memory to achieve the one-handed rib stuff and other handed ribcage push that got the protestor off the stage. I was greatly helped by the eater to my left, an amateur turned pro, "The Douche" (no actual name). The Douche is actually a lovely sweet fellow who just plays the part of a bodybuilding sleeveless meathead because that is what the Windy City wants. His beautiful girlfriend and stunning Mom were in the crowd and made up a DNA dynasty of the future of humankind. The Douche has a young Ahnold-like body, but wouldn't flex for the crowd until his attractive girlfriend gave the OK. All I saw as the protestor went flying was The Douche's tricep, defined like Mt Rushmore below a triumvirate of deltoids which weren't even flexed in the mild effort to push the protestor off stage. We returned to our primary purpose and focused on the ribs. Michelle Lesco would win her first outright title and first novelty giant check (seriously where do you cash those?) with 3.21 pounds in 8 minutes. I would place last in the prize money covering enough for three cases of Old Style canned beer and two of Miller Lite which I would consume responsibly with friends over the following 30 hours (is playing laser tag while drinking a six-pack responsible? My moral compass may be slightly off.) The Douche sadly, would not place, perhaps the loss of those 18 seconds, like the missing 18 minutes of the Nixon Tapes (all excessive lunch orders from what I can surmise) would cost him a place on the prize money pantheon. I know in my stomach, that The Douche will fight to live to eat another day.

My adrenaline was pumping as the BBQ was digesting and the afterparty was at Taco in a Bag. There I learned that the unknown protestors were going for total animal liberation, which if you've followed the Tbilisi, Georgia Zoo escaped animal story it really doesn't work out in the short term. A wiser man, Sam Barclay, pointed out that everyone had their moment - eaters, fans, and protestors alike - and no-one got hurt. It was a fine contest and one for the upcoming Major League Eating book series, "Profiles in Stomach Courage."

Despite my 1.5 pounds of ribs and copious Old Style beer I had room enough for the unicorn poop from Taco in a Bag. I have previously written about "The True American Food Outlaws," Gravy Brown and Deepdish Bertoletti. Gravy and Deepdish own and operate the fast food mecca that is Taco in Bag. After debuting a food truck titled, "Glutton Force Five" and a year's lease won on Food Network's "Food Court Wars" in a distant mall, they opened a downtown location for all the drunks, punks, soccer moms, and Bill Murray at 4603 N. Lincoln Avenue. The place is decked out in Gravy's graffiti style, an R rated John Hughes world - a Shermerville taco joint worthy of all the accolades that Deepish's wonderful food gets. They even have salads although bacon vinaigrette may not catch on with the Lululemon crowd (they're stretch pants - go ahead indulge yourself.) The next day I would volunteer to work an eight hour shift at register one as a thank you to the hospitality of Gravy and Deepdish, but mostly so I could try every menu item.

Finally now - the unicorn poop - it starts with the texture and taste of a fine Italian pignoli cookie giving way to the non-cloying but sugared sweetness and pull of salt water taffy and did I mention it's rainbow colored and has rainbow sprinkles? It was magical and pairs nicely with the bottles of Unicorn Tears also sold exclusively at Taco in a Bag. Oh sorry, does drinking unicorn tears offend you? I suppose you can join the TULF - The Unicorn Liberation Front, but if you choose to protest my consumption during my consumption, please do so with a modicum of dignity. Let's keep unicorn poop eating classy.

WHEN PIGS FLY (into the Mouths of Competitive Eaters)
(June 24th 2016)

Most folks assume Upton Sinclair's seminal work, "The Jungle," about the Chicago meat-processing business, is the current state of affairs regarding hot dog production, but they would be as wrong as pink slime. I am one of the few civilians to tour the SFG Specialty Foods Group, Inc's not-open-to-the-public Chicago factory which formerly made 98% of the Nathan's hot dogs in the world. As a fourteen year Major League Eater, I was allowed to visit this hallowed hall of cased meat - like a gustatory gladiator in a non-filmed reality show titled, "America's Next Top Dog!" I can unequivocally claim that it was professional, stunningly clean, and a wonderful processed food facility. I wore three lab coats, a hairnet and even a goatee net and all I will write now (until I write my digestive memoirs), is that it was a cross between a dry cleaners and a car wash, that churned out pure beef dogs on three floors of production. Nathan's hot dogs are currently made by the John Morell company who know what pesky gluten is and how to get rid of it like an unwanted house guest. John Morell has a connection to Nascar and in the lead up to this July 4th hot dog eating contest, Joey Chestnut has been touring Nascar events featuring Nathan's hot dog qualifiers. Some say the 8-time chomping champ is getting pointers from the race cars to use in his own ingestion engine, but I believe that he is simply spreading the good love (and mustard) regarding the John Morell recipe. As for me, I have been buying packs of the John Morell produced Nathan's dogs hoping to find "The Golden Weenie" - the invite to tour their factory. If any Morell reps are reading we can discuss the factory dress code at the unofficial official hot dog after party (July 4th, 7:33 pm, Professor Thoms at 219 2nd ave, the password is, "Swordfish.")

American hot dog production is on the level meaning that the creation of NJ's beloved Pork Roll is below the level or perhaps below the belt. From the ubiquitous hot dog to the niche specialty meat, pork roll, we are talking about two different animals - the God-like revered cow (at least in India and David Duchovny "Holy Cow" novel) and the lowly swine (other than the three little, the one at the market, the one from "Charlotte's Web, and Babe. I believe Porky is on the fence and may be an anti-hero) Speaking of, "The Babe" in George Miller's, "Beyond the Thunderdome," pigs in shit-produced methane to run Bartertown ("Who run Bartertown? Not Master Blaster, not Tina Turner, but the pigs) but eventually Genius George turned his productive pigs into a superfluous farm cute who smiled a lot and went to the city. I can't remember if Orwell was pro-piggy, but there is something Orwellian in the pork roll production. Granted, I am no stranger to the potted meat genre of food. I worked for the film company that produced Billy Bob Thornton's "Sling Blade," and got to sample all the potted meat critical to the plot (most people remember the french fried per-taters.) I went to college in B'More and ate my share of Scrapple, the Maryland and PA regional breakfast side. If Scrapple is poor man's head cheese, than Pork Roll is the destitute down-and-out Liverwurst. NJ claims that Pork Roll is in the Bologna genus or a distant cousin of Spam, but I feel it's more like a pate of all the pig parts that people assume hot dogs are made of. Pork Roll is the foie gras of farm unmentionables and this coming from competitive eater who once did a dog food taste test for the "Dig and Scratch" newspaper (Alpo Chophouse T-Bone with Gravy had a couple bone chips but was tangy with hints of sandalwood.)

Before my dislike for the pork roll discipline gets me suspended from Major League Eating (poo poo'ing a sponsor's food is big no no), The World Pork Roll Eating Championship held at the Meadowlands Race Track and Victory Lounge was a stellar event. The people were kind (there was only one fist fight between fans over who got to sit nearest top ranked female eater Miki Sudo), families were out at the harness racetrack (betting on the trifeca in the fifth race is cheaper than a babysitter), and the production of the contest was top notch (I liked that they advertised the eating event on the backside of an Ostrich and Camel race billboard.) I do have some issues with NJ Transit and perhaps the State of NJ in general. I am very pro public transportation, but the NJ transit driver chose not to mention that the bus would go to a proper drop off, instead, everyone attending the contest was let off at the closed old racetrack instead of the new human-attended one. What could we do a mile and half from the event, but trudge forward watching 400 pound Badlands

Booker (an MTA conductor and flagger no less; Go MTA yeah!) sweat through his "Hungry and Focused" clothing line.

I've written about harness racing and competitive eating before in, "They Shoot Wild Harness Horses, Don't They," so I knew how to bet on the trotters versus the flats and indeed, just before the pork roll contest commenced, I bet the three horse to show in the sixth race. I could see the three horse pulling ahead and then winning outright. The eating contest started and I was secure that if I didn't take home any of the top five prize money (each with a big novelty check) I had a winning betting stub…for how much, I did not know. I was tearing into the harsh Portuguese roll and the 5 thick slices per sandwich pork roll. (Later Wild Bill Meyers would insist his third sandwich had 7 slices in it and I would respond that if he was counting slices, he wasn't eating fast enough.) It was a dunking contest, but it seemed no amount of liquid could penetrate the dense almost meat-and-bread football. We were eating jockeys, riding a run away pork roll mudder and then mid-contest, deja vu replaced digestion as I recalled a previous Meadowlands eating contest and the worst event in Major League Eating history.

The Pork Roll contest seemed to blur in time and nitrates. I could hear fill-in MC Diamond Dave Keating work the mic but he was only present because MLE founder George Shea had called in sick, his first time in twenty years of the pro-eating circuit. George's claim was laryngitis but I don't believe it. George Shea is the guy in the Italian boater hat on the 50-ft riser on stage July 4th, the blazer wearing gent popping and locking with the bunnettes, the announcer who screams to the Stillwell and Surf Aves 40,000 person crowd that, "Competitive eating is the battleground upon which God and Lucifer wage war for Men's souls." George is the best in the ballyhoo business, a caloric orator, a raconteur of the reversal of fortune, but even the finest chowdown commentator couldn't return to the scene of the World Pigs Feet Eating Championships, held at the Meadowlands, NJ over a decade ago.

I was there, driving up the Jersey Turnpike, leaving a wonderful Eastern Maryland hippyish party titled, "Love Fest," to attend what was the saddest, most incomprehensible eating event ever. The Italians know what to do with the swine hooves - cook them for 8 hours in sweet tomato sauce, until they are palatable. These pigs feet were boiled, white, with giant toe nails and some hairs still clinging to the calloused hooves. The prize money was for four places but only three eaters showed, Erik the Red, Arturo Rios, and myself. Pat from Moonachie was in attendance but claimed he could not eat pigs feet or would have to seek medical attention. Hungry Charles, the MLE commissioner convinced Pat to simply take the stage and he could have the 4th place prize money. Pat from Moonachie did, and simply put the pigs feet on his bald head (making all the News cameras perk up.) The pigs feet were impossible to eat, all skin and cartilage. It was like trying to eat a flip-flop. Post contest, George Shea's wingtips would be sloshed with pigs' feet cooking juice run-off as the scales malfunctioned. The eating event was preceded by a Sparkle Motion Dance Troupe, 13 year old girls in synchronized spandex outfits shaking their under-aged stuff in unsynchronized fashion. The Meadowlands staff was hurrying Hungry Charles and George to weigh the pigs feet because an ugly baby contest was suppose to take the stage and that was the evening's biggest draw. In the end, we guessed that Arturo Rios ate 1.1 pounds (the lowest total in MLE history until pork rinds would top out at .9 pounds and everyones gums were cut to bloody ribbons.) Arturo earned his only world record and title and I raced off, driving back to the welcoming party, cursing NJ the whole way until I could open a can of Natty Boh beer on a dock on the Chester River.

From feet to skin to roll, Major League Eating has waged a scarfing battle against the porkers in every form, fashion, and butchered part. How many records are there in the other white meat category? According to Major League Eating's record keeping department and my digestive track there are over a dozen pork or pork-related world records including Baby Back Ribs (5.24 lbs in 8 mins), Sliced Ham (2 lbs 10 oz in 5 mins), Pork Ribs (13.76 lbs in 12 mins), Pulled Pork neat (9 Pounds, 6 Ounces Smoked in 10 mins), Pulled Pork on Bread (45 sandwiches in 10 mins), and Pulled Pork Sliders (62 in 10 mins) where clearly smaller buns yielded a 38% increase. I am not even including Vienna Sausage (8.31 lbs in 10 mins), Bologna (2.76 lbs in 6 min) and Ham and Potato (6 lbs in 12 minutes). However, I don't know where to put Pork and Beans since the 84 ounces of baked beans was quaffed in 58 seconds on Oct 8, 2008 by Wing Kong Collins so perhaps it only counts as a drinking contest?

At the Buffalo Chicken Wing Festival George Shea has announced that the war between humans and poultry stands at not one human life lost, while millions of chickens are on crutches. Pigs are craftier than fowl though. I think the Pork Roll event was finally, "The Pig's Revenge." It may have started with the feet 10 years ago, knocking George Shea out this week, and then hammering the last eater standing into satiety submission. Matt Stonie the world bacon eating champion (182 Bacon Strips in 5 minutes) would go on to win agains the pork roll beast, but I believe the pigs, via pork roll, had their revenge on me. I finished run-through and hurting and in sixth place, just outside of the prize money. But I had my winning three horse ticket and I cashed it in thinking of fortune and gold doubloons. My three dollar bet paid three dollars and thirty cents. That's right, I won three dimes. That, and an aching belly, was my take for the night. Upon exiting The Victory Lounge (not as aptly named in my case), NJ transit was late. I smoked a non-victory cheroot and lamented being stuck in one of my least favorite states. Yes, they have The Boss and Kevin Smith (I think exalting Bon Jovi is like saying Canadians pride themselves on Justin Bieber) but NJ is just not for me.

Somewhere in the distance the "What Trenton Makes the World Takes" sign was lighting up but isn't that slogan a bit defeatist? Still rumor has it that come late September only one of the two different and separate competing pork roll festival will have a Major League Eating event. Perhaps I'll be banned for trash talking NJ and their love of the pork roll delicacy. That said, I insist the state motto should be, "New Jersey: Why Bother?" As the delayed NJ Transit bus careened toward the Holland Tunnel to return me to my New York snobbish breakfast patty lifestyle, the bright jumbotron billboard advertised the pork roll festival as if to taunt me - your belly might steal our pork roll, but NJ has taken your soul.

LET THEM EAT CAKE (SERIOUSLY)
(April 19th 2015)

After Matt "The Megatoad" Stonie quaffed 14.5 pounds of vanilla buttercream birthday cake at the Palm Beach Outlets World Birthday Cake-Eating Championship, West Palm Beach mayor Jeri Muoio mentioned on the microphone that it would be a long time until she ate birthday cake. At which point she was presented with a birthday cake, as it was also her actual birthday. This might be called synergy or irony or something that ends with a "y" (it was a Sunday in case that matters), but on the Major League Eating circuit, it is an common occurrence that a public official is both impressed and mortified at competitive eaters' consumption and that The Megatoad, all 110 pounds of his skinny jean-clad body, could hold a stomach that can expand to eat $7\frac{1}{2}$ Whole Foods cakes.
I ate a respectable 5 pounds, but it was only good enough for a fifth place finish. At the buzzer I was fairly deducted two plates due to the glove of frosting that coated my right hand.

Later at the after-party at Tootsies (all nude, all friction dances) while I smoked a large Cuban exiled South Florida cigar brand and dealt with some buttercream issues, I thought about those dense cakes. My good friend next to me, in conversation with "Princess" (she was bejeweled in dazzling cubic zirconia and not much else.) He explained that we do not need to live in an "either/or" world - that a man need not be a breast or an ass man - I assume he was referring to chicken and pork butt. I agreed, however, one area that confounded me in the haze of thick cheroot smoke and three-dollar Miller Lites was that it seems that most of the world is divided into either cake people or frosting folk. I have always been a cake fan, but dislike the hardened sugar of frosting. While on the show Cake Boss, I unfurled the iced fondant searching for the fluffy yellow sponge cake (spoiler alert - their cakes also have PVC piping for structural purposes but if you are polite to the Hoboken baking gang, pastry genius Big Frankie will show you how sfogliatelle is made.) While eating a cab-shaped cake at the NYC car show for The Jay Thomas Show, I peeled the yellow frosted doors off to get to the backseat of chocolate loaf. However, never have I had to deal with so much frosting as it spackled my extremities and later my lower intestine. Tootsies was enjoyable despite the dyspeptic dilemma and as my glazed eyeballs stared at the toned body of yoga porn perfection on the main stage, I, like Palm Beach Mayor Muoio, thought it would be a long while before frosted cake graced my lips or stomach. (Note - it is an election year and the yoga-porn enthusiast vote cannot be dismissed lightly.)

Marie Antoinette would have made a terrible competitive eater - for more on this please consult with Henry "The Historian" Hatau (13 bowls of Hutspot in ten minutes) who has meticulously compiled a list of all major historical figures and their chances on the pro-eating circuit (i.e "Marco Polo strong in ice cream, weak in dense meats", "William the Conqueror a casual diner only, good with drink", and "Amelia Earhart ravenous except for large crustaceans.") Marie Antoinette, despite movie portrayal, preferred simple bread to cake. The bread she chewed might have been kipfel (Austrian bread similar to a croissant) or kaisersemmel (fancy-schmancy name for a Kaiser roll) but was nothing made by Sara Lee. Also at swanky dinners she was known for simply pushing her food around the plate. Still, she really went for thick chocolate so perhaps she was a frosting girl after all.

History was made at the West Palm Beach Outlets upon their first-year anniversary (hence all the birthday cake). The Megatoad won $2,500 enough for the slim fit chaps at Wilsons Leather Outlet or some plus-sized lingerie at Torrid (it was Valentine's Day) while my $200 could be spent buying Speedos at Aqua Beachwear or perhaps a really high-end crock pot at Le Creuset. (It is South Florida.) The Whole Foods which supplied the cakes doesn't open for a couple of weeks, but one can predict with certainty that never again will that much buttercream be decimated in a ten-minute sugar frenzy - that is until The West Palm Beach Outlets' two-year anniversary in February of 2016.

OYSTERS CHAMPION RAIN, OYSTER CHAMPION REIGNS
(June 3rd, 2014)

"Sonya, Sonya, Sonya," was heard, not from the fans at the Acme Oyster Eating Contest during New Orleans' Oyster Festival, as they had absconded from the pit in a pouring deluge of rain right at the eight-minute contest's end. No, this was not the usual rabid chanting that follows Sonya "The Black Widow" Thomas from coast to coast on the Major League Eating circuit; These were the disappointing cries (much like, "Marcia, Marcia, Marcia," on The Brady Bunch) from Adrian "The Rabbit" Morgan's very attractive fan base. The Rabbit had placed second, valiantly slurping thirty dozen oysters (and drinking interesting flavor-changing beverages), while Sonya, The Baroness of the Bivalve, The Mistress of the Mollusk, the... anyway, Sonya ate forty dozen. Her smiling visage, her slender arms holding aloft the bejeweled oyster belt would make the front page (the whole front page) of the Times Picayune's Monday edition. I was once the Oyster King in 2002 but was relegated to page 2 (wearing a jaunty Goorin Brothers Hat as I have for the last ten competitive eating contest — how many until I get a sponsorship deal?)

Speaking of the Times Picayune, my goal this year was to beat beat reporter James Karst, who had shown promise in the Rouse's Crawfish Championship and decided to turn pro in Oysters. Karst had done finger-tip push-ups to improve his manual dexterity. Karst had chewed frozen Hubig's Pies to increase jaw strength. Karst had watched video tape, picking up on Sonya's economy of motion, where she spears four mollusks at once and gulps them down anaconda-style. At the end of the contest, when the skies opened and poured rain down onto the fans in the spray zone, I thought I had Karst beat by a dozen. Later, the Major League Eating Twitter Feed would list us as tied at fifteen dozen. Instant replay has yet to be implemented in competitive eating and there was certainly no recount as the band the Mulligan Brothers had to take the stage just after the contest (Hey, Styx played after a chili eating contest and they didn't complain). I consider this reportage yellow journalism or maybe battleship grey after the oysters' hue. Regardless of Sonya's greatness, Adrian's focus, and the epic Karst/Conti "Uno Mas Oyster" battle of 2014, the day belonged to the oysters. I assume it rained because the oysters wanted that weather. Oysters thrive in the intersection of fresh and salt water, perhaps rain is nice intermezzo? I should have asked Sal Sunseri, the public face of P&J Oysters, a distribution company that has been in his family for over 100 years. I tried to talk to Sal, but he wanted to show me a photo of the current Ms. USA slurping a giant mollusk. Lest you think otherwise, Sal's gaze was firmly rooted on the oyster. He wants to make the photo into a billboard. Each year Sal team-leads a civilian group that goes oyster harvesting via one of Sal's providers. Last year, I was the guest of Captain Wilbur Collins and his sons as we hit Area 15. You ask a New York foodie where the best coal oven pizza is, prepare for a dissertation. However,

NOLA foodies far surpass the NYC pizza snobs. I overheard this actual statement from a Oyster Festival bystander
— "You know we had some oysters from Area 4 and they were big and creamy." Who Dat who knows oysters — New Orleanians do. I am 86 Netflix episodes in on the 202 X-Files shows and wish that Nola had an Area 51 to harvest Alien Oysters.

The Heritage Tent houses the closest thing to extraterrestrial oysters as each year it runs a largest oyster contest. Some of the finalist weigh 2 1/2 pounds as a single oyster (shell included) and are sometimes a foot long or as large as a flattened volleyball. If and when I retire from competitive eating, I would like to do it at the Acme Oyster Contest, coming full oblong, as my first pro-event was the first contest in 2002. However, I would ask that instead of mounting the largest oyster on a commemorative plaque, I get to eat that champion oyster during the eight-minute contest. One man, one stomach, one oyster. Would the oyster feel it?

According to Mary Roach's informative book Gulp: Adventures on the Alimentary Canaland the footnote on page 175, Oyster expert Steve Geiger says an oyster's emotional state is low on the scale, but could possibly switch to an anaerobic mode (no oxygen) and survive for a few moments in the belly. I believe in the oyster consciousness — my stomach communes with them, like a beacon welcoming them back into the bosom of the Gulf. My enteric brain, the one in my prodigious gut, has a psychic connection to the mighty mollusk. Hence my belly rumbled and the bivalves telepathed, "Let it rain."

So when the rain stopped, but Sonya's reign continued, Adrian announced where the afterparty was going to be — a bar titled, "The Upper Quarter." Normally, I would dictate where the afterparty is held, however, as I am in my Fat Elvis stage of competitive eating (I need a navel-gazing jumpsuit to distract from my crumbling eating ability) and Adrian Morgan is in the Elvis, teen idol, hip shaking phase of his, we went to his bar. And what a bar it is. There were all of Adrian's co-workers from Delmonico, the giant TV was replaying the contest, and Adrian has his own signature drink, "The Dead Rabbit." It is a bloody mary mix, vodka, cucumber ears, and the secret ingredient — Sheffield, England's favorite relish, Mr. Henderson's, which is really more of a malt vinegar/soy sauce liquid. Adrian was swigging it during the oyster contest (along with fruit punch) to change the flavor profile. I was using Abita Amber... perhaps I should pay attention to the young guns of eating after all. The Upper Quarter was hosting a wedding, the ceremony and reception in ten minutes. I was hosting an oyster-eating warm-down — twenty five pounds of Superior Seafood crawfish and two orders of Fiorella's red beans and rice. A wedding is fine and dandy, something that people should do three or four times in their lives, but Louisiana seafood is forever.

Assault, Profanity, Prize Money and Why Major League Eaters Always Finish Their Veggies (April 30th, 2014)

Over the weekend, in Rome, a crowd of 800,000 watched as two former Popes were canonized into sainthood. Meanwhile, at the South Florida Fairgrounds during the Sweet Corn Fiesta, a couple thousand folks watched two hefty men nearly come to fisticuffs over the results of the corn-on-the-cob eating contest, thus permanently eliminating them from sainthood consideration.

Major League Eating celebrates the wildness from the wilderness with two coast-to-coast vegetable contests — Stockton, California hosts the Deep Fried Asparagus Festival and in West Palm Beach the Sweet Corn Fiesta at Yesteryear Village celebrates an earful of yellow gold. Just to keep their carnivore rep solid, Major League Eating also squeezes in a Nathan's hot dog qualifier in Las Vegas.

Pablo Martinez, a respected marriage counselor, won a berth at the July 4th contest in Coney Island by eating 26 franks in 10 minutes. Pablo's couples therapy skills were needed in West Palm Beach as the Notorious B.O.B., the alter ego of Humble Bob Shoudt on the pro-eating circuit, charged me moments after the corn-on-the-cob eating contest ended. He had won last year, beating me by a half-ear, but this year, I had bested him by a full ear and he was not happy.

He had been haranguing Miki Sudo (more on her later) whom he thought also beat him. B.O.B was yelling and gesticulating that his ears were much cleaner. Miki, ever the lady, was polite to B.O.B, claiming that it was her first time in corn competition and she used mixed techniques. B.O.B.'s technique was, "the rake" where one rubs the ear downward on the jaw, blooding the lower lip, and spraying corn kernels everywhere. B.O.B switched this year to "The Florida Stripper" where one sends the ear upwards towards the front teeth. This technique is titled "The Florida Stripper" because it virtually guarantees that no food actually enters the mouth allowing for a svelte pole dancing figure.

My technique is the, "manual typewriter," a left to right motion without the ding sound; however, this year due to larger and crunchier ears, I had to "type" for six rows of kernels, as opposed to five as in previous years. Sean Brockert, former competitive eater and casual bow-tie wearer had the thankless job of sifting through eaters' eaten ears and deducting raccoon chomped ears. I received a deduction of three, B.O.B only two; however, I spent the last 30 seconds of the contest eating four large handfuls of kernels that had sprayed the table in front of me. B.O.B left a Mt Everest of kernels at his station that were not counted against his total (and likely would have constituted two or three ears of corn). In the end, I ate 43 ears of corn, B.O.B and Miki Sudo tied for second at 42. I won the corn title for the fourth time in seven years, replicating such dynasties as the 1912-1918 Red Sox and the NEWMAC quarter finals results for the Mt Holyoke Women's' Field Hockey Teams of the late 2000s.

B.O.B. charged me brandishing an uneaten ear of corn from my area of the table. "What is this?" he screamed in my face and pushed the leftover ear towards me. I yelled back, "It's an uneaten ear of corn that didn't count towards my total" and slapped the ear away. It hit B.O.B. in the face. He turned towards Major League Eating founder George Shea and screamed, "That's assault." George, still wearing the league mandated Italian boater hat but not being a member of law enforcement ignored us both and resumed trying to get a car rental upgrade on his computer (He was successful and recommends Hertz as a premium car rental agency).

I yelled at B.O.B., "Let's take this backstage." I was referring to the argument, but I can see how this might be construed as an invitation to a donnybrook. B.O.B. said he didn't want to fight and violating my MLE code of conduct contract, told B.O.B. to, "Fuck Off!" B.O.B mentioned something about his preferred sexuality and that was pretty much the end of it. Elsewhere at the same moment, John XXIII was excused from the miracle requirement for Sainthood, because he founded the landmark second Vatican Council, although I don't know why they didn't just make the guys eat as much corn as they could for 12 minutes and then duke it out.

Regardless, the true hero of the day was Miki Sudo, who did, "the double" competing in both MLE veggie contests. Saturday, she quaffed over seven pounds of deep fried asparagus in Stockton to finish third and Sunday she tied for second in corn. She faced travel delays, sleep deprivation, and the fact that those two veggies affect digestion in ways that are anathema to social interaction. However, this year on the pro-eating circuit she faces a bigger challenge — her past and an egregious error of judgment that led to 10 months home confinement and four years probation. An internet search of Miki will lead one to back-to-back sites from the FBI and the working mothers of America, both with negative conations.

Miki, reeling from a boyfriend using her credit card to purchase an airline flight and spending hours on hold with the credit card company to no avail, called in a bomb threat to the airplane her now ex-boyfriend was on. Miki did not take into account that the date was 9/11 and the 10th anniversary. Miki never wanted to harm anyone (and no one was) and she regrets her transgression greatly. She has paid her time, fines, community service and is now trying to put her misdeed behind her — she would like to represent the best of America in Coney Island on July 4th, our country's start date, in the Nathan's Hot Dog Eating Contest. She is likely to win the women's division and perhaps set a new world record, but she wants to do that difficult task without a heavy heart, just a full belly. She hopes for forgiveness and this Q and A shows that.

CLC: What happened and why?

MIKI: It was a different part of my life and I am not proud of my actions that day. I meant no danger to anyone but was frustrated that my credit card was used without my consent and that after 12 hours of trying no one could rectify the situation. New York holds a special place in my heart — I was born there, I went to college there. People who know me best, know my actions that day were out of character and I have tried to live each day since appreciating people more.

CLC: What did you do during the 10 months of confinement?

MIKI: I finished my degree, I volunteered with Opportunity Village, a charity which works with the disabled. I still do that today.

CLC: How did you get into competitive eating?

MIKI: I ate a 12.5 pound serving of Pho, the Vietnamese soup. I won some prize money and I love food so I kept doing it.

CLC: Why the double this weekend?

MIKI: I always ate my vegetables as a kid and I love competing plus the travel. For corn, I get to hang out with Michelle Lesco — another great female eater. I am her #1 fan. In Buffalo this year, three women beat all men in chicken wings!

CLC: How do you feel about the Nathan's Hot Dog competition?

MIKI: With hot dogs there is so much more on the line and it's not all based on capacity — there is taste tolerance and one has to be more focused, well-hydrated, and well-rested. I've eaten 40 in a qualifier last year, but I know I can do more.

CLC: Are there male groupies for the female eaters?

MIKI: I have gotten a few marriage proposals so I do have that to fall back on...

As the South Florida sun set, a golden maize hue on the horizon, one had to reflect on the corn eating championship. It was more than the usual competitive eating contest — it had fights and forgiveness, despair and hope, bad behavior and magnanimity. As Miki Sudo looks forward to hot dogs and a forgiving return to NYC, the Florida crop growers can only hope that next year's harvest will have more fat guys fighting over their produce. We are left only with song... amber waves of grain but also aureolin half-eaten ears of corn... America the Beautiful.

I'm the Bartender at the Corporation Bar; Do You Remember Yesterday?
(April 16th, 2014)

Leslie, the aforementioned bartender of the Corporation Bar in New Orleans, probably greets a lot of people with the above salutation. The Corporation Bar, or "The Corp" as it is known resides in a squat ramshackle building in the Warehouse District. First, a word about dive bars: "Martini's Place," makes an appearance in "It's a Wonderful Life" as George Bailey's bizarro world bar — a place, in Nick the bartender's words, "Look mister, we serve hard drinks in here for men who want to get drunk fast and we don't need any characters around to give the joint atmosphere." Basically saying a dive bar is a place you cannot order a flaming rum punch or a mulled wine, heavy on the cinnamon and light on the clove. If every time a bell rings an angel gets his wings, perhaps every time a shot glass is emptied a devil gets his horns. I think a simpler dive bar definition is an Edwin Meese notion of I know it when I see it (or drink in it.) The Corp is a dive bar through and through. Are the wedding collage photos above the cigarette machine people known at The Corp or did they come in the frame? The kitchen closes at 5 pm, but if you are a regular they might hold a fully dressed baloney and cheese po-boy for you around 11 pm. They have very poorly executed taxidermy. They also have two dollar shot specials, which Homer Simpson would regard as the cause of, and solution to, all of life's problems. I think you understand The Corp and realize it's a drinkers' Heaven and a teetotalers' Hell..

Back to Leslie greeting me at the Old Mint stage for the Rouse's Crawfish Eating Contest at the height of French Quarter Fest. Rich Shea, Major League Eating's President and MC is revving the crowd through the media round where James Karst of the Sun Times Picayune is attacking the mudbugs like he types 900 words a minute. I make sure Leslie has two beers and a front row seat for the crawfish eatathon. Sonya "The Black Widow" Thomas is a four time champ, but Adrian "The Rabbit" Morgan is a local hero and tied her last year before losing in an eat-off. Adrian's very attractive fans all wear bunny ears and the crowd, still reeling from Dr John returning to French Quarter Fest after a twenty year hiatus, wants a local win. The Rouse's crawfish, 400 pounds in each boil, has corn, sausage, and garlic, but for Major League Eaters, we each get twenty pounds in the shell, and eat for ten minutes in a shuck and awe campaign to determine whom ate the most tail meat (and occasional shell, despite it being against the rules.) My fans are not dressed in bunny ears, but perhaps droopy hangovers — the crew from Superior Seafood and the band, The Bare Handed Bear Handlers, are out in force as Team Crazy Legs. The Bunny Ears would take it — The Rabbit would edge out the spider with 2.7 pounds. My hung-over cheerleaders would settle for third with 1.9 pounds and enough prize money for me to pick up the bar tab at Molly's on Decatur.

Like sitting at the Old Point Bar in Algiers, serenity settles upon me. Granted, my hands are cut from speed shelling crawfish and my lips sting from spice, but I present 60 pounds of Rouse's crawfish in two giant platters (it's good to be a Rouse's VIP) and my fans present me with several Abita Strawberry Draft. I am content because I am in New Orleans — besides being the greatest food city in the United States, it has a spirit that is uniquely its own. Defiance, respect, ridiculousness, and love all form the bouillabaisse that makes New Orleans, N'Awlins. You got dem shoes on your feet and it's the best way to make your way. You see it in the faces of the folks that line the streets for a parade, you hear it in the brass of hundreds of bands ringing the sky with their instruments, you taste it in the smoky red beans and rice with alligator sausage burned perfectly on only one side, you smell it in the night jasmine that fills your nostrils, you feel it in the hip-shaking movement of the second line. The bumper sticker is true, NOLA puts the fun in funeral. In a place that can celebrate silly death, you know they know how to live. True dat!

Green Egg Substitutes and Un-Ham
April 1st, 2014

I eat professionally but write as an amateur to maintain my Olympic status. With apologies to Theodor Geisel...

That Satian-I-am!
That Satian-I-am!
I do not like
That Satian-I-am!

Do you like
Green egg substitutes and un-ham?
I do not like them,
Satian-I-am.

I do not like
Green egg substitutes and un-ham.

Would you like them
Fair trade or "near?"
I would not like them
Fair trade or "near."
I would not like them anywhere.

I do not like
green egg substitutes and un-ham.
I do not like them
Satian-I-am.

Would you like them
in a retrofitted, repurposed, refurbished house?

Would you like them
with an endangered species-protected mouse?
(like the Perdido Key beach mouse?)

I do not like them
in a retrofitted, repurposed, refurbished house
I do not like them
with an endangered species-protected mouse
(not even the Perdido Key beach mouse)
I do not like them
fair trade or "near."
I do not like them anywhere

I do not like green egg substitutes and un-ham
I do not like them, Satian-I-am.

Would you eat them
in a locally sourced, 100-percent-made-of-recycled-materials box?
Would you eat them with an endangered species-protected fox?
(like the California Channel Island fox?)

Not in a locally sourced, 100-percent-made-of-recycled-materials box.
Not with an endangered species-protected fox
(not even the California Channel Island fox)
Not in a retrofitted, repurposed, refurbished house
Not with an endangered species-protected mouse
(and still not with the Perdido Key beach mouse)

I would not eat them fair trade or "near."
I would not eat them anywhere.

I would not eat green egg substitutes and un-ham.

I do not like them, Satian-I-am.
Would you? Could you?
In an electric car?
Eat them! Eat them!
Here they are.
I would not
could not,
in an electric car
(not even a sporty hybrid with airbrushed flames.)

You may like them.
You will see.
You may like them
in a saved-from-logging-by-chaining-a-hippy-to-it tree!

I would not, could not, in a saved-from-logging-by-chaining-a-hippy-to-it tree.
Not in an electric car (or a VW bus for that matter!)
You let me be.

I do not like them in a locally sourced, 100-percent-made-of-recycled-materials box.
I do not like them with an endangered species-protected fox
(not even the California Channel Island fox)
I do not like them in a retrofitted repurposed refurbished house
I do not like them with an endangered species-protected mouse
(and still still not with the Perdido Key beach mouse)
I do not like them fair trade or "near."

I do not like them anywhere.

I do not like green egg substitutes and un-ham.
I do not like them, Satian-I-am.

An environmentally safe, "green" train! An environmentally safe, "green" train!
An environmentally safe, "green" train! An environmentally safe, "green" train!
Could you, would you,
on an environmentally safe, "green" train?
Not on an environmentally safe, "green" train! Not in a saved-from-logging-by-chaining-a-hippy-to-it tree!
Not in an electric car (especially those Tesla things!)
Satian! Let me be!

I would not, could not, in a locally sourced, 100-percent-made-of-recycled-materials box.
I could not, would not, with an endangered species-protected fox
(not even the California Channel Island fox)
I will not eat them with an endangered species-protected mouse
(and still still still not with the Perdido Key beach mouse)
I will not eat them in a retrofitted, repurposed, refurbished house
I will not eat them fair trade or "near."
I will not eat them anywhere.

I will not eat green egg substitutes and un-ham.
I do not like them, Satian-I-am.

Say!
In the dark (because we turned the lights out for green week!)
Here in the dark (because the lights are out for green week!)
Would you, could you, in the dark (it's really dark because the lights are out for green week!)

I would not, could not,
in the (turn the lights back on right now) green week dark.
Would you, could you,
in the non-acid rain?
I would not, could not, in the non-acid rain.
Not in the green week dark. Not on an environmentally safe, "green" train.
Not in an electric car. Not in a saved-from-logging-by-chaining-a-hippy-to-it tree!

I do not like them, Satian, you see.
Not in a retrofitted repurposed, refurbished, house
Not in a locally sourced, 100-percent-made-of-recycled-materials box.
Not with an endangered species-protected mouse
(and still still still still not with the Perdido Key beach mouse)
Not with an endangered species-protected fox
(not even the California Channel Island fox)
I will not eat them fair trade or "near."
I do not like them anywhere.

You do not like green egg substitutes and ham?
I do not

like them,
Satian-I-am.

Could you, would you,
with a responsibly farm-raised goat?
I would not,
could not,
with a responsibly farm-raised goat!
Would you, could you,
on a zero emissions boat?

I could not, would not, on a zero emissions boat.
I will not, will not, with a responsibly farm-raised goat.
I will not eat them in the non-acid rain.
I will not eat them on an environmentally "green" train.
Not in the green week dark! Not in a saved-from-logging-by-chaining-a-hippy-to-it tree!
Not in an electric car. You let me be!
I do not like them in a locally sourced 100% made of recycled materials box.
I do not like them with an endangered species-protected fox
(not even the California Channel Island fox)
I will not eat them in a retrofitted repurposed refurbished house?
I will not eat them with an endangered species-protected mouse?
(and still still still still still not with the Perdido Key beach mouse?)
I do not like them fair trade or "near."
I do not like them ANYWHERE!

I do not like
green egg substitutes
and un-ham!
I do not like them,
Satian-I-am.

You do not like them.
So you say.
Try them! Try them!
And you may.
Try them and you may, I say.
Satian!
If you let me be.
I will try them.
You will see.

Say!
I like green egg substitutes and un-ham!
I do! I like them, Satian-I-am!
And I would eat them in a zero emissions boat.
And I would eat them with a responsibly farm-
raised...
Yeah, yeah, yeah... before all that blather, you owe me
26 dollars for the green egg substitutes and un-ham.
Cash or credit?

THE WOLFING (DOWN) OF WALL STREET
(May 12th 2014)

Eat this, Scorsese! I've read Jordon Belfort's book of excess, greed and over-consumption yet I felt it paled in comparison to the same qualities, but on the Major League Eating circuit. I could talk of the eater who "palmed" a crab cake after the buzzer causing a $1,000 loss to a fellow competitor, or the money grab of negotiating all the prize money as an appearance fee in a Vegas extravaganza TV show. But like Quaaludes, it's been long digested. However, MLE eating and Wall Street did collide and collude albeit its greed turned towards altruism, its consumption turned towards charity. Due to the Byzantine nature of SEC regulations involving trading floor conduct and cake with a 60/40 frosting-to-cake ratio, I have had to obscure the names of the executives and their banks in the following post. All alleged payments were made in newly minted Canadian nickels and stock options in Axis 3 (a mail-order antacid).

Several months ago, Eater X and I joined a lunchtime crowd of 600 bankers on their trading floor — let's call the place Nacho Bank (no affiliation with Nacho Bank Street — the underground queso cheese/wrestling club in the West Village). I emceed while Eater X demonstrated Nathan's hotdog eating technique from "Double Japanesing" (two dogs at a time lined up with the molars) to "The Peter Criss Cross" (while wearing face paint, eating the buns first, but holding them like drumsticks before each dunk). Then several executives (and I believe someone in a teddy bear onesie) had an eat-off for charity. Side bets of thousands were made regarding reversals of fortune and the "buy low, eat high" capacity of an exec who had to follow his dozen hotdogs with a meeting with the Germans (can you belch weltanschauung?). Everyone at Nacho Bank was amazingly cool and kind, and it was one of the most fun lunches ever — sort of Mad Men meets La Grand Bouffe.

Then, just a few nights ago, I was asked to serve as a celebrity food judge at a function to raise funds for the Cystic Fibrosis Foundation. I was joined by two high-ranked Morton's Steakhouse execs and a lawyer who has Cystic Fibrosis to judge seven teams' appetizer attempts. The open bar had been flowing for two hours and I noticed one team was made up of my trading floor buddies from Nacho Bank. The only sauce they were working with was from the open bar but we were thrilled to see each other. They were the last team to deliver their food offering and while all other teams had made enough for the crowd, Team Nacho Bank made only enough for the four judges. First, however I tasted salmon wontons (high score for appearance) and nori wrapped sweat socks (low score for indelibleness). Just as I reached for the ceviche spoon from Nacho Bank, one of the execs yelled, "Don't eat it Crazy Legs, we had no citrus." I've eaten my way out of an eight foot box of popcorn (The popcorn sarcophagus) and chowed down on sticks of butter, live octopus and loose meat sandwiches — A little poorly prepared ceviche was not going to kill me (but it might do in the other judges). I was told the fish was tilapia, which I don't think is sushi grade, but the add-on of Cheeto dust to the dish made me wonder how bad could it be? It was not bad... it was terrible. It tasted of low tide, ball bearings and armpit with an aftertaste of Drakkar Noir and turpentine. SEC regulations regarding collateralized loan obligations and dry rub seasoning be dammed — I gave my Nacho Bank comrades a perfect score (ignoring that battleship grey is a bad color in food presentation). Nacho Bank would lose to the wonton team, but didn't seem bothered in the least. The event raised a ton of money for the Cystic Fibrosis Foundation and as far as I know, the Morton's executives are still alive.

Perhaps this is the new Wall Street — no hookers and blow but just philanthropy and a little booze, plus a lot of eating. When you overhear a mogul at the Regency power breakfast order a two dozen egg white omelets with side of a trough of oatmeal or a fellow Alton Lane bespoke suit customer ask for elastic pants with his three-piece, well, just wink and point and say, "Nacho Bank never sleeps... but always eats."

INDY - MY KIND OF TOWN!
(February 14th, 2014)

I have always relied on the kindness of strangeness, so 24 hours of shrimp cocktail, beer and whiskey in Indianapolis required a stumble to the dark side, with some nice folks along the way. As a city on the competitive eating circuit, Indy has often confounded me.

In 2002 at X-Fest, a thrash death metal concert, I was slated to eat oysters before Mudvayne played. I took to the stage and was immediately pelted with cellphones, sneakers and full beers — all objects I assumed the five thousand mosh pit fans would need to get through the day. Later in the evening, MLE MC Rich Shea and I tried to find, "the regular bar," but were befuddled by each downtown bar having strobe lights, a dance floor and a crumbling disco vibe.

Finally, two years ago on the Hooters circuit, Gravy Brown, who had lived in Indy for five years, brought me to the promised land of wonderful dive bars. I am at a loss for the name of a single one, but the Fountain Square area seemed to have several worth quaffing local brew and hanging out with toothless bartenders and hippie girls. I was also introduced to Indianapolis' native sandwich, The Pork Tenderloin. If a traditional Weiner Schnitzel is a Blu Ray, then the Tenderloin is a Cassingle (for those readers of a certain age, a "cassingle" is a cassette single song, played on boom boxes to keep the Dinosaurs away).

The Tenderloin has a following, indeed, documentaries and blogs exist, but my sampling left me extremely disappointed. The Tenderloin is a flattened cut of pork, breaded and deep fried, served overhanging in a burger bun. The one I had was similar to eating a Dr. Scholl's foot insert and not a new one out of the package, but one used by a recreational jogger with gland issues. As someone who tries to never give Philadelphia any credit whatsoever, the cheese steak kicks the Tenderloins' ass.

I returned to Indy for the St. Elmo's Steakhouse shrimp cocktail eating contest, preceding the Big Ten National Championship game at Lucas Oil Stadium. The stadium has a roof, leading Ohio State and Michigan State fans to under dress in jerseys only. The Mejier Trail Greater party on beautiful Georgia Street, does not have a roof. Indeed, the low teen temperature might be great for shrimp, but for humans, it was the coldest outdoor contest in MLE history. Joey "Jaws" Chestnut said after that he had to visually inspect his hand to see how many shrimp he was holding because he couldn't feel his hand. Despite the fact that shrinkage is not limited to a guy in a Speedo winter dipping, Joey's stomach showed no sign of cold contraction, as he ate $9\frac{1}{4}$ pounds of St. Elmo's shrimp cocktail in ten minutes. I ate a respectable $4\frac{1}{4}$, finishing third, and staved off hypothermia by relying on the six ounces of shrimp cocktail sauce in each 1 pound bowl. St Elmo's cocktail sauce is 50 percent horseradish, leading two amateur competitors to suffer a Brassicaceae belch, removing them from competing. Indeed, their sauce channels the 80's movie (no relation) as truly, St. Elmo's Fire.

I cannot say enough kind things about our St. Elmo's hosts. When their 1933 Lounge was overcrowded, they let us use their conference room, complete with a rolling keg-o-later. Like the movie, "Slacker" where one follows one character into each scene and leaves with another, the MLE eaters followed the keg-o-later to a kind beer distributor's suite inside Lucas Oil stadium (due to NCAA rules, suites are the only place one can get booze). I may have been a division three, 2nd string punter, but I am still a collegiate 1st team all-American drinker. With a goblet of Macallan Scotch, I enjoyed a Spartan's upset among the company of the owner of Brad's Brass Flamingo, a venerable peeler joint (oddly enough the owner's name is Jerry. I never met Brad). Jerry insisted that we have a night cap at his place of business. We had a four hour night cap without a tenderloin sandwich in sight. I was deposited at the airport just passed 4 am. Thank goodness for the kindness of the Delta rep who woke me for my 6 am flight with the words, "Are you on this flight, or do you need to go directly to the morgue?"

The Indy kindness was the kinetic energy that allowed me to live 24 hours on solely shrimp cocktail, beer and whiskey - a diet that would kill most people, but one which Neitzsche and I revel in. Indy, you are my kind of town. Please mail my liver back to NYC and send me some St. Elmo's cocktail sauce to put on my breakfast cereal.

Is Twinkie the Kid a Zombie or a Vampire?
(October 25th, 2014)

I have kept the same heroes since the eighth grade and it has been a great month for my own personal hero worship. Those heroes are still active and working — I read Billy Crystal's latest book about his trouble with turning 65, I watched a midnight screening of Arnold Schwarzenegger's "Escape Plan", where he makes up for his 1980's grudge with Sylvester Stallone (like Arnold's goatee, the movie bristled with action), I saw my beloved Boston Celtics play a preseason game against the Brooklyn Nets (where many of my favorite Celtics now play). Next week, I will take in a reading of my favorite actor, Corey Feldman, as he presents his memoirs (Coreyography — which, thanks to a Strand Bookstore reviewer's copy I read in one sitting. You might assume his writing is as flighty as his later roles in "Meatballs 4", but you would be wrong. The book has the gravitas of his "Stand by Me" performance or the wishing well scene in "The Goonies."). I will also hear my favorite band, The Tubes, play in Times Square. I have seen the Tubes over thirty times in thirty years, starting at EM Loews in Worcester, Mass in the eighth grade. A Deadhead could travel to hundreds of shows, but a Tubeshead has limited chances, as the northern Californian based rock-n-rollers don't play as many shows. I have a ritual that I present Fee Waybill with a bottle of Canadian Whiskey on stage. I have done this for the last decade of so, even after bass player Rick Anderson told me,

"We don't drink as much as we use too. We kind of save the whiskey for holidays now." No matter, The Tubes have been the soundtrack to my life and any thanks I can give back is small compared to the joy their music has provided me. Former founding member, Michael Cotton is working on a Tubes documentary (check out www.thetubesproject.com) and I was interviewed for the film, but forgot to say that I've always thought, "The Tubes are the greatest band in the history of recorded music, why no one else knows this is beyond me?'

For a 42-year-old, the chance to return to the vivid emotions of a 16-year-old, does not come along very often. To have a month of my favorite team, band, and actors is a walk down childhood lane. That lane, however, was sprinkled with homemade pies and non-processed desserts. As I approach the world Twinkie Eating Championship at Tunica-Bally's Casino, I have no childhood memories to lean on regarding the yellow spongy crème-filled mini brick. I have eaten Twinkies competitively as an adult and not been kind to the Hostess iconic snack (I once joked that the $\frac{1}{2}$ life of a Twinkie is seven years so I am still digesting the 30 I ate at K-Rock's radio station in Boston). I followed the bakery conglomerate's bankruptcy and the masses flocking to supermarkets to buy the last of the cupcakes and sponge cake that formed food memories of the consumers' childhoods. I had no such compunction, but was glad when the factory baked goods came back from the dead (hence the title of this post — is it Twilight Twinkie or the The Walking Diet?) I consider Twinkie the Kid, the rooting tooting mascot of the space cake, to be someone I have dueled with on occasion. I bear him no ill will, but when challenged I will eat him to his hat, boots, and resilient crumbs.

I first ate Twinkies competitively at a Boston radio station, early in my Major League Eating career. I ate fifteen very fast to crush their intern, when the portly EMT said he could do better. I ate the next 15 just barely faster than the EMT. I was on the radio station with guest Joe Millionaire who was one of the first reality show personalities and was there to promote an in-store appearance at Filene's Basement. I figured eating thirty Twinkies was the better gig. My dad picked me up in his pick-up truck and lit up a stogie. Somewhere along Route 2, I urged him to pull over. In an industrial complex parking lot, I threw up a mass of foamy yellow that looked like the soufflé come to life in Woody Allen's "Sleeper." I am pretty sure that yellow biodome is still there. I also ate Twinkies as my stunt to qualify for Wing Bowl in Philadelphia. Wing Bowl is run by two cantankerous radio hosts and is held the Friday before the Super Bowl, as a conciliation rally (of drunkard and strippers) for the Eagles. I describe Wing Bowl, as as close as one can get to the apocalypse without it being the actual apocalypse. I ate twenty-five Twinkies in five minutes and one of the hosts called it, "one of the greatest Wing Bowl eating stunts in history." I also quaffed Twinkies for charity at the now defunct dive bar Red Rock West. Nearly the 20th Twinkie in, my then girlfriend tried to rub my belly for help, but she was rebuffed by the giant bouncer. Twinkie eating is apparently is a solo journey. All these attempts were dunking (in coffee or water) and at the world championships dunking is ver botten. The only time I haven't dunked Twinkies was at an impromptu pro-am contest at the single sailor lounge at Yokosuka Naval Base in Japan. However, each team had to open the Twinkie boxes and remove each individually wrapped Twinkie from the plastic. Trying to remove the plastic from a Twinkie, while one's hands are covered in Twinkie mush is like trying to hot wire a bomb while wearing oven mitts. At Bally's Tunica Casino, the Twinkies will be naked as the day they were molded.

Will all this childhood nostalgia help me or hurt me when I face the yellow foam and white filling? Will I be able to channel a 16 year's old dream of all the Twinkies one can eat and no vegetables? Black and Red aren't the only colors you can bet on at Bally's Tunica this weekend — me? I'm putting it all on Yellow.

The Assassination of Twinkie the Kid by the Coward Crazy Legs Conti
(October 27th, 2014)

I intended to kill Twinkie the Kid. I was going to macerate, masticate and mash the cowboy themed foam filled Kid. I had arraigned to meet the yellow bellied sponge cakester at an hour past high noon at the World Twinkie Eating Championship at the Bally's Tunica Casino. The Casino has a weathered barn look and the folks there were all glad to see me and have a Twinkie shoot out (or stuff in).

The clock started and down the table Joey Chestnut was slamming three Twinkies at a time into his mouth, until the foamy whiteness leaked onto his cheeks. It looked like yellow waves crashing into a saliva soaked cave. Joey would consume an astonishing 121 Twinkies in six minutes. Matt Stonie, aka "The Stone Ranger," would crush 111 Twinkies, finishing just behind Joey. I would finish a couple of bites behind in a close 6th place, eating 28.

I know I was leading in the early three seconds. The truth is, I had it out for Twinkie the Kid, but he whipped my behind, stomach and various other body parts to make the me the laughing stock of the Bally's Tunica Casino. The $5 high rollers slot machines were swallowing faster than I was. For me, it all past in a yellow blur. I really didn't hit my stride until the six and half minute mark when the contest was over.

Since our sport doesn't have a Gatorade bath, I took a plate of ten Twinkies and did the, "Twinkie stuff" into winner Joey Chestnut's face. He was not happy. I thought the stuff would go viral and other contests (perhaps not chili) would feature the winning Major League Eater getting face-stuffed with the victorious food. I had a shirt from the generous Hostess sponsors that read, "Prepare your cakeface." I thought that was what it meant. Did I mention that Joey was mad? I had to buy him beer from Clarksdale to Memphis to make up for that faux foam pas.

Despite my pitiful "just desserts" finish, I had an amazing 24 hours in Clarksdale, Tunica and Memphis. I went from down home Delta BBQ at Ground Zero (Morgan Freeman's graffiti covered bar) to giant Canadian burgers at Kooky Canuck in Memphis. I wandered Beale Street and got some of the 100 year old grease on me from Dyers. I tuned into AM stations playing scratchy blues as I sped down Highway 61. I spoke to high ranking Hostess executives about the bakery braintrust that thinks up and creates new desserts (they are self admittedly very good at flavors). It was a great, albeit exhausting trip. Tunica, perhaps I'll be back. Twinkie the Kid...you won this round, but I'm already prepping for the next go round at the OK Corral...Buffet.

THEY CAN SHUT DOWN THE GOVERNMENT, BUT THEY CAN'T STOP THE CHILI
(October 15th 2013)

In 1968, as Washington, D.C. was overcome by riots, Ben's Chili Bowl on U Street not only stayed open, but served the rioters on one side and the police on the other, proving that governments may be protested, chaos may reign in the streets, but chili brings only peace.

The streets of D.C. this past October 12th are very quiet: The usual hum of government activity silenced due to the shut down. However, at the Taste of D.C., 30,000 vocal locals have gathered, not in protest, but in celebration of the great food and drink of the district.

Food trucks, like the Cajunator, line the fenced off streets while pop up stands from El Tamarindo, Woodlands Vegan Bistro and the Thunderpig Confectionary offer their signature items. Puposas mingle with samosas, pizza with pho and donuts with dessert wine. Ben's Chili Bowl has two pop up tents serving their signature chili cheese dogs, half-smokes and bowls of their presidential approved beef chili. The center stage bears the banner that is the backdrop for the World Chili Eating Championship and each 32-ounce bowl contains the chili that will make or break a competitive eater's day and stomach.

Two years ago I slogged my way to three-quarters of a gallon of chili while Joey Chestnut bested my total by a gallon, wiping his victory stained hands on the back of my jersey, as if to say, "Better luck next time, chili chump."

That day was special because a mystery military eater, nicked named "Tomahawk" graced the stage. In a previous Huffington Post blog, I wrote about my trips with Navy Entertainment and the joy of interacting with the armed forces while eating quickly overseas. The C.O. of the U.S.S. Fitzgerald had worked with Tomahawk carrying the nuclear football at the White House. Tomahawk introduced me to four of the seasoned White House photographers who had shown up with cameras in tow for the 1st Chili Championship. The photos that they produced were not dissimilar from presidential portraits in their mise en scene, their composition and clarity... they were beautiful, except of course, that they were all of competitors with chili dripping from chins, ladling in more chili to open mouths. It was as if Richard Avedon and Jackson Pollock split duties on a photo.

The other highlight of that day is that the chili eating contest opened for the band Styx. Backstage, as the rock gods and eating gods mingled, I mentioned to one of the band members that Paradise Theater was the first cassette I owned. He paused and then asked how messy the chili contest would be on the stage so I excused myself by simply back peddling out of the tent.

In 2012, Tim "Eater X" Janus set a new chili world record with two gallons in six minutes. Chili is too dense to be a soup, too solid to simply be a stew, so Eater X's record sits (heavily) by itself in the "other" category of food consumption. Despite the government shutdown, Eater X, clad in face paint, not dissimilar to Mel Gibson's William Wallace, would yell, "They can take our livelihood, but they will never take our free chili!"

The 2013 contest would go to overtime as Eater X and Bob Shoudt would tie at the two gallon mark. An overtime in competitive eating is about as much fun as water-boarding on the weekend, but both competitors dug into a frenzied "first to finish" another 32-ounce bowl. Bob won by three seconds or 14 beans and a bay leaf.

The highlight of the contest for me, was when 400-pound Badlands Booker, whom I was eating next to, couldn't produce a burp and instead shot a wad of chili shrapnel onto myself and Miki Sudo (who despite her dry cleaning needs, would finish third). Technically, not a reversal as the chili spittle was more of a spray than, "an urge contrary to swallowing." It didn't hit the table and as someone who once shot half a chewed oyster onto Ms. Louisiana, I was glad to see Badlands recover. I rubbed his back, eliciting a large belch and Badlands dug into another bowl.

I never made it passed my second bowl. Was my second bowl a cornucopia that magically refilled itself with every scoop? I didn't know. In the first bowl I encountered giant balls of beef that a casual diner would look upon as gold nuggets in their chili, but proved to be roadblocks towards my progress. The second bowl simply would not empty and sat half full at the buzzer.

In an earlier military round, Ronnie Hartman would eat two bowls in under two minutes. My total was good enough for last place and as I continued to stare, searching for my reflection in the chili, I wondered how this had happened? MC Sam Barclay saw my befuddlement and motioned me to the side of the stage. He gravely said, "Major League Eating did not want me to tell you this before the contest, but your stomach is currently owned by the U.S. Government and due to the shutdown, the stomach you ate with is not your own." Science be damned, I asked, "Whose stomach did I eat with?" Sam replied, "You ate with the stomach of Millard Fillmore, the 13th U.S. president who looks a lot like Alec Baldwin on a bender and has the capacity of only three pounds of mutton stew." I was shocked. I asked Sam, "Where is my stomach? Will I get it back in time for the Twinkie Eating Contest at Bally's Casino Tunica on October 26th?" Sam paused and then said quietly, "Your stomach is at Area 51, and if the government is back up and running, you'll have it in time to stuff it with newly minted Twinkies." Sam then disappeared behind the J. Edgar Hoover FBI building business entrance. I wiped some errant chili from my beard and wondered how much canned beer would fit in Millard Fillmore's borrowed stomach?

TAKE THE GUN, LEAVE THE CANNOLI
(November 12th 2014)

I have previously written about cannoli. I wrote a six thousand word opus titled, "Moby Cannoli" that though rejected by The New Yorker was selected for publication at my second choice, the "On The Plate" section of Crazylegsconti.com.

The cannoli is the perfect Italian dessert and its most unforgiving. It must have a crunchy jagged shell pockmarked like the moon. Its shape is an open cornucopia allowing filling from both sides. The filling is both firm and creamy, either the swanky mascarpone or the traditional ricotta cheese blended with sugar, cream, and slight spices. In the cannoli's perfection lies its difficulty in the competitive eating field. The shell can break like daggers as if the pastry is trying to shank one's gums and mouth roof. The cream, so dense it can require chewing, builds like stucco in the cheeks. There is no rhythm in cannoli eating, only the fortitude that six minutes requires. For eleven days the Feast Di San Gennaro celebrates sausage, beer, zeppole, paint-on-nails, and chest hair, but the six minutes of the cannoli eating contest may be the closest link to the religious aspect of the patron saint of Naples as one's faith is needed more than jaw strength to win this grueling event.

Labor Day weekend, Buffalo Jim Reeves stepped to the plate at the world chicken wing eating championship for his twelfth consecutive appearance at that event - longevity a rarity in our sport. I will be eating for my twelfth cannoli contest in as many years, also a record. Unlike wings however, the cannoli discipline has required more post-contest dental work than any other discipline. Eater X, whom at one point was getting buy back dental fillings from his Connecticut dentist, retired from cannolis because of chipped teeth. His dentist wept. I have continued to chomp, despite the pain on the teeth, the peeling of the gums, the crystal meth like sugar rush, and the fact that one will smell like a dairy barn for three days, as the cannolis reverse osmosis out one's pores. The cannoli totals will differ year to year depending on the cannoli sponsor - Café Roma on Broome Street makes the hardest shell, Ferrara's on Grand the most copious filling, and Bella Ferrara's off Canal on Mulberry the perfect mix (and sponsor the year that Eater X ate 28).

I did win the cannoli championship in 2009 with twenty cannolis in six minutes after almost a decade as a marscapone bridesmaid, but this year I feel an urgency to silence the critics who say I am in the twilight of my career. Why have I been performing so poorly (Not qualifying for Nathan's, second place in corn, wing totals comparable to casual diners)? If the saying that the way to a man's heart is through his stomach is true than the inverse is also just - put simply, I am heartbroken. A relationship of eight years ended and a girl I had hoped to spend a lifetime with, moved overseas. Life (and competitive eating) has simply not tasted as sweet.

I don't know the cannoli sponsor this year, nor who my competitors will be. I do know that cannoli eating has not gotten the recognition it deserves, either in competitive eating or gangsta rap (one mention - Chappaqua's hardest rapper, Awkafresh dropped, "You're in the club popping bottles with models, while I'm at San Gennaro snapping cannolis full throttle.") I am announcing ahead of time, that instead of phallically front loading the cannoli (ala Linda Lovelace) I will be snapping the cannoli (ala Lorena Bobbit) and keeping the filling drool to a minimum. The snap, perhaps symbolizing the heartbreak, but also will break the Herculean cannoli for easier mouth stuffing.

A win this Thursday, Sept 12 at 2 pm at the corner of Hester and Mott won't make the heartbreak dissipate, but perhaps it can reenergize my love of professional eating. Perhaps there is still time in 2013 to show the world that competitive eating is more punishing than the NFL, more intestinally circuitous than Nascar, and more intense than Kevin Garnett in warm ups at the Barclay Center. Football season is underway in New York. The US Open of tennis just finished, but I submit that the Ultimate Fighting Championship of competitive eating is on Thursday and it will be for all the marbles of mascarpone. Please come out to the feast of San Gennaro where you can chew ziti thoughtfully, eat zeppole slowly, and wonder if the cannoli kid has one more notch in his belt to unbuckle?

The Buffalo Wing Festival in Two Bites — Part One:
From Sage Daiquiris to Chicken Feed
(September 3rd 2013)

Over a decade ago, I went to my first Buffalo Wing Festival in Buffalo, New York. Hungry Charles Hardy and I spent a half week enjoying the greatest bar food city on the planet. Wednesday at happy hour, everyone left their offices to enjoy $2 Molson Lite and listen to forgotten rock bands (in this case, April Wine).

Thursday we hit the Anchor Bar, where in 1964 an Italian woman named Teressa Bellissimo invented the modern day chicken wing when her drunken kids came in late and wanted something to munch on. All she had was chicken parts and tomato sauce but the kids flipped for it. The Anchor Bar serves a larger style chicken wing, so Hungry Charles and I ate history (also a 50 piece bucket).

Friday, we heard Joan Jett play a free concert on the Erie Canal and Saturday and Sunday, at the minor league baseball park, we enjoyed the Buffalo Wing Festival and all it's saucy glory.

The notable Bill Murray film, "Osmosis Jones" (far better than "Garfield 2" but no "Quick Change") featured a fictitious wing festival in Buffalo. Local businessman and raconteur Drew Cerza decided the city deserved a real one. Like Clark Kent abandoning his mild mannered disguise, Drew became, "The Wing King" (magenta cape and all) and got local wing places to set up in the outfield of the park showing off their signature sauces. He had cooking competitions (Coondog O'Karma's Pineapple Jerk Chicken Wing was an early winner in the nontraditional category). He had bobbing for wings (folks donned goggles and dunked their heads into a small swimming pool of blue cheese, taking wings out with their teeth and smelling like a dairy farm for three weeks after). He contacted George Shea of the International Federation of Competitive Eating and sanctioned the first World Wing Eating Championship. For wing connoisseurs, the Wing Festival was like nirvana with hot sauce or a Burning Man, but with chickens and less drugs. The festival was a hit and 2013 welcomed its 12th installment.

It is Friday night before Labor Day and I am laboring at my first shift bartending a new joint in the Meatpacking District in NYC. Underfed girls in too tall high heels are shepherded by promoters to the bar because the Gastropub is sandwiched by two night clubs, above and below it. A whole table of male models looks bored and like vampires, while tourists pay $15 for cocktails and look for famous people (all out of town in the Hamptons this weekend). I am making sage daiquiris as the bar manager hates mint. I am not serving boozy manhattans, but girly concoctions, and I realize I may be getting too old to bartend as my back hurts and everyone looks fourteen.

Twelve hours later I am in Buffalo with my college roommate Matt "Ups" Jennings. His nickname comes from his jumping ability, and although Ups is more sedentary as a father of two, he still has a spry step. I rub my sore back as we do more manly activities before noon, than I do all year. Matt and his wife Jen recently bought chickens (fifteen, down to a dozen due to coyotes). Yesterday, after three months of growth and acclimation, the first eggs started dropping. He had a $1000 dollar omelet, but each day the cost will amortize as his chicken can produce 180 eggs a year which he plans on selling to the neighbors. We let the chickens out of the coop, feed them, and then watch the roosters preen and prance. We then drive a tractor and go to a sporting goods store and buy a gun (for coyote deterrence). A mere twelve hours previous, across the bar was a couture wearing priss while today, across the counter a grizzled gun salesman utters, "Here's a pamphlet on gun safety, blah, blah, blah…just sign it and I'll go set the scope for your firearm." With the gun in the trunk of the car we stop at Duff's for some wings and beer. My testosterone levels are higher than they have ever been and there isn't a sage daiquiri in sight. The only thing left on the manly list is too tear into some meat with my bare hands.

As luck would have it, at 6 pm I am at the competitive eating table for Saturday's main event, the buffet bowl. In front of each competitor is a five pound tray containing 2 slices of pepperoni pizza, three beef on wecks (a Buffalo tradition of a roast beef sandwich on a hard roll dipped in it's own au jus), and a mountain of boneless chicken nuggets. The crowd surges forward, the countdown begins, and two minutes later I have the two pieces of pizza down. I am enjoying my third beef on weck two minutes after that, when it is announced that Miki Sudo, the female wonderkind of competitive eating (see my previous post on her kimchi victory) has finished her 5 pounds. Joey Chestnut finishes a minute behind Miki and Sonya Thomas and Michelle Lesco battle for third place. I convince myself that because I spent the day with 12 lovely chickens, I was reticent to eat the nuggets in my tray. Or perhaps the beef on weck was so good; I simply savored it as the clock wound down. The truth might be that like bartending; I may be getting to old for competitive eating…my esophagus muscles becoming recalcitrant and my manual to oral dexterity becoming arthritic.

Luckily, I have the liver of a much younger man and as the social director for the pro-eaters I have the entire field head to Liberty Hound, a bar near two decommissioned cruisers. Liberty Hound is owned by another college friend of mine, Mike Shatzel. Shatzel was a fierce basketball player in college but was kicked out for drinking and fighting. He moved back to Buffalo and took over his father's bar Cole's. In Buffalo, if you can drink and fight really well, it almost makes you the mayor. Cole's is perhaps America's finest bar…all the trophies and softball photos fall off in the 70s, the place has the smell of wood, wings, and stale beer. The clientele has elevated drinking to Olympic levels. Cole's is a like a museum of a great bar that serves drinks in its lobby…it's old school and modern, rolled in parmesan and baked at 350 degrees. Shatzel did become the unofficial mayor of Buffalo, and as a responsible bar owner (Soon after the success of Cole's he opened his second bar, The Blue Monk bringing Belgium food to Buffalo, but double frying it) the city approached him to open Liberty Hound. All the Major League Eaters are digesting their buffet bowls with Canadian Beer as the Buffalo sun sets au jus, and I realize that this city is a place where one can reinvent oneself - a college brawler can become a model citizen, an all-star hoopster can become a farmer, and perhaps a broken down competitive eater can become a champion once again. Tomorrow is the Buffalo Wing Eating Championship of the World and I intend to wing it!

DESTINY AND PIG RACING AT THE NEW JERSEY STATE FAIR
(July 2nd, 2013)

Friday, 6:43 am
The donut hole filled morning smells of hay, whether from the petting zoo a few stalls down, or the "big cat" tiger exhibit across the way, it is hard to determine. Mixed with the animal aromas are heavy notes of deep-fried everything — grilled cheese and PP&J sandwiches, pop tarts, Oreos, and buck-eyes (peanut butter balls rolled in chocolate, coated in tempura batter and oil fried until they look like a witch's eyeball or a sci-fi created planet) — welcome to the scent of the New Jersey State Fair. Technically, it is the State Fair Meadowlands, but after taking a subway, a train, and a $30 taxi to a NJ off ramp stadium I prefer to call it where it is, not what it is, since instead of a meadow a crappy flea market fills the vista ($2 sunglasses, $15 daggers, $22 gas masks, $3 lemonade.)

I am inside the chain link fence among discarded go-cart wheels and the guy who cleans out the port-o-potties at night. He's had three energy drinks and coffee and is eyeing the uncooked hot dogs for my first media hit of the day. I have left him in charge of the dogs, knowing a few will go missing, and wandered over to Rosaire's Royal Racing Pigs where a camera crew films the racetrack. Rosaire's has been the go-to pig racing outfit for 26 years, racing three varieties of pigs from Yorkshires to Piney Wood Rooters to Vietnamese Pot-Bellied; The last who waddle to the delight of the crowd, all racing for one single crème filled cookie. Today, Miley Swinus (as popular as the pop singer, but with a different fashion sense) is unstoppable. The crème filled cookie is all hers, leaving crumbs for the losers. She is ready for Saturday's big event, sagging stomach primed, with the mental focus of Zoltar, whose prognosticating booth is a few feet from the racetrack.

Saturday, 2:49 pm
I should have gotten Zoltar to predict the outcome of the final Nathan's hot dog eating qualifier, but that would have ruined the surprise. Badlands Booker, the only eater with a career longer than mine, has eschewed his Citi Field qualifier and come to the fair to try to earn that last spot at the final table for the July 4th weinerfest at Coney Island. This is bad news for the rest of us. Also eating is LA Beast, Jim "Buffalo" Reeves, and a host of new comers. I do alternate nostril breathing to focus as I watch the long line for the elephant ride noticing that not one soul is waiting for a camel ride. George Shea, the MC, is raining down metaphor on the crowd, "I have seen signs of the apocalypse...a girl holding a limp doll, a monkey riding backwards on a poodle...the four horsemen of the esophagus gather..." For twelve years I have followed George around the globe as he has extolled the world of competitive eating verbally, while I have championed it orally, mouth full, cheeks stuffed. It seems to always come down to this, one's final chance, the last shot...sometimes the hot dog Gods smile and sometimes they smite. George has been traveling the intestinal highway of competitive eating for twenty five years, opening for junior beauty

pageants, food vendors' conventions, even a health fair (Badlands ate 9 pounds of peas in six minutes to my 5 pounds). He is sole judge and executioner, whose gloved hands have to sort through bun detritus, hot dog greased liquids, and stained paper plates...some stained with fruit punch, others with tears.

In the last two minutes, I muck up my fifth plate of hdbs, as Badlands is on his sixth. I try to outrace peristalsis, spilling buns and niblets of dogs, in a vain attempt at victory. Badlands finishes with 28 1/3, I with 24 (deducted to 22). My cheering section of Maria Edible, Marcos Owens, and Pat from Moonachie is aghast. Badlands, whom is my competitive eating brother, hugs me a in sweaty embrace. My playoff grown beard is dripping fruit punch, my hands stained like Lady Macbeth's, but my stomach feels void. I will not be at the final table on July 4th, my Major League Eating ranking will drop, and there will be those who feel I should waddle away from the sport and retire.

Miley Swinus was 0-3 on Saturday, the crème filled cookie eluding her each time. To be a competitive eater, or I suppose a racing pig, one must believe, like Jay Gatsby in, "the orgastic future that year by year recedes before us. It eluded us then, but that's no matter — to-morrow we will run faster, stretch out our arms farther. . ."

I'll take all of Sunday to digest this thought and then on Monday, perhaps I'll jog, eat a salad, and wonder what Zoltar will predict next.

THE TIME I TRIED A 36-HOUR FRUIT PUNCH DIET
(August 19th 2013)

Sometimes one attempts the strangest things to achieve victory — Bill "Spaceman" Lee appearing in full uniform, while pitching for the Red Sox, drinking a beer during the 7th inning stretch. That's right, The Spaceman was currently playing in the game and decided he needed to up his hops count at the concession stand at Fenway; The Fans loved it, management not so much. William Hurt's Edward Jessup in "Altered States" takes a tincture of Banisteriopsis caapi root while floating in a sensory deprivation tank to achieve physical and psychological breakthrough.

In the spirit of the strange, I decided to digest only fruit punch for 36 hours prior to my Nathan's hot dog qualifier in Pittsburgh. Planning to dunk my hot dog buns in fruit punch at the ten minute contest, I fathomed that if my body was awash in crimson powdered liquid, my digestive system would assume everything coming down the gullet was fruit punch and the wieners would disappear, leaving only a stain of day-glo red and sugary garlic burps. I was very wrong. I'm pretty sure The Spaceman lost the game while quaffing suds, and Edward Jessup turned into an ape, so perhaps my day and half diet of fruit punch caused biological devolution, not simian, but heading towards the Kool-Aid Man, "Oh yeah."

I was between my fourth and fifth dog at the 48 second mark, when it was announced that Marcos Owens was on his ninth. At that point an eater chews thoughtfully, hoping that the stomach speed demon will suffer an urge contrary to swallowing (we use euphemism in place of the V(omit) or P(uke) word to avoid the mind-body connection between the two.) When Elvis didn't leave the building, but Marcos finished with 30 hdbs, I was at twenty. I took out what was left in my mouth, leaving the bitter taste of defeat, and self deducted my way to 19.5 hdbs. My fruit punch experience put my consumption into the gerbil/hamster range. The ten minute debacle left me shaken, but having eaten so little, I still had room for a Primanti Brothers sandwich and a few Iron City beers. The sandwiches come loaded with french fries, cole slaw, and one can request double meat. If hemlock was a condiment, I might have ordered it.

I have one chance left to qualify for the Nathan's finals on July 4th and the adjectives improbable, unlikely and near impossible come to mind. I've taken the weekend off the pro-eating diet (falling between a horse jockey's pack of peanuts a day and a Sumo wrestler's cauldron of ramen) to decide if I was going to subject my mind and body to weeks of tubesteak preparedness for my next, and last qualifier. Years ago, I had a cameo on "Wife Swap" where pro-eater Badlands Booker was paired with a female professional boxer. The boxer was very much against competitive eating, which befuddled me, since boxing's rules are basically, "punch someone in the head until he or she falls down, preferably unconscious." Over-eating seems a lot healthier than that, but the recent circuit has delivered me a series of body blows, narrowly missing the head shot that would put me down to the canvas. I am fruit punch drunk, wobbly, and against the ropes, but not mathematically out yet. Neither ape nor Spaceman achieved victory through the strange, but it's the only place for me. When the chewing gets tough, the tough get strange. I'll see you on the circuit, "Oh yeah."

THE MAGNIFICENT MOLLUSK
(June 4th 2013)

"Madame Lily Devalier always asked, 'where are you?' in a way that insinuated that there were only two places on Earth one could be: New Orleans and somewhere ridiculous." - Ken Robbins, Jitterbug Perfume.

The thunder sounds, but no rain comes on this grey sky Nola afternoon. The breeze picks up, but not enough to shake the tangled, Mardi Gras beads from the tree in the front yard. Leaving New York in a blaze of smoky mescal margaritas was not the wisest course of action before coming to a place where drinking is as natural as breathing. A fried oyster salad with bacon lardons and roasted corn along with a strawberry Abita beer and I am beginning to feel human again. My morning was spent sipping Rue De La Course iced coffee and reading all of Shaq: Uncut. Shaquille O'Neal has a much deserved statue at LSU, where I'm located (side note: Early in his one year with the Boston Celtics, Shaq froze himself, as a human statue in Harvard Square). The Uptown of New Orleans is lot like a breathing still life statue — the flowers imperceivable growth in the muggy air, the empty streets with the threat of rain and I walk alone wondering what night jasmine looks like during the day.

Since 2002, I have competed in every Acme World Oyster Eating Contest that Nola has held. The mighty mollusk now has its own festival devoted to it, the first weekend in June (a month without an "r" leading some locals who only eat "ersters" in proper 'r' months to declare the festival blasphemous while the rest of us have a pretty good time). Each year, the Tuesday before the festival Sal Sunseri, who with his brother runs P&J Oysters, takes a bunch of civilians out on an actual oyster boat to dredge not for gold, but for grey. P&J has been around 100 years, weathering hurricanes, oil spills and politics. Sal is a walking oyster museum with a mollusk knowledge so vast that runs the gamut from science to gastronomy to gluttony. Last year, I finally made the oyster boat (I've been to the Nathan's factory to see how hot dogs are made, I figured I should see where my other favorite pro-eating food comes from). Captain Wilbert Collins and his sons took 20 or so of us out on his boats. The map of the family owned oyster beds was Chinese arithmetic to us, but the Captain Wilbert Collins, with 75 years of oystering, looked like a man who knows where he is going; Picture Martin Sheen meets Jimmy Stewart, although wearing a light blue Cuban shirt with a gold oyster pin in its collar. We dredged a lot of shells and tiny crabs, but very few salvable oysters — still we ate them right from table. A fresh oyster taste unlike anything else you've had — first you get the salinity (like a good marriage, an oyster thrives where the salt water meets the fresh water) — it pops in your mouth like a Roman Candle firework. Then, one gets the viscous texture that requires no chewing, but floats down the throat like a Viking Ship, pillaging every taste bud. Finally, like a good scotch, the warm oyster leaves a wonderful aftertaste — slightly leathery, more salt with just a hint of metal. It is as if an ancient alchemist got hungry trying to turn things into gold, and simply turned gold into an oyster.

Oyster harvesting is a tough business and as resilient as the oyster is, to stay in business, like the mollusk itself, requires a hard shell. You wouldn't know this judging from Captain Wilbert's smile nor the photo that adorns his dining room wall (opposite an entire wall's oyster plot map of Louisiana). In the photo, one of his boats is so loaded that every spare surface is covered in piles of grey and white shelled oysters. His voice becomes low as I hear him say, "I remember that day..." He feeds us oyster spaghetti, oyster fricassee, and pimento cheese until no one can move. It is a magical feeling, pleasantly plump, perhaps opposite from the belly I will have at Sunday's contest as I try to break my record of 32 dozen oysters in eight minutes. Even after all those oysters, I always have one to simply taste it, to appreciate what I consider the perfect food. In this blog post, Tom Robbins had the first word, so I will let him also have the last:

"Every passive mollusk demonstrates the hidden vigor of introversion, the power that is contained in peace." - Ken Robbins, Jitterbug Perfume.

BUT IS IT ART?
(May 12th 2014)

Tilda Swinton has been making a kerfuffle in the art world for her exhibit at MOMA titled, "The Maybe" where she naps in a Plexiglas box for an entire day. Perhaps that is why the 24-hour news cycle missed my performance art at Pratt as part of Lucia Pedi's senior thesis exhibit. I sat at a table with a box of cannolis and an alarm clock. Each time the alarm went off I ate a cannoli. I did this for two hours and then went home and took a nap — so perhaps Tilda Swinton is on to something.

Lucia's other exhibited pieces were mostly religious themed — a statue of Mary that cried once a day (the miracle happens at 5:30 pm due to an installed water pump), a video of a guy in a suit carrying a massive cross through midtown and a plaque that recounted how she paid an actress to cry on the High Line for two hours. The last was a reference to Italy, where she informed me that people pay women to weep at funerals. I found that amazing, melancholy, but also life-affirming. Lucia is a petite pixie, but has a presence that makes you know she is going to do big things in the art world (Tilda, perhaps a collaboration?).

My role was to wear a suit, not smile, and eat cannoli at each buzz of the preset alarm clock. There were cannolis for the art goers and I could talk to them about whatever I wanted...art, pro-eating, or my preference for sfogliatelle. It was sort of competitive eating deconstructed and I found it harder to eat 20 cannolis over the two hours than in the six-minute contest at San Gennaro each year (I finally won in 2009 after so many attempts, shedding the impression that I was the Susan Lucci of the pastry world). I began to hate the sound of the buzzer and my taste buds grew tired of monotony of mascarpone. Sisyphus would have made a terrible Major League Eater. At the end of the event, no cannolis remained and Lucia hugged me profusely ("gentler please"), sending cannoli crumbs from my goatee like a leaking snow globe. Her smile was better than any antacid and I walked out a belt size bigger, but also happier.

My mother is an abstract artist so I felt inclined to help Lucia out. It was easier than my last foray into the art world, as a nude model at the Fashion Institute of Technology (It really is cold in those rooms!). I don't paint, sketch, or doodle, but I grew up around giant canvases and paint splatter, so I have a healthy appreciation of art. George Shea, the head of Major League Eating, has often compared our sport to, "a ballet of the buffet." He is often ridiculed for comparing traditional art to, well, stuffing one's face for prize money and a trophy. However, what most gustatory gladiator fans don't know is that George is an artist himself despite his art neither exhibited nor shown to the public. It is rumored that George has been working on a single painting for years — a large canvas, brushstrokes in oil, of the crowd and eaters at the July 4 Nathan's Famous Hot Dog Eating Contest. One single painting for over 20 years.

I picture George with a beret and palette saying, "No, puce just isn't right, let's try eggplant," but perhaps George sees himself more as a poor man's Matthew Barney. Barney left an Ivy League football scholarship to pursue art, while George abandoned his Ivy League high diving scholarship, ending up not with a career in art, but rather, public relations — highlighting others talents before his own. One either makes a splash in the modern art world, or drowns in its whirlpool. But perhaps George is simply a modern-day Henry Darger — he doesn't need Art Forum to recognize his work, nor a gallery, or people to stare at it. Each stroke of his brush holds off the sand filled hourglass, pointing to one moment, high noon on July 4. Perhaps artists like George, Lucia, and yes, even Tilda are telling us something very subtle about time. Try as one might, either sleeping, eating, or weeping, no artist can compete with the clicking clock or in the poetic words of Andrew Marvell, "Thus, though we cannot make our sun stand still, yet we will make him run." Run, artists, run!

IS COMPETITIVE EATING A YOUNG MAN'S GAME?
(May 8th 2013)

The Naples, Florida sky turned from pink to azure and a zephyr swirled, sending cocktail napkins at the Alice Sweetwater's Bar and Grill, into a mini white-out as if anticipating the tears for the one lone Celtics' fan at the bar. On screen, NBA vets Paul Pierce and Kevin Garnett hugged, despite the first round loss to the Knicks. Would this be their last moments in Celtics green? Would they hang up the sneakers and call it a career?

A lot of competitive eaters wear open-toed shoes during competition, a fashion faux pas, I find both disturbing from a social etiquette issue to a health department concern. Perhaps, that's why Major League Eaters refer to retirement as, "hanging up the esophagus." Twenty four hours later, on a connecting flight from Atlanta to NYC, 23 Nathan's Hot Dogs and Buns churning in my stomach, less painful than the third place finish in the Naples qualifier, I would face the inevitable question — has my stomach aged beyond the sport?

My two main competitors had much more loftier goals than I. The LA Beast, with Jim Carrey's wacky personality contained in a man mammoth body, is trying to turn his YouTube popularity into a career in Los Angeles' full throttle world of television, fame and money. Juan "More Bite" Rodriguez, the eventual winner with 27 hdbs, is trying to become Henderson,

Nevada's most famous bodybuilding trainer. The Vegas strip, known more for a six-pack of beer at the card table, than on one's stomach, would be the physical frontier this muscled two-armed bandit, would attempt to change from fat to flex. Me, I just wanted to win a spot at the Nathan's July 4th Hot Dog Eating Contest in Coney Island. I'd spent a decade's worth of America's Independence Day at the final table and wanted to return for my 11th appearance. One gets three chances to qualify at the contests around the nation and I thought I had a good shot in Naples. Of course, the Celtics thought they had a good shot at forcing an improbable game seven too. I wore a Paul Pierce jersey to my first Nathan's qualifier 12 years ago in Boston. His nickname is, "The Truth" and the most honest journey a pro-eater can take is the ten-minute hot dogs and buns quaffing quest at a qualifying table. The qualifiers don't separate the men from the boys (Major League Eating has a women's division), but perhaps separates the future from the past. LA Beast and One More Bite were the future of competitive eating, which makes me a relic of the trophy era — there are no rewards for longevity, only stomach capacity. Perhaps you can't teach an old hot dog, new tricks?

Sure, I've had a famed career — a couple asked me to hold their infant for a photo while they told their four-year-old that I was the one he played so often in Major League Eating: The Game on his Nintendo. My video game avatar doesn't age though — in real life, it's not crow's feet on my temple that reveals the years, it's chicken wings on my stomach.

The Atlanta airport use to be home to both a Nathan's Famous Hot Dog stand and a Krystal Hamburger Outlet, but I couldn't find either as I scanned the listings. With the gurgling 23 hdbs in my belly, I couldn't eat at either, but I thought a walk from the famous tubesteak to the iconic burger would be a nice stroll down digestive lane, as both fast food places represented the two major contests on the Major League Eating circuit (the Krystal Square Off sadly defunct, and last I heard, the burger executives moved to an ice cream conglomerate). Nostalgia can cause heartburn, if not heartbreak, so I decided to look ahead to the next Nathan's qualifier. I scanned prices for flights to host cities as I thought about Paul Pierce returning to the Celts for one more year. Another year for Kevin Garnett, "The Big Ticket", whose intensity I had been channeling as, "The Big Stomach" on the pro-eating circuit? With a spring in my step and a belch from the belly, I headed to Jamba Juice — I think papaya acts as a digestive — The Smithsonian will have to wait to receive my stomach, it's got a date with destiny. Well, destiny and Oliver Powers, the Nathan's rep who will be grilling the dogs at my next qualifier.

THE TRIPLE CROWN OF THE CHOWDOWN
(April 29th, 2014)

The Iditarod may be sports' most grueling race, where competitors eat whole sticks of butter for their calories, but Major League Eating has its own Iditarod and butter is not on the menu. It's known as The Triple Crown of the Chowdown — three eating events in three days and only the strongest weapons of mass digestion survive. This weekend, the triple including Alabama Gulf Oysters (5 minutes), Creek Indian Corn Tacos (8 minutes) and corn-on-the cob (12 minutes). Its caloric intake rivaled only by the intestinal (and highway) miles travelled by several competitors. In the end, the triple would claim victim to the top ranked female gurgitator, cause a Boeing Executive eater to rely on shots of hot sauce to keep him awake for a 14 hour drive through the night, and cause me to lose the corn crown, the title of King of the Kernels, and push me to the brink of satiety and sanity. The triple is not for the faint of stomach.

Atmore, Alabama is a quaint town just over the Florida state line whose entertainment depends on the Wind Creek Casino and this year's first annual Foodabaluza Festival. BBQ, Blues, and competitive eating would provide the high rollers and slot pullers with life long memories long after the potato salad was digested. Kenny Wayne Shepherd may have had reservations about having a taco contest as his opening act but the casino crowd was all in (hey,

Kenny, Major League Eating opened for Styx with the Ben's Chili Bowl Eating Championship and there was no on stage slippage from the Paradise Theater boys). Before we get to the culinary mash-up that is a Creek Indian Corn Taco, Friday night featured the salty goodness of the Gulf oyster. Each gurgitator had catering trays of ten dozen mollusk in front of them, stacked three high. Sonya "The Black Widow" Thomas, the Acme Oyster reigning queen with 47 dozen in eight minutes, was concerned that the short form contest of five minutes, would not allow her to overtake competitors down the stretch, when her "economy of motion" technique (four oysters to a fork, a dozen downed in roughly 12 seconds) would propel her to victory. Her concerns were unfounded as she quaffed 37 dozen to become the Baroness of the Bivalve. I had a good outing, downing 21 and $\frac{3}{4}$ dozen for a fifth place finish and $200 in prize money to be spent on a sizable Rusty Nail bar tab at the casino. Unnoticed by the crowd that night, was the petite soccer bodied Michelle "Cardboard Shell" Lesco who, lost out on the prize money by one oyster. Her face snarled, as if the salinity of the oysters literally rubbed salt into her wounded pride. She vowed revenge the following night, shaking her tiny fist into the purple Alabama twilight, as if to say, "I am a woman eater, hear my stomach roar!" Revenge, as it turns out... is a dish best served with sour cream.

A Creek Indian Corn Taco — what is it? Take a doughy piece of fried bread and the contents of a sloppy joe sandwich and then add an overstuffed amount of taco fillings (tomato, cheese, lettuce, salsa, and sour cream) and have the three collide in a caloric three-car pile up weighing in at $\frac{1}{2}$ pound each. This was going to be the messiest contest in history as each taco could barely be picked up without a firework explosion of fillings. If Jackson Pollock had eschewed the brush for the guacamole gun at Taco Bell, this is what he would have created. Eating all the fry bread first and then mashing the toppings into a mound and diving in was Nasty Nate Biller. Sam Barclay, the MC noticed that the mound on Nasty Nate's plate was bigger than his head (but not his stomach). Nasty Nate channeled Richard Dreyfuss' Close Encounters character and made a mountain out of a Móle hill. As she predicted, it would be Michelle "Cardboard Shell" Lesco who would eat with the fury of a jackal chasing its prey on the Serengeti. A brief pause to explain her nickname: She would often order out pizza delivery only to call and complain that each pies' slices 9 - 12 tasted terrible. Her local pizza joint insisted that each pie only had eight slices and it seemed that she was consuming the bottom of the cardboard box after the pizza was gone. The overall winner was Tim "Eater X" Janus, as his six-pack abs became a one pack with 10 plus pounds of taco and 1st place. Shockingly, for the first time in Sonya "The Black Widow" Thomas' 11-year career, she would lose to a woman. In 2nd place overall "Cardboard Shell" would beat Sonya by a pound and $\frac{1}{2}$ with 16.5 tacos. Michelle, asked post contest if she wanted to rebrand herself as "The Brown Recluse" or "The Noir Widow" or "Widow, Black" she deferred and said she would stick to "Cardboard Shell" and promise to only eat the first eight slices of each pizza. Sonya, reeling from a loss and a sinus head cold, would bow out of corn the next day. The unrelenting triple would claim its first victim.

Erik the Red Denmark would drive through the night heading to the South Florida Fairground's Yesteryear Village for the corn-on-the-cob eating championship. He would arrive with a torn ACL, a dopey gaze of unfocused hallucinations, and if pro-eating refs could throw in the bib before the contest, ETR might have been counted out. ETR would finish third in the corn discipline changing his technique mid-contest from the "toilet paper roll" (circular eating) to the "woodchipper" (unfortunately similar to the Linda Lovelace method of eating corn). Despite me being a three-time champ and previous two-year-in-a-row winner, I would feel lockjaw at the eight minute mark and never recover. Notorious B.O.B with his wife yelling encouragement at him and heckling me ("He's looking at you BOB, he's worried") would use his weekends rest and "the Rake" to eat 35 ears of corn. My "manual typewriter" method would get me within one ear or 216 kernels away from victory. Emily Dickson described the moment in her poem, "Success is counted Sweetest." Its last lines are, "As he defeated — dying — on whose forbidden ear the distant strains of triumph burst agonized and clear" It seems all the scholars had missed that Emily was talking about an ear of corn.

The wrath of corn complete, I stumbled off stage as the triple crown of the chowdown claimed its final victim.

THE MAGNA CARTA OF MEAT
(April 25th, 2013)

The symbiotic relationship between a man's fingers and a chicken wing is at its best when the sauce covers both, camouflaging a melding of man and bird as one. That is, until the wing is shoved into the mouth, meat in cheek, leaving only bones and cartilage, like ruins of an ancient civilization, discarded and spent. At least the first wing is like that, but what about the 208th in 12 minutes. That is how many wings Joey "Jaws" Chestnut ate at the first ever Eastern Shore Wing War sponsored by Mountaire Farms in beautiful Wicomico County, Maryland. This post is neither about Joey's latest world record, nor the gigantic succulent Mountaire Farm wings (competitive eater Wild Bill Meyers — "These are the largest wings I have ever faced in completion — did they come from hawks?"). This post is about dissecting the classic chicken wing — the drumstick and paddle (or flat). Reading this you will get no sauce on your shirt, but you may have a few chickens on crutches very mad at you. Continue at your own peril, but know that in the end, you can beat every $\frac{1}{2}$ priced wing night at your local bar and earn the respect of men, the fear of poultry, and be treated by women pretty much the same as before.

The Pork in the Park event had it all including a $300 Cornhole contest (despite its ominous sounding name, Cornholing is a benign bean bag toss game — like horseshoes but softer). It had BBQ trophies as large a small children in front of award winners

Smokin Dudes BBQ, Phat Boyz Catering, and Jacked Up BBQ where candied bacon counted as a vegetable option if piled on pulled pork. Not even my Major League credentials could get me into the competition tent. I stuck my head through a hole and now know what Heaven smells like. In the tent, like Willy Wonkas of Poultry, folks were creating waffle battered fried chicken wings and something called, "the eggplant parm wing" (Wild Bill Meyers, upon eating that piece of chicken announced that it tasted, "just like eggplant parmesan.") The Pork in the Park event is the largest BBQ festival on the East Coast and has turned the Q world on his head, or on the spit, or some other metaphor — how did Wild Bill get into the cooking competition tent?

Before Joey's 208, I was unexpectedly handed the microphone by MC George Shea and asked to riff on the chicken wing for the six minute amateur undercard. It was all there on stage - the crowd favorite in his "Risky Business" glasses double fisting wings with the fury of Prairie Prince on drums - and the girl to his left, cleaning the bones as if her mouth was a vacuum, turning her tray into tiny archeological dinosaur offerings. I launched into something I learned in Buffalo New York at the Labor Day Buffalo Wing festival in 2004. I presented Drew Cerza, the Wing King, with a sauce stained torn loose leaf paper forever known as the Magna Carta of Meat. Here is the shocking news: The drumsticks, despite visually appearing larger than the flats, have only a .49 meat-to-bone ratio, while the flats have a .66 ratio. I had dissected 100 wings in batches of 20 in the back of a Tiki Bar and yes, it was very scientific — I wore latex gloves and safety goggles.

The amateur contest was no contest as the cleanly lass beat the messy boy handily. The pro round would feature similar results but adding a pro-eaters speed to the equation changes the results. Sonya Thomas, with by far the fastest manual to oral dexterity, would clean the wings 65 percent but her speed would lead her to 159 and second place. By comparison, from the Drexel Hill, PA Wing Bowl circuit, Wing Kong would clean his bones 98% (Wild Bill - "They looked petrified when they came out of his mouth.") Plus Wing Kong stacked them neatly in his 24 pound bowl, adding OCD to the long list of alleged disorders at the competitive eating table. Wing Kong finished 5th in the 140 range, proving that it takes just as long to make a good bite as a bad bite. Honestly, I was overwhelmed by the meatiness of the wings and instead of cleaning them ala Wing Kong, cleaned them only 53 percent and slowly, finishing in 10th place. Wild Bill, perhaps cleaning at 59 percent finished just below me (Wild Bill to me: "I almost beat you this time, you still have to buy the funnel cake though"). As the confectionary sugar settled on Wild Bill and my now substantially increased girth, as Sonya lined up for pictures with fans, as Joey was interviewed on TV holding a two-tiered trophy, I thought about the Magna Carta of Meat. Could I have been wrong? Is the wing simply both the perfect and impossible competitive eating food at once? Before I could doubt myself and my fowl research, Eater X approached and said, "I think we need to twist the wing, pre-masticate, split the bones, and meat umbrella at 79 percent and we can catch Sonya and Joey." I nodded in agreement and handed him the rest of the funnel cake.

THE GREATEST PLACE ON EARTH - NEW ORLEANS
(April 23rd, 2013)

Can you name the three things in the world that always make you happy? I can. In no particular order they are:

1. The movie "The Goonies.

2. A burger at the Corner Bistro.

3. Joan Jett singing "Love is All Around" (the Mary Tyler Moore theme song) live.

I have decided to add a fourth — the Crescent City, the Big Easy, New Orleans, LA, or for short, NOLA. Since 2002 and that year's Acme Oyster Eating Contest I have been returning to New Orleans for the music, the food, the people, the madness of the quarter and the solitude of the Garden District. I owe much of my competitive eating career to Nola — they have even named a street after me. Truthfully, the street was there first, but when in NOLA people call me "Con-Tie" instead of "Con-Tee." Nola has a special place in my heart as well as my stomach. I may not have changed much in the past decade, but NOLA has, however, it's indomitable spirit, it's celebration of life and death (A second line is simply the way I want to be remembered), it's red beans and rice on Monday, it's oysters and crawfish, the smell of night jasmine and even the stale beer dirty stench of Bourbon Street at five am... I love it all.

My standard travel schedule is to leave NYC at 3:33 am, giving me a half hour in the bars if I need a nip for the road. With New Orleans awaiting I simply nap instead of nip, knowing that spicy bean laden bloody marys and Abita beers are acceptable breakfast beverages. At 11 AM, I am in the warehouse district at Cochon Butcher eating Boudin (the pate of the sausage world), brussels sprouts, and head cheese along with a pecan beer. The day would unfold in a well traveled pattern that I have perfected over the years. There are two bars I drink in on Bourbon Street, but first I stop at the Acme Oyster House and give shucker Stormin Norman a hug. Norman shucked the 34 dozen oysters during the 2002 Super Bowl that I ate, setting a restaurant record, and changing my eating habits for life. I pop into the Jean Lafitte Old Absinthe House for NOLA's original cocktail — the Sazerac. A Sazerac starts with an absinthe rinse, followed by a substantial pour of rye and pechauds' bitters (some places also add Angostura bitters too, but I am a traditionalist). A lemon rind follows in the glass because one could simply live on Sazeracs for weeks and it is important to avoid scurvy at all costs. The Sazerac is like a good short story, with a beginning, a middle, and an end. It's starts like the morning's first sip of coffee or skinny dipping, an eye and liver opener. The middle makes the impossible happen, a feeling of both burning and melting at the same time, until the wisp of rye sublimate in one's mouth. The end might be the best part — a lingering bitterness not dissimilar than when an attractive girl insults you, but winks at the same time.

My Sazerac starts in glass, but ends in plastic as New Orleans is the most civilized place to drink; one can walk into any bar with a drink and walk out of any bar with a drink, as long as it in in a plastic cup. And amazing, this has simply helped the booze business, not hurt it. I avoid Hurricanes, Hand Grenades, and other beverages that are literally named and aimed for one's gut, but it is hard to argue with the joy that is strolling the sunny streets with a beverage in one hand and a world of possibilities in the other.

I stop for my second sazerac at the Old Blacksmith Shoppe, a place that claims to be the oldest bar in America. Depsite the proliferation of electricity over the years, the place is darkest during the day, and does feel like an Alcoholic time machine. Two sazeracs and I usually switch to Abita beer, except for one other drink — the frozen Irish Coffee at Molly's on Decateur which comes with coffee grinds intentionally sprinkle on the frothy foam of the greatest adult milkshake. Pre- and post-contest, my folks know to find me at Molly's and I finally saw Tera, the wonderful tattooed bartender make the Frozen Irish Coffee from scratch... it was like watching a cow be created from alcohol. I won't reveal the secret ingredients that go into the five-gallon container but it has more booze than I would have thought. It is the perfect beverage post competitive eating — a digestive dairy delight.

On to the pro-eating and the Rouse's World Crawfish Eating Championship. Northerners have trouble understanding what mudbugs are (two people in NYC asked if I use crackers to open the crawfish shells). On a swamp tour years ago, I learned that crawfish are harvested three times a day at 3000 pounds each time. That's a lot of mudbugs.

Rouse's is a supermarket chain, that seems more like entering your Grandmother's kitchen. The slogan is, "You're either local or you're not," and it's easy to become a local in New Orleans. Crawfish are a socially consumed food, families and folks, sit and eat for hours, sucking the heads for the spicy boil and then popping the meat of the tail into their maws. Suck, pinch, repeat. The contest, during French Quarter Fest at the Old US Mint, is ten minutes and as a debris food is weighed before and after. Each eater gets twenty pounds and discard dish. Backstage, I weigh five crawfish which comes to .2 ounces. I eat the tails and re-weigh the debris... still .2 ounces. Sonya "The Black Window" Thomas has won the previous three years by simply eating the entire tail, shell and all. Adrian "The Rabbit" Morgan, a Baton Rouge born eater is always close behind her, eating crawfish the way a Vegas dealer flips cards. This year would be no different as Sonya would eat two pounds for victory, and Adrian would eat 1.9 pounds for second. The numbers were about a pound off last year, due to the larger mudbugs. Despite my promise to refocus, I would finish fifth — next to me Nasty Nate Biller would say that I looked slow. Despite my sloth like pace, Nate would draft off me for third place. The truth is, every eater is a winner in NOLA and with free Abita Purple Haze and an extra 40 pounds of crawfish for my fans, it's hard to feel competition as a necessary part of sport. As the distant strains of Kermit Ruffin's mischievous trumpet play, I look out into the crowd and realize that New Orleans is the world's hometown and it's great to be home — it makes me happy.

MOBY CANNOLI
(March 24, 2010)

You approach the ramshackle stage on the corner of Baxter and Grand. The Feast of San Gennaro decorations in red, green, and white, are draped over the street. The sloped asphalt, the tilting stage, the heavy decorations give the impression that something very large has dropped, crushing everything into a collapsing wedding cake. Ten feet away, you see Cookie Jarvis. He stands with his feet wide, his black Velcro strapped sneakers bulging beneath his cankles. Short white socks give way to his monstrous calves that, like the moon, have ripples and craters. Despite the warm September air, he is clad in a long black trench coat, buttoned from top to bottom so you can clearly see the spray painted image of a little Cookie Jarvis holding a spoon on the front of the jacket. His midsection extends, stretching the image of himself like a carnival mirror. The New York Times referred to his gargantuan overhanging belly as, "Shaped like a water balloon pinched at the top." You see it as Kuato from "Total Recall;" a separate entity fused to Cookie's endomorphic frame with a mind of its own. That glorious gut, which some look upon with disgust is Cookie's greatest asset. His stomach is a world champion stomach. That stomach is responsible for Cookie's many titles which are embroidered in gold onto the trench coat sleeves: Fastest Pizza Consumed (17 inch pie, 3 minutes), Most French Fries (2.8 pounds, 8 minutes) Zeppole Eating Champion (15.5 in 4 minutes), World Champion Ice Cream Eater (1 gallon, 9 ounces, 12 minutes). Cookie must sense that you are looking at his stomach and he taps on his belly like a drum, thumping his fingers, quelling the beast. You approach and greet him. Cookie snorts out a dismissive hello. He cranes his head above you, searching the distance for camera crews and reporters with notepads. Finding none, he returns his attention to you.

"Hey rookie, you know Cannolis have a really really hard shell. Not to mention the sugar, oh boy are you in trouble when the sugar hits. Are you sure you want to eat in this contest, this a rough one, rookie."

Your eyes move to a white bag that Cookie is holding in his right hand, cradling it as if it were a football. Cookie sees you studying the bag and tries to move it closer to his body. It would be hidden from view if not for Cookie's love handle which protrudes like an inner tube. Cookie claims to see a news camera and waddles off as fast as a 400 pound man can. Behind the stage, you find Badlands Booker. Equal in size to Cookie Jarvis, Badlands is a man mountain; however, his demeanor is diametrically opposed to the Ice Cream Champ. Badlands' shadow is the size of a small island, but he is followed by the sun. His warmth and easy laughter give credence to his moniker, "The Gentle Giant." He is the nicest guy in competitive eating, a kind word for every fan. He often stays long after a contest discussing the difficulties of the food stuff or chatting about future events. Badlands man hugs you, his lat fat solid in your open hand. Is his pleasant demeanor a detriment at the table? Cookie maintains an "Eat or Be Eaten" killer mentality, while Badlands often simply answers, "It's all good." Badlands has but one title, World Burrito Eating Champ (15.5 six ounce burritos, 8 minutes) but says of the cannoli contest that he is, "Hungry and focused." You mention to Badlands that Cookie is holding something in a bag. Your theory is that it is cups of hot coffee. Once in boastful conversation Cookie told you that he consumed 68 double stuff Oreos in two minutes, an astounding number. When you asked how he did it, he said dipping them two-at-a- time into a coffee. You confide in Badlands regarding your suspicions about Cookie's game plan. Badlands eyes go wide and he decides to get coffee for himself. Badlands lumbers towards The International, a greasy spoon coffee shop a block away. He returns with a white paper bag of his own and offers you a large coffee. You decline. You decide to stick with your practice sessions with water and eschew the coffee. You've made a tremendous rookie mistake.

You crunch down on the last bit of your thirteenth cannoli and feel the shell poke at the roof of your mouth like a potato chip point up. You shove your fingers into your mouth to correct the shell placement, swishing the crushed shell and creamy mess from the roof of your mouth, to the front, then to the back where you gulp a swallow as your mouth opens for needed air. Your hands are covered in white froth and drip to the table into the cups of water in front of you. You pick up the water, the cups rim is covered in caked on cannoli and take a tiny sip. You reach for the next plate of five cannolis, the small paper plate sags under their weight. You lift another five inch cylinder to your mouth like a log heading into a woodchipper. 3/4th in, your mouth is bulging again and you reach for the water. In the fifth minute of the contest, with just sixty seconds left, your mind wanders, your eyes focus on a woman whose can't contain her flabbergast look of disgust - mouth open, one eye wide, the other cocked in disbelief at the vile gluttonous display before her. The announcer, George Shea, boater hat, blue blazer has a different take on the proceedings,

"Oh my friends, this is a glorious display, this is ballet. A ballet of the belly. I look upon these men, nay these athletes and I am filled with pride. They are filled with Cafe Palermo cannoli, but I am filled with pride that I have not felt since the birth of my first child - a son. OH MY GOD, Cookie Jarvis is onto his fifth plate. His fifth plate, ladies and gentleman - he is a gustatory gladiator. But Badlands Booker is right behind. Badlands is onto his fifth plate. Badlands will not yield; there are no white flags in competitive eating!"

The crowd, an entire street block deep, surges forward towards the collapsing stage. The Coliseum has transported itself to 2002 but the crowd cries out not for blood, but for cannoli. "Eat. Eat. Eat. Eat." They yell, fists wave, cameras click, the stage sags under the bouncing weight of the eight competitors. On my 16th cannoli, I feel a different surge, one from my esophagus heading the wrong direction. A snake of mushed cannoli is shooting upwards, heading towards my mouth. I pause and bring my clenched messy fist to my mouth and Louis Armstong the mass into puffed cheeks, and then I swallow it down and lift my 17th cannoli. The only rule that matters in competitive eating is "The reversal of fortune", i.e. Throwing up. When a competitor literally loses his lunch he or she is disqualified not to mention embarrassed and ridiculed by fellow competitors. The mind over stomach matter that is required to suppress the gag reflex from automatically dispelling what one has already consumed is formidable. Perhaps, that is the reason that the reverse action of eating is mentioned only in euphemism. The "P" word, the "V" word banished from verbal mention, replaced with "Urges contrary to swallowing", "A Roman Incident" or "Elvis has left the building." The body's natural response to overconsumption is to alleviate the fullness as quickly as possible. A solid competitor must contain the food in his or her distended belly and move beyond the point of satiety and sanity, avoid adverse reaction, and bite, chew, and swallow continuously. The league's motto is for moments like these "in voro veritas" - in gorging, truth. Chew faster. Feel less. The cannoli is the king of Italian pastries. Its tube-shaped hard crusty shell, pockmarked with dried grease spots is the perfect conduit to delivery the rich creamy insides made from ricotta or mascarpone cheese and sugar. So much sugar. Cannolis can run you $1.75 at Rocco's on Bleecker (your favorite) to four bucks in Little Italy. Everyone wants a firm fresh product, except if you have to eat as many as you can in six minutes. In competition, you hope for three day old cannolis that have been refrigerated until the shell has softened into damp chewy taffy. The taste of the insides or the outside matter not, but the shell is the killer in the competition.

The sponsor is Cafe Palermo with a store on Mulberry Street. The contest kicks off the eleven day Feast of San Gennaro. The Feast each September is the primary money maker for Little Italy as each store and restaurant extends their storefront to a crudely built open air wooden shack. Italian flags and novelty tee shirts, cigars and cds fill the pop-up stands. But the prime draw is the food. The smell of fried dough mixes with Italian sausage and peppers until the air is thick with hunger. Cafe Mela on Mulberry has four kinds of pasta including tri-color tortellini with Romano cheese. Umberto's off Grand has clams on the half shell, and DiPalo's has aged sopresetta. Some nondescript carnival stand has zeppole, six soggy sugar coated fried dough balls in a grease stained paper bag. The narrow streets congested with gawkers, locals, Jerseyites, and actual dark haired, fake-nailed, clingy sweatsuit wearing Italian women and their comb-haired paramours. The feast welcomes all, as does Vinny Vella, self-appointed Mulberry Street mayor. His slick backed silver hair and wandering eye for the ladies is well known as he is king of the Mafioso wannabe actors. A made man only from scattershot TV and film appearances, Vinnie is a fixture on the scene, greeting wrinkled old ladies and yelling at kids to listen to their Mommas. Even Vinnie, shaking hands, kissing cheeks has heavy eyes this year. After the roughest September in NYC history, the Feast of San Gennero is meant to add some levity and saturated fats to lower Manhattan. The International Federation of Competitive Eating, run by the high profile public relations firm of Shea Communications has been called upon to add that levity - the first World Cannoli Championship.

George Shea and his younger brother Rich are the unknown faces of commercial real estate public relations, but the very visible principals of the only competitive eating league on the planet and have concocted this foray into the Italian pasty discipline as their culinary pro bono. Normally their clients from Nathan's hot dogs to Ben's matzo balls would pay handsomely for the services of arriving on the front page of the newspaper or with their brand mentioned on TV, however this is a freebie; a gift back to the city. Akin to the ballyhoo showman PR agents of old, who would put an elephant on water skis or have someone sit on a 100 ft pole for a week, the Sheas have brought PR spin into the 20th century. After inheriting Nathan's and the annual 4th of July frankfest from mentoring PR guru Max Rosey, the Sheas realized that like the NFL, a league could be formed as the defining overseer of records and sanctioning of all food groups. Who can deny the historical fair crowds that gather to watch pie eating contests? The Sheas wanted that crowd. Their expertise in wrangling real estate newspapers stories lead to a simple formula. If the locks at Stuyvesant Town were to be changed from keys to electronic locks, calls to every news outlet would never be returned. However, if the

Sheas added that a 100 pound woman was going to eat as many chicken wings as she could against two 400 pound men (and likely win) every camera in town shows up for a photo. The news cameras are here now; You can see them beneath you pushing against each other for the perfect angle of cannoli stuffing mayhem. Over a fateful and fortuitous but with slow social dining etiquette, the International Federation of Competitive Eating was birthed. The Sheas placed calls to their lawyer for trade marking purposes and almost immediately blue tee shirts with large block letters, IFOCE, were printed in sizes medium to 4X. Their forward thinking bordered on genius despite grossly underestimating the tee shirt size limit. George Shea, whose blue blazer is free of cannoli splatter has his arm raised, mic shaking in his hand. He is like an Evangelical preacher channeling the spirit, passing it on to the swelling crowd,

"There are thirty seconds left in this the world championship cannoli eating championship...of the world. Competitive eating is a battleground as God and Lucifer wage war for men's souls and you are seeing it here today. Cookie Jarvis and Badlands Booker are neck and neck, cheek to jowl, count down with me now from ten, nine, eight, seven...

You hear nothing at this point but your own thoughts. You remind yourself that you know the rule - what is in your mouth at the buzzer counts as long as you clear it in a timely manner. You are chugging water to clear your mouth of parts of cannoli sixteen and seventeen. At five seconds you are clear and begin to stuff a pristine cannoli, closing the back of your throat and crunching down on every inch, your palm flat as creme oozes out between your fingers. The final cannoli is in. Your mouth is closed, you cannot breath, you tilt your head upwards eyes to the sky searching for solace, seeking closure. You begin to work the mess in your mouth trying to find the strength to swallow, trying to avoid any thought that might cause your gag reflex to trigger a reversal. You are on the brink, like a marathon runner whose hamstrings have cramped duck-walking across the finish line. George, exasperated, excited, spent: "Put down your cannolis."

The beige wooden table sags under the weight of eaters resting their elbows, their fists clenched on it. The table is an impromptu Jackson Pollack of broken brown shells and smeared white ricotta. Three undamaged cannolis sit on a paper plate below you like bobbing lifejackets among a turbulent foamy sea. Beside you, Cookie takes a towel from his back pocket and wipes his face. He blows his nose with the force of a clogged drainpipe coming loose. Badlands is sipping the dregs from a crinkled coffee cup, his 6X shirt is a mirror of the table, the shadow of an avalanche of cannoli extends from his neckline to the cusp of his hefty belly. Cookie belches in your face, takes off his glasses and polishes them with the cannoli snot rag and says, "Not too bad, huh rookie?" He turns to Badlands and says, "I'm not even full." Badlands absentmindedly retorts, "It's all good." George grabs both Cookie and Badlands stout arms and stands between them. He shouts,

"One of these men, one of these athletes has eaten twenty and one half cannolis in six minutes. The other has eaten twenty-one. In first place, for no prize money but simply eternal glory with twenty-one Cafe Palermo cannolis in six minutes The World Cannoli Eating Champion is Ed "Cookie" Jarvis. Ed "Cookie" Jarvis!"

Cookie's stump like arms raise breaking George's grasp and flecks of cannoli detritus fling off of them spraying in every direction. The cameras flock to Cookie, snapping furiously as he pumps his meaty hands in victory. George continues to announce albeit his voice forgotten amidst Cookie's messy victory wave. You've finished third with eighteen, as Badlands tell you, a very respectable 18 cannolis. What was once overpoweringly sweet in your mouth has turned sour with the realization that you should have trusted your gut, not your brain and retrieved coffee for the contest. Your remaining water cups filled to their plastic tops sit still on the table. Your stomach does back flips. Long after the eighteen cannolis digest, the painful memory of your coffee folly will remain.

The following year, the league grows adding new contests and uncharted forays into different food titles. The IFOCE Adds to the venerable hot dog and matzo ball circuits, with championships in Chicken Wings (Oleg Zhornitsky 74 in twelve minutes), Russian Dumplings called Pelmeni (Dale "The Mouth from the South" Boone -274 in six minutes and oysters (you, 14 dozen in ten minutes). The cannoli contest returns untouched untarnished and with the same busted table on the sloping stage at the corner of Grand and Baxter. The sponsor changes to Ferrara a pastry shop known for the iron hands of its Italian baker, Nunzio. Each cannoli shell reflects its maker, hard and unsmiling. Badlands is relentless, dipping his cannoli into coffee cups with such force that a tsunami of liquid erupts from each cannoli plunge. Despite his efforts, Cookie holds onto an early lead and emerges the victor with 16.5 cannolis to Badlands 14.5. You are again in third but tied at fourteen with two other gurgitators. A half-hearted two cannoli eat off ensues, with you finishing in the middle, behind the formally attired Gentlemen Joe Menchetti but ahead of the wisecracking Dale "The Mouth from the South" Boone. Cookie immediately points to his right sleeve wondering where his next title can be embroidered. He chortles, "Not much room left on the jacket boys." We sneer behind his humped back and curse Nunzio's jawbreaking shells.

The 2004 contest is filled with precontest media. Competitive eating has hit the big time, Badlands holding a matzo ball is the cover story of the life section of US Today. Elevated from talk show fodder (Coondog O'Karma eating donuts in a dunk tank on Sally Jesse Raphael) pro-eating gains some respect. Actual news shows cover the build-up, radio show phone ins fill the week before the contest. You join a new eater, Tim "Eater X" Janus for the morning slot on The Larry Hoff show. Eater X, his face painted in disguise either as George Shea posits to hide his inner turmoil or more likely to hide his identity from his day trading employer. Larry Hoff is a fireball of energy stirring the 5 am confectionary sugar at Bella Ferrara, the new cannoli sponsor. Hoff is talking for three people and you have no idea if he is directing you to start eating for the camera or talking to Tony the camera guy or actually bantering on air. His sidekick is the raven haired Jill Nicoletti, fresh from a stint on "Married by America", Jill is divorced by herself but paired to Larry like a rabbit to a hedgehog. In between wondering what Larry is doing or who he is talking to, you convince Jill and Eater X to exchange phone numbers, which they do, scrawled on Bella Ferrara napkins. You finish the show with your mouth stuffed with cannoli for the 9 am live bump. As Larry runs around congratulating everyone on the best morning bit of his career, you spit out the cannoli and wonder if what you've ingested will affect your performance for the contest later that day.

Five hours later, Cookie is being serenaded by the crowd. Proclaiming to be on a diet, he has graciously backed out of the contest but will remain on stage in an official capacity as the head judge. George Shea proclaims Cookie to be a great American. The day is rainy and for once you are glad to be under the crude roof of the jimmy rigged stage. A swarm of folk from High Def TV are buzzing about and George is introducing them to everyone, "Yes, yes, this is Alan "The Shredder" Goldstein so named because his incisors simply rip the food apart - Alan show the HiDef TV folk your teeth." George's tone indicates that he is trying to sell the HighDef folk on the wise decision to cover competitive eating with a series despite the network having no name brand recognition. The TV folks are not easily hoodwinked and keep explaining that they would have brought the cameras, but the rain would be problematic. You could care less, instead wondering if the outcome of this year's contest, without two time champ Cookie, might fare better for you. Badlands has gained weight but that's not why the stage feels cramped. To your left is Eater X stoic under his rodeo clown get-up. To your right and jostling you for room is Alan "The Shredder" Goldstein, a muscular registered nurse from Long Island who spends his weekend drumming in a wedding band. The Shredder is a protege of Cookie Jarvis. He recognized Cookie while dining at J&R Steakhouse (Finish the 76 oz steak, a salad, a baked potato, and a beer and it's free). Cookie invited Alan to join him at his table and then put on a competitive eating clinic for the starry eyed fan. Cookie devoured the entire meal in seven and half minutes, a record that stands to this day. The Shredder spent the rest of the circuit following Cookie event-to-event, learning as he went. This event marked the first time that The Shredder would eat without his mentor competing with him at the table. Cookie's watchful gaze would be focused on his young hopeful but due to the tight stage area, Cookie's protruding belly would be at Allan's back. Literally.

The Shredder tears the sleeves off his shirt which seems to act as a starting gun for the contest. Cannoli number one is in your mouth within seconds. The shells are more pliable than the year before, but not by much. You don't make it past your third plate of five. Badlands ekes out victory from Eater X, 16.5 to 16. You tie The Shredder at fifteen. George calls for a third place eat-off. Cookie is rubbing down The Shredder's back like a corner man. The Shredder flexes to the crowd. George loves it. You refuse to be the hopeless confetti covered sap in this parade and pick up the two cannolis off the plate and begin to consume them as if you've not eaten in weeks. It seems that you are ahead, but the Shredder methodically loads in his second cannoli after clearing his first. You both chew like beavers and open your mouths, empty at the same moment. "Again" cries George Shea. Two more cannolis are placed in front of each competitor. Your mouth moves like a drowning man's fighting to the surface seeking air to breathe, life from death. A tie in the second overtime occurs. The crowd groans in disbelief. "Again" cries George Shea. The Shredder dumps a cup of water over his head. You fight through sawdust mouth and swallow the second cannoli, your sixth of the overtime period. You think you have it, but the Shredder's empty mouth opens a second before. Despite eating 21 cannolis, almost five more than the actual contest winner, you are left licking your mascarpone wounds. A napkin, pressed to the roof of your mouth produces red splotches that look like a scarlet Milky Way. You've eaten through the pain - blood, sweat, and dessert. The HiDef folk can't believe they didn't bring the cameras and now say the rain wouldn't have been a problem. "What drama!", they exclaim, "Who knew?" they ask. You knew.

You know it as you walk with Badlands who is heading to the sausage and pepper stand. After 16.5 cannolis Badlands is grabbing a sausage sandwich. He offers you a bite. You pass. To the victor, goes the sausage. The following year, Badlands backs out citing weight gain. Cookie pounces on the opportunity and opts in. Palermo is the sponsor and their shells are the Seabiscuts of the pastry world. With dunking de rigueur Cookie keeps a coffee below his bottom lip like a spit cup, however, instead of going out, the coffee drool and cannoli goes in. By the time the dessert tube hits Cookie's molars it is the texture of cereal left too long in milk. Cookie runs away with the title and sets a new world record with an astounding 26 cannolis in six minutes. Eater X places second with 22 and you finish close behind with 21. The Shredder, perhaps still coasting on the accolades of the previous year's 3 OT spectacular, dubbed, "The Thrilla with Vanilla," is a no show. Big Brian Subich, formerly known as Yellowcake, comes in third with 18. How many more years can you compete with this ricotta albatross hanging from your neck?

In 2006, Cookie and Badlands both decide they have nothing left to prove in the cannoli discipline and sit out the contest. The stage, the same sagging stage as always, breathes a sigh of relief that the duo, close to 900 pounds total, will remain in the pit with the media. Will the asphalt hold? The story this year is that Eater X has moved into your apartment as a roommate three days prior. Years before at the

Buffalo Wing Festival, Eater X would be walking to Duntire Park for the wing eating championships as you, Badlands, and Hungry Charles Hardy would be driving by in a free rental car. When offered to bunk at a free room at the Holiday Inn, Eater X declined, instead opting to stay at the youth hostel. His reasoning is that he wanted to pay his dues on the circuit. After tying Cookie Jarvis with a solid 4th place finish in wings, Eater X got the respect that he so wantonly craved. Appearance fees, comped accommodations, black cars for morning media followed. Now, many years later, the media world buzzed with the notion of two competitive eaters living together. What is in the fridge? Who does the shopping? Endless camera crews and print reporters would slog up the 4 floor walk-up asking the same endless questions. You begin to double book media, inviting The Village Voice photographer and an inept film crew from Al Roker Productions at the same timeslot. You even double book live appearances, bringing a Canadian camera crew to the 5 am Larry Hoff show. Larry loves it, even putting the Canadians on camera.

The 2006 sponsor is Bella Ferrara but the shells remain as pliable and pillowy as the previous year. It's a lopsided affair with Eater X tying the world record at 26. You place second with 22 and a rookie, Justin "Me so Hungry" Mih clocks a messy 18. The Shredder is nowhere to be found. The league office actually produces a trophy this year, a gold spray painted pedestal with a plate on top for cannoli. The trophy comes home with you, but sits on Eater X's side of the apartment. In the following year, it collects dust and grease while what sticks to you cannot be seen in the shafts of window light - failure and disappointment sway in the air. Palermo returns as a sponsor but in a cruel twist of fate, the shells are double baked. They resemble Taralli, the hard donut Italian pastry that old men without teeth dunk in coffee and gum to death. The league outlaws dunking. However, Eater X makes a game day decision to participate despite mounting dental concerns. His Connecticut dentist is his sugar consigliere. Advising him through cavities and chips, fillings and bondings. Eater X's visits are so frequent that his dentist often doesn't charge in a perverse Tooth Fairy buyback program. Eater X does chip a tooth and accepts the victory with the frustration that he has to head to Connecticut again. His 21 is a long way off his co-world record. Your 17 also falls off the mark, but is enough to outdo a returning Alan "The Shredder" Goldstein and rookie "Nasty" Nate Biller. Those two, despite tying for third with 16, wave off the notion of OT. Everyone retires to O'Neil's for beers at the black oak bar. Fitzy, the bartender welcomes the competitive eaters as a break from the "Sex in the City" tour bus crowd who arrives promptly twice a day, three times on weekends. He has a monster jug with premixed Cosmo and offers the eaters the remains of the last tour bus leftovers. We stick to Guinness, which mixes in our belly with the cannoli like cement churning in the barrel.

In 2008, the circuit is changing, becoming darker. Prize money has tainted the scene and with it comes a new breed of eater - reckless, young, and stupid. Great foils for George Shea's comic skewering, these nineteen and twenty years olds care only for victory no matter what price their body pays. Brad "Psycho" Scullio is emblematic of the problems facing Major League Eating (rebranded from the clunky International Federation of Competitive Eating). He subscribes to every training ritual no matter how ludicrous: swallowing whole ice cubes to enlarge the esophagus, eating uncooked rice hoping that it will swell in his belly, and the water method. Perhaps the most dangerous thing ever to appear on the circuit, the water method involves chugging gallons of water as quickly as possible to get the stomach to expand. Despite the dangers of electrolyte cleansing, Hyponatremia aka "brain float", and passing out, Psycho Scuillo trains with water twice a day. At a pretzel contest in Miami, Scuillo confides in Eater X that he has been to the emergency room twice in the past month, both times with an irregular heart beat after powering through two gallons of water. Eater X tells him to be careful, that no prize money is worth risking one's life for competitive eating. Scuillo waves him off, insisting that he now takes potassium supplements to ward off the ill effects of over water consumption. George Shea barely knows Brad Scuillo's name but the dark haired youngster in an "Italian Stallion" tshirt, stained with all his previous victories, is honored to be the same stage as the eaters that he has admired for so long. The Shredder is back at the table and Cookie has returned in a judging capacity. You have black electrical gloves which Cookie studies carefully mentioning to George that you made a big mess last year. George talks of judges deducting cannoli due to excessive debris but you can see in his eyes that he wishes he was in a conference room, high above midtown, discussing commercial real estate. George's personality is like those conference room windows, reflecting whatever is in front of him in slanted jagged vision. At the moment, Cookie's decision to ride your cannoli mess has George over your shoulder, shouting, "Clean it up!" You ignore them both, perhaps unwisely, but you know the rules and know that you don't have to worry about the mess until just before the final buzzer. You feel it is necessary to keep stuffing cannoli after cannoli because you and Shredder are very close. You pull ahead late in the contest but your gloves are dripping white. The Shredder looks possessed and George urges him on, calling him, "A jackal loose on the plains of the Serengeti!" The crowd counts down as you stuff cannoli number twenty-one in at the buzzer. It explodes into your mouth like a firecracker in the mud; the paper plate below you is a quarter inch high in cast off creme. Cookie whispers in George's ear and you are deducted from 21 to 19. A two cannoli deduction is a bit overzealous you feel, but can't voice your displeasure because your mouth is still full. Nineteen puts you even with the Shredder, but before an eat-off can be announced, unbeknownst to the principal players, Brad "Psycho" Scuillo has steadily eaten to twenty cannolis and the win. George holds the trophy facing backwards because it is inscribed as a Nathan's Florida hot dog qualifying win, an unclaimed trophy plucked from the office at the last moment. Later, online blogs will claim that the Sheas were so confident in your imminent victory that the trophy was already engraved with your name on it. As George peddles Cafe Roma, the sponsor's name, Brad Scuillo breaks into tears. Genuine tears of emotion. George, ever the showman, puts the tears front and center and the cameras capture the moment.

Later E:60, the venerable sports show, will display a ten minute puff piece that opens and closes with Brad's tears. Jimmy Kimmel will replay the moment for laughs, quipping that one should never cry after winning a cannoli eating contest, that is unless, your dying father's wish was for you to win a cannoli eating contest. None of it matters to you. You think back to the moment of loss, your black clothes stained with cannoli. You leaned over the rear of the stage and tossed your water bottle into the sewer. Your anger, not at yourself or George or Cookie, but at the cannoli itself...all of them from all the years you've competed, like a giant white whale that you harpoon time and time again. Seemingly without injury it submerges, gone for another year. You blink in the harsh sun, trying to picture where it has gone, but find yourself unable to see farther than the International Coffee Shop whose cardboard sign "Best Coffey in NY" clearly mocks you and the many years you've stood defeated on the sagging stage while the distant strains of triumph break agonized and clear.

September of 2009 would be the most lucrative prize money month in Major League Eating history, an unthinkable $95,000 from chili spaghetti to chicken wings to burgers to burritos. The only contest listed as a zero gain except for eternal glory, is the world cannoli eating championship. You have made your peace with this contest. Eight years and eight consecutive second or third place finishes; Always the mascarpone bridesmaid, never the bride. Your compiled losses provide you with a Stockholm syndrome where you see honor in defeat. You would be fine never winning the contest and in fact a rookie Sean "Flash" Gordon is getting a lot of traction as a favorite in this year's event. Still, you take a collared shirt and write down the results of the past eight years on its back. Jesus had his cross, you have your cannoli loss chart to bear. With a heavy heart and an empty stomach you mount the busted stage to face your destiny with dessert. 2009 is a new world, Larry Hoff's morning TV contract goes unrenewed and Rich Shea is sure that he spots Larry drinking Scotch at 9 AM in terminal four at LaGuardia Airport. Rumors abound that the league is going to be sold for millions of dollars. In a final sign of foodie apocalypse, Don "Moses" Lerman, the once great butter champ (7 1/4 quarter pound sticks in eight minutes) returns to the table in unsanctioned contests run by imitating amateurs. His butter record and legacy tainted like steroid assisted statistics in Cooperstown. Et Tu, "Moses" Lerman, Et Tu?

Still, the September day is crisp and sunny and the creaky amusement rides on Grand street glisten. The Shredder has announced his retirement and you find yourself as the last cannoli eater standing. It is you,

George Shea, and the table as the only leftover remnants from the first cannoli championship eight years prior. You have six cups filled with lukewarm water, one for each minute. Eater X is below the stage yelling out Flash Gordon's numbers. It seems you have him until late in the contest when he mounts a surge. George rides the crowd, his face contorted, red with passion "This is it!" he screams into the microphone as if the balance of the world will be determined by the cannoli contest outcome. Record numbers line the street and the scaffolding erected on Grand street allows for office workers to gather behind barbwire on the second story of a building that overlooks the crowd. You are eating in a pit, the Thunderdome of consumption, and George has the crowd in a frenzy. "This is it!" he keeps screaming as children cry, the crowd roars louder. Each bite reverberates like an echo, a bone-cracking crunching ripple across the crowd. George pleads for more cannoli and the sponsor Ferrara answers with more plates. The table strains to its utmost breaking point and then suddenly everything stops. You gently massage the table with your gloved fingertips and look into the crowd. You strip off your shirt and throw it to the masses. Your gloves and hat too. The crowd wants more, but you have nothing left to give. "Flash" Gordon, holding his six year old son, has eaten 19.5 cannolis. You have eaten twenty.

There is no trophy, no championship belt, no prize money, but you are named the world cannoli eating champion. All you can do now is digest.

Fear, Loathing and Chicken Wings in Panama City, FLA: The Hooters World Wing Eating Championship — Part One

They say you can't go back to spring break, and they are right. Yet, spring break seems to symbolize the collegiate American Dream — no picket fence, 2.5 kids yet — we want to party with no consequence, no limits and no tan lines. At the age of 42 — older, but no wiser — I returned to spring break for 14 hour run in Panama City. A rental car — no hotel room to crash in — and destiny in the form of the first qualifier of the Hooters World Wing Eating Championship, awaited me. But it was Friday, and there was business to take care of first.

Most folks find it strange that there is a league for competitive eating. Would they find it stranger that every ranked Major League Eater signs a three-year contract with the organizing body — the I.F.O.C.E — The International Federation of Competitive Eating (the only stomach-centric sports league in the world). The contract is to ensure that each gurgitator competes only in league events and eschews the non-paying restaurant challenges (made famous by certain TV shows, giant hockey puck tasting burgers and massive pizzas that taste worse than the cardboard they are served in). I have a confession: I have an eating Achilles heel. My local Boston bar in NYC is Professor Thoms — they do Monday night lobster specials, serve beer named after Bill "Spaceman" Lee, show all the wicked Beantown teams and even welcome New Yawkers. They, like most bar food establishments, serve nachos. I have never finished an order of their nachos — a waste for the casual diner, but a colossal embarrassment for the 20th ranked eater in the world (An autographed poster displaying my eating prowess hangs behind the bar, but not for long after they read this post). The nachos are delicious, served on a pizza tray, and despite last year's entire Celtics playoffs, Pats, and Bruins games, each attempt left me pawning off some sour cream stained chips to the folks seated next to me. I am now freed from this albatross of cheese and jalapenos as recently Prof Thoms has offered a "Nachos for one" served on a football-like plate, but clearly, my pride and dented stomach capacity will prevent me from ordering the puny dish. Restaurant challenges are out, but the loophole in the MLE contract is the all-you-can-eat buffet. Since my contract had recently expired, I planned on resigning and celebrating at a half-price sushi all-you-can stomach joint on 1st Ave.

The contract was easy, most eaters have a boiler plate agreement, but I have a special rider that provides if a crab cake eating contest occurs, I am allowed three National Bohemian beers as my dunking liquid. No alcohol is allowed during eating contests, but it's a dealbreaker for me if I can't double fist Old Bay seasoned crab and Natty Boh beer. The league wasn't happy, but it's not like there is an M&M eating contest and I refuse to eat the brown ones. The contract is printed, signed and faxed — it was time for some stomach fireworks. For several months I had been researching half-priced sushi places until

arriving at one that has a catering party platter selection voluminous, reasonably fresh, and tasty.
I had arraigned a platonic dinner date with a fellow competitive eater, Maria Edible. She is of the new breed of pro-eater, young, sexy, and capable of consuming over a gallon of chili in six minutes. Maria dates the number two eater in the world, Pat "Deepdish" Bertoletti, and he with his mohawk and her with her tattoos make for a more benign Sid and Nancy of Punk Eating. Maria, who recently had been wrestling with the idea of vegetarianism, was willing to help me decimate the ocean's economy for all-you-can-eat sushi. When I discovered that my place offered all the beer and sake one could drink with their voluminous meal for only 33 bucks, it was like being handed a preview of Heaven. Granted, this is not the wisest meal one should have the night before a wing eating contest, but I was going on spring break so stretching my liver's capacity, along with my stomach's seemed like a Masters Degree like idea. As I settled into my first round of sushi (6 Ikura, 2 Eel, 2 White Tuna, 1 Kani, 1 Saba, 1 Inari, hand rolls of spicy crunchy yellowtail, spider roll, and black pepper roll) I told Maria about my first trip to Spring Break, back in 1991.

My junior year of college with barely 100 dollars to my name, meant I would be staying in Baltimore, spending my limited budget on Natty Boh and a bushel of crabs. I did own a beat up pick-up truck, so when two females I knew reasonably well, offered to pay gas, tolls and oil to Ft. Lauderdale, visions of multiple viewings of VHS copies of "Hot Moves,"

"Spring Break" and "Hardbodies" made my answer, "when can we leave and where will we stay?" One girl had a grandmother who would house us, rent free and we left that afternoon. Twenty-two hours later, sputtering gas fumes into Ft, Lauderdale, Grandma said, "No chance." I found myself staying in a room with nine other sorority girls — it seemed like a movie — until the first morning, the manager unlocked door and threatened to charge per person or boot all us. I secretly moved to the balcony and slept under a folding chair for the rest of the week. Spring Break on such a limited budget was not quite like the movies I loved, but I'll give you the highlights. I bought a week's worth of hot dogs and sour kraut, a case of Wegman's Beer, and a bag of briquettes. I got drunk on left over green beer from St Patrick's Day at every skinny bikini, naughty lingerie, or wet tee shirt contest (where they give away the leftover green beer). Friday I discovered and all-you-can-eat peel and eat shrimp special in a strip club. Peelers and peelers, except all the strippers had gone to the beach. I discovered one could get down a lot more shrimp without the peeling part of the equation. I may still be digesting those shells. After seven servings, I was asked to leave. Saturday, I took the bag of briquettes' and lit a BBQ (first on the balcony and before moving to the more approved concrete parking lot). I sent folks to the grocery to bring back whatever they wanted me to grill. I ate a third of everything I cooked for eight hours straight while drinking warm Wegman's. Then we drove back to Baltimore. Not a fun drive back with spring break in the rear view mirror, but I had joined the countless ranks of America's collegiate youth — I had even hooked up on the beach one night (cue the music from "Fraternity Vacation.") — spring break had become spring broke, but I was unfettered, free, inebriated, and content.

Maria Edible: "You would be able to eat a lot more half-priced sushi and drink a lot more beer and sake if you didn't talk so much."

Me: "Duly noted. Let me tell you about the next time I went on spring break over round two"

TO BE CONTINUED

Fear, Loathing and Chicken Wings in Panama City, FLA; The Hooters World Wing Eating Championship and 42 Year Old Returns to Spring Break: Part Two

When we last left off, Maria Edible and I were on round two of all you can eat half-priced sushi and talking about spring break in Florida. For round two, I ordered 1 masago, 2 smoked salmon, 2 spanish mackerel, 2 red clam, Ikura, two handrolls of yellowtail and salmon skin, and another pitcher of beer. As I have blogged before, competitive eating takes one to some interesting places. In 2006 GoldenPalace.com sent myself, my girlfriend, and two MLE announcers on spring break to South Padre Island, TX and Panama City, Fla to search for the greatest collegiate eaters in the huevos rancheros and key lime pie disciplines. Four contests in total — two for aspiring college gurgitators and two of the gustatory gladiators known as Pro-Eaters. Off-shore gambling, prior to being shut down in the U.S., was competitive eating's greatest sponsor due to their inability to use traditional advertising. What better place to influence today's youth towards recreational gambling then when today's youth is nearly black-out drunk, shouting either "Whoo Whoo" (the ladies) or "Show me your Whoo Whoos!" (the fellas).

Golden Palace was sending us in style with our own driver and we were slated to travel in the vehicle known as, "Golden Palace Casino's Museum of Oddities." In reality, an oversized Winnebago, storing all the incredible items that the gambling chain had bought at auction to make headlines. We would be riding and sleeping next to items such as the pope's cane and the grilled cheese sandwich with Jesus face on it. Godly items on Earth would seem to be enough for most online casinos, but just in case, Golden Palace boldly bid where no man had bid before and acquired William Shatner's kidney stones. Beam me to Spring Break, and give it all you've got, Scotty we've got the Captain's kidney stones and there is no stopping us. Well...

Who would have guessed that no one would insure "Golden Palace Casino's Musuem of Oddities, making the caravan not quite street legal and Shat's stones to be left in storage in Canada. We rented an SUV and drove hellbent to spend a day in New Orleans (where it is always spring break). There are many highlights (and lowlights) of four adults running competitive eating contests on spring break, but I will relate only two.

South Padre Island — College Contest — Huvoes Rancheros, sixth minute.

In a word, spring break in South Padre Island, could be described as, "sloppy." I didn't think that it would carry over into the competitive eating events, however, at minute six of the collegiate Huveos Rancheros contest, something happened that I had rarely seen before. The crowd was huge, pushed up to the front of the raised platform — it was like a Rolling Stones concert, except instead of music, we had 12 college "eatletes" scarfing down platters of huveos rancheros. One eager gurgitator rushed to the front and put his finger down his throat. Before I could react or reach him, a stream of yellow and brown spurted out from his throat — the breakfast geyser he produced didn't scatter so much as land on the shoulder of a guy in a football jersey in the front row. It sat on his shoulder, closely resembling a parrot, while he gave the puker the finger. I realized, the guys were buddies and the eater had gone for "the vanity puke." It is a technique only seen at Philly's Wing Bowl (more of an early morning stripper parade than an eating contest). I described Wing Bowl 13 as, "as close the apocalypse as one could come, without it being the actual apocalypse." Occasionally, one of the 30 eaters, chowing down on ice cold chicken wings, would decide to go for the vanity puke. The most famous, by an eater known only as, "Sloth" was a projectile vomit that put the "Exorcist" to shame. Each year, if the action lags, they show Sloth's reversal in glorious slow motion on the Jumbotron. The crowd loves it.

Back to "Elvis leaving the building" in South Padre Island. I escorted the eater to the back of the stage, but little could be done for the omelet parrot guy. In all future MLE event, the front row is referred to a, "the spray zone." Now you know why.

Panama City — Pro Contest — Key Lime Pie — Post Contest

I am often asked, "What is the worst you've felt after a contest?" An easy one — after almost 5 whole Key

Lime pies in six minutes, my stomach felt like Mike Tyson was taking swings at it. We had a short flight from Panama City to Orlando and a tight connection to get us back to NYC. I was hunched in my seat at a 90 degree angle, moaning the entire way. In Orlando, I decided to do the unthinkable — attempt to evacuate my key lime overload. I am always thankful to the sponsors and the food which they put forth; digestion is a part of our sport plus, we usually are on stage for interviews or wandering the crowd signing autographs so the food naturally settles. In my case, I felt 10 months pregnant with a key lime baby pushing against my belly button. In the rest room, I decided to attempt to take a crap, hop up, smell my crap, and inevitably throw up. Everything went fine, until I hopped up and the automatic flush quickly disposed of my feces, the aroma, and my hope. Tim "Eater X" Janus yelled into the bathroom that the plane was boarding. I yelled that I wasn't going to make it. He returned moments later with a large Perrier bottle. I chugged it, Eater X cheered me on, and I exploded like a pipe bomb. It turns out that poorly made key lime pie will expand in one's stomach and the tripled amount of greenish mush and graham cracker filled the toilet to overflowing. The automatic flush could not keep up, and like a low-production value Terminator movie, man won over machine again. I've never been back to the Orlando airport and I really owe whoever discovered the key lime volcano an apology, but hey, I was still on spring break.

Still eating and drinking $\frac{1}{2}$ priced sushi with Maria Edible. For the third round, I request the dealer's choice plus a piece of Ikura. I get a roll with real crabmeat and six pieces of deep sea or back row sushi. I also order another pitcher of beer and we return to Spring Break in sunny Florida.

Saturday, March 30th — a slight breeze blows in from the beach, where 50,000 Panama City breakers drink, boogie, and drink some more. It appears to me that Panama City has fallen on hard times since my last spring break — evidenced by the shuttered Club Latitudes and Breakers Bar. However, Hooters seems to be leading a revival. Their bright orange logo serves as a beacon to the spring breakers and the eight dollar pitchers of Miller Lite as the nectar reward. A stocky clean-cut guy makes his way across the balcony. His swagger and protruding muscled jaw mean it can only be the number one eater in the world, Joey "Jaws" Chestnut. Described as, "an American Hero," Joey rise in pro-eating has been majestic. In the 2013 Hooters finals, he ate 144 wings in 10 minutes as Super Bowl veteran (and former Hooters oyster shucker) Jon Gruden looked on slackjawed. In competitive eating, Joey is a man of firsts. He created an appearance market previously unknown to Major League Eating. He booked bar mitzvahs, birthday appearances and frat parties. He cut the starting line tape at San Jose bike races. While most eaters had what he called gimmicks — Mohawks, face paint, or outlandish hats and suits, Joey said his only gimmick was winning. He became the first rock star eater after a fan offered drugs off stage (he declined) and by trashing two hotel rooms. (Note: He didn't throw any televisions, but post contest enjoys a nap in the bath and often leaves the water running). In Major League Eating, we pay our way to the qualifiers and then the sponsor pays for travel, accommodations, and generous prize money in the finals. However, Joey became such a commodity that it is said, he doesn't open his mouth for less than thousands. The Hooters qualifiers have $500, $300, and $200 in places one through three and last year I recouped my travel costs to Indianapolis. This year was spring break and Easter weekend. My flight alone cost more than any other competitive eating trip in the last decade. Joey will be lounging on the beach while I will be confined to a rental car with Yasir "Doggie Bag" Salem. My exit strategy has me driving two hours, flying out of Tallahassee at 6 am, taking three planes, and arriving in Newark 13 hours later. A rock star eater I am not; Even celebrity short order cooks travel better than me.

Joey and Hooters have had a symbiotic relationship for many years. He has appeared in one of their commercials and if rumors are to be believed he has dated no less than five Hooters waitresses. Hooters Panama City was reviving spring break but also going more upscale — granted the uniforms were not going to change. One Hooters rep called the pantyhose and orange shorts, "unforgiving." But really why go upscale when one looked at the 15 girls assembled to be "wingettes" for today's event. The girls worked at Hooters up and down Florida and I kid you not, they all loved their job (but probably not their uniform). With 15 beautiful Hooters girls cheering it is easy to get distracted, but Joey gets into a wing eating rhythm (his manual to oral dexterity is unparalleled). Joe wins easily with 140 wings. His technique is so good in the future I will publish a blog on Joey's chicken wing technique titled, "The Magna Carta of Meat. Did I qualify for the finals? I did not. My technique was flawed. My new mantra is that it takes just as long to take a bad bite as a good bite — Joey Chestnut's 20 pound bowl was a mound of bones as if consumed by one of the dragons from Harry Potter. My 20 pound bowl was filled with wings with tiny holes in them as if consumed by Ron Weasly. I was clearly eating only the middles and that might fly at the Indianapolis Hooters, but in Panama City one needs strip meat from bone. $800 bucks in credit card debt at this point would deter some from the rigors of the pro-eating circuit, but I have adopted a Dude like attitude towards the whole thing. Strikes and gutters, hot dogs and chicken wings or to quote directly from The Stranger: "Sometimes you eat the bear, and sometimes, well, he eats you." The bear in my case was Neil Seabree, a rookie from Freeport, Florida in his first contest. Sam Barclay, the MLE MC often has to think of pro-eating nicknames on the spot and pre-contest proclaimed the heavily bearded, fuzzy haired Neil Seabree, "The Bear." His name and incredible wing total of 128 was read second, only behind Joey's victory. It's not unheard of for a rookie to shock the pros — Seabree's totals were weighed four times before the announcement to be sure of the result, but this was a flabbergasting 1st performance. A closer look at Seabree and one realized he was the spitting image of one of today's hottest comics. The beard, the hair, the girth — formerly Neil Seabree, now forever known on the MLE circuit as, "Snack Galifianakis" A gig playing musician (Snack: "I grew up playing Guns and Roses covers, but now I am way into bluegrass.") was reborn as a pro-eater. His wife and two week old daughter (two weeks old and already on spring break?) looked on amazed. I wondered how he didn't get any wing sauce on his shirt. (Snack:"They gave me this nice white tee-shirt, I didn't want to get any sauce on it."). Hooters also gave him $300 and after signing an MLE contract, Snack Galifianakis is heading to Clearwater, Florida on July 25th for the Hooters World Wing Eating Finals 2013.

I was heading for the bar — first Hooters, for a cool down milkshake — and then with Joey, Doggie Bag, and the rest of the gang in tow, several bars that exist in liquor stores (we visited Ms. Newbies, Ms. Newbies Two, and Packaged Liquors, owned by the Ms. Newbies franchise). When you have that much food in your belly, you can pretty much drink as much as you want. Setting competitive eaters loose on your city can be dicey, and we often find ourselves winding down in a strip club (they have the nicest restrooms), but we tip well and don't drool much.
Several hours later, at 4 am central time, I find myself screaming down the desolate Florida highway, heading towards Tallahassee and 13 hours of airport travel. Doggie Bag is passed out in the passenger seat and with only the hum of the wheels on the highway, the solitude gives a man time to think about his wing technique. It's true that there were four more Hooters qualifiers in Augusta during the Masters (last year John Daly showed up not for the golf, but for the

wings), Las Vegas, Dallas, and city TBD, but I had busted my budget traveling to spring break. Fortunately for me, the pro-eating circuit allows do-overs of sorts. In two weeks at the Pork in the Park event in Salisbury, Maryland would be the Eastern Shore Wing War presented by Mountaire Farms. In Wicomico County, I would again face the dreaded chicken wing — this time the paddles would have no flaps the drumsticks would appear. I passed into Eastern Standard Time and it occurred to me it was Easter Sunday. For this competitive eater, there would be no family ham, no chocolate bunnies, and the only resurrection occurring April 21st at the next wing eating contest. As Easter dawn broke through the dirty windshield of the rental car, I had only one thought, "How would Jesus eat the drumsticks?"

THE MAGNIFYING CREDIT UNION WORLD ICE CREAM EATING CHAMPIONSHIP: TOO BIG TO SCOOP
(April 12th, 2013)

I scream, you scream, but at the Magnifying Credit Union World Ice Cream Eating Championship, how do you avoid screaming with brain freeze? (Answer below). As a competitive eater, I do a ton of media — perhaps you've seen me on TV or heard me on the radio? I hold a few world records, but I am best known for plugging the sponsor's name incessantly. On the New England Sports Channel, I said, "The Verizon Voice Wing Battle of the Wings Chicken Wings" 87 times in a three minute spot. I ate three pounds of watermelon and plugged MLE: The Game in one minute, forty-seven seconds with Kathy Lee and Hoda (When my video game avatar threw up in glorious Nintendo color, they were mortified). When a great sponsor name comes along, like the Magnifying Credit Union, in conjunction with an ice cream contest, well, I just can't help myself. National and local media — consider yourself warned.

What do the names John Daly, David Wells, Dennis Rodman, and Crazy Legs Conti have in common? All legends in their sports until they began to rely on their outsized personalities in lieu of talent and became known as buffoons, has-beens, and former greats. The night before an eating contest I should not be at Showgirls in Plant City downing seven Coors lights in twenty minutes to beat the happy hour special. I shouldn't be at Louie Mack's steakhouse ordering both the porterhouse and rib eye along with a few Manhattans and a few smoky whiskeys. The harsh Florida sun would be my hangover's wake up call and perhaps my career's death knell. In the morning, I nearly had a, "reversal of fortune," and this was hours before the contest. What had become of the once great oyster king of 2002 and when did he start to refer to himself in the third person? Was it time to hang up the esophagus? I scream indeed.

Lakeland, Florida was the scene of this first ever ice cream festival and when top ranked Major League Eaters show up to consume record numbers of partially melted vanilla pints, 25,000 people show up to see if they can lick the leftovers. Baskin Robbins and Hershey's jostled for tent space along with local favorite, Working Cow Ice Cream. Despite exotic flavors such as, "Smurf", "Butterscotch Explosion", and "Garbage Can," the contest would feature the mundane vanilla, but make no mistake; ice cream is an unforgiving discipline.

I had eaten ice cream in competition once before — at the venerable Water Club in NYC, Major League Eating held an ice cream eating contest open only to the press. As Pat "Deepdish" Bertoletti, Tim "Eater X" Janus, and I battled, no cheering was heard. It was an odd contest and with only the combination of slurping sounds and camera shutters, I suppose it was a lot like filming pornography. In porn, rarely does one freeze themselves from the inside out. Eater X had the best gimmick and used a silver marathon heat blanket to avoid hypothermia post contest.

Brainfreeze, or spenopalatine ganglioneuralgia if you are playing scrabble or trying to impress the ladies, can be avoided. If you hold the spoon upside down and don't let it touch the roof of the mouth — no brainfreeze. In a six minute all you can wolf down, it is pretty much a sure bet that you will be chilling your mind at some point. What do you do? Power through, drink warm water, or realize that Joey "Jaws" Chestnut to your right has eaten three pints in one minute and you should have studied harder in school. However, the darker side to competitive eating can also help. The last time we ate ice cream, I covered my gums in ambasol, an oral painkiller. However, due to the cold and hot combo, my gums peeled for a week. I am heading to Nola for the Rouse's Crawfish Eating Championship next weekend and no way could my mouth stand the spicy boil with any cuts. No ambasol in Polk County for me. One unnamed eater used Percocet with caffeine pills. Drug testing has yet to come to pro-eating, but rubbing the clear or Winstrol V on your stomach, won't help anyway.

Six minutes later and The Joker Marchant Stadium was awash in vanilla ice cream run-off. It was like a milkshake river parted the competitors. My goatee probably had a few dripping ounces in it as the empty pint containers were counted. Joey edged out Adrian "The Rabbit" Morgan (the Justin Beiber of our sport) with 1.81 gallons. The Rabbit's 11.5 pints were just a Sundae away from the win. I placed 5th with just under a gallon. Perhaps my night before activities are starting to catch up to me although at the moment I felt a reversal coming up the esophagus, I Louie Armstrong it, and swallowed. I was not going to lose that $200. Next weekend is New Orleans, a city with a special place in both my heart and stomach. Despite my penchant to eat and drink amazing amounts in that city, I will refocus my energies from bacchanalia to athletic achievement. The Rouse's World Crawfish Eating Contest awaits and I intend to be Master of the Mudbug and return to gustatory glory and if I win any prize money, what better place to put in than in a Magnifying Credit Union money market checking account.

GET HIMS A BODY BAG FILLED WITH FROZEN YOGURT, JOHNNY!
(September 30th, 2013)

It's 4 am and I am peddling a NYC rental Citibike towards Penn Station while singing the Standells' "Dirty Water." Actually, I am singing the Dropkick Murphy's cover of the Standells' "Dirty Water" because that is the only version they have on the Coyote Ugly jukebox. After fifteen hours bartending, one shower, and two episodes of "Girls," I decide to stagger to the bar for an hour and then head towards my ride to Boston. Wing Kong and Wild Bill Meyers are meeting me in Secaucus and we are road tripping to Beantown's Phantom Gourmet Food Festival and the Yogurtland Frozen Yogurt Eating Contest. The Phantom Gourmet Food Festival is in its tenth year, under the shadow of Fenway Park, with fifty vendors giving out food from The Sausage Guy to Uppercrust Pizza to beer. Lots and lots of beer. The event sells out because Boston is a town that likes to celebrate anything without pretension. Show up in your Celts, Pats, Sox, or Bruins gear and eat and drink and talk sports among Titletown's folk. The Phantom Gourmet and its local TV show (investigating Boston restaurants in a complementary way) are run by the three Andelman brothers — Dave, Dan, and Michael. It makes sense that the three would turn to TV, as the natural progression from their father, Eddie, who is one of Boston's most iconic radio hosts. The

Andelman's have been linked to competitive eating from the early 2000s as Eddie's annual hot dog safari hosted a Nathan's qualifier each year (and was my rookie hot dog performance site). Now, the Nathan's qualifier is held at the Phantom Gourmet BBQ festival, where two years ago, an underage Matt "Megatoad" Stonie had to eat his hot dogs separated from the rest of the field due to the 21 and over rule. He was locked in a fenced off cage. It looked like a Blink 182 video or a zombie film as 19-year-old Megatoad ate to prison victory.

Megatoad is now 21, and on Sunday eschewed the Shocktop Pumpkin Ale and instead ate 10 $\frac{1}{2}$ pounds of pumpkin (and vanilla tart) Yogurtland yogurt to claim a new World Record, a giant trophy spoon, and $750 in coupons for more yogurt.
Despite Megatoad's impressive performance, the Phantom Gourmet Food Festival belonged to two men. The first is one of the kings of 1980s teen films - William "Billy" Zabka. From his roles in "European Vacation," "Back to School", and "Just one of the Guys" he always played a smart aleck, usually a villain. However, his role as Johnny Lawrence in the first (and for purists, the only) "Karate Kid" is the role that still has people yelling lines at him and asking if they can join the Cobra Kai Dojo (you can't, but you can buy a souvenir t-shirt or headband). Billy looks much younger than his actual age and is kind to everyone who does the crane pose or yells, "Sweep the leg," or "Get him a bodybag, Johnny." Billy is actually an Oscar nominated filmmaker who does five "Johnny Lawrence" appearances a year to satisfy fan's needs for

a time when villains were just human bullies. It's odd that Billy was always cast as a bad-guy, because in real life, he couldn't be nicer. Billy is introduced prior to the yogurt eating contest and the crowd goes bonkers.

The day also belonged to Wild Bill Meyers, whose second place finish with 8 pounds of Yogurtland yogurt is akin to Brian Scalabrine shutting out Larry Bird in one-on-one. Wild Bill, formerly a table-ender and known only for driving extreme distances to contests and eating challenges, became Greg Kite blocking Magic Johnson, but in yogurt eating. While I was slogging through four pounds of pumpkin yogurt (think of turtleneck sweaters, large piles of dead leaves, a roasting fireplace), Wild Bill was doubling my total eating only Vanilla Tart (the eating equivalent of those ice sports at the Olympics with the long skates). He even beat Wing Kong - the mighty Kong falling from Boston skyscraper-like height victory (Kong won the Uppercrust pizza contest at this venue three years prior and remains the only Yankees fan to emerge from Fenway with pats on the back instead of punches to the belly). Wild Bill had found his groove and over a few wind down wings at the Cask and Flagon, he simply said that he felt at home with the yogurt and that he felt more brain freeze at his office IT job, than in the eating arena.

My all-nighter and poor performance at the yogurt table (I shouldn't have had that free Sausage Guy grinder) left me spent, but I sat with my nephew, 9 month old Simon as he tried to liberate my beer bottle from me and thought that perhaps casually dining with family and friends is the true meaning of the Phantom Gourmet Food Festival. As Wild Bill drove off to the Allentown sunset and Billy Zabka flew back to LA, I simply sat digesting autumn yogurt and smiled. And then I fell asleep.

The Buffalo Wing Festival in Two Bites. Part Two: I Am Woman, Hear My Stomach Roar!

Asking someone where the best chicken wings in Buffalo, NY are is like asking them to pick their favorite child, but year after year, the discussion continues with no clear winner in sight. I'll add my favorite three in no particular order, Gabriel's Gate in the Allentown section serves a wing that sings in perfect pitch, elevating the wing form to fine dining. Duff's serves its wings in wooden bowls with sauce as a dipping soup as if the wing can be a solid, a liquid, and by the process of sublimation, a spicy mist that hits the nostrils with Pavlovian longing. In the non-traditional sauce category, no one does it better than Cole's on Elwood. They have a baked parmesan wing that brings tears to my eyes and napkins to my shirt.

On the Major League Eating circuit the hot dog is the toughest food in competition due to the meat and bun combo, but the chicken wing is the most difficult. The chicken wing, both the drumstick (or bat) and the paddle (or flat) requires jaw strength, rhythm, and in a twelve minute contest — capacity. The World Chicken Wing Eating Championship is not for the faint of heart or stomach. Coca-Cola Arena, home of the non-edible minor league baseball Bisons, is filled with 35 venerable wing specialist from across America like North Dakota's Parrot's Cay (signature sauce: North Dakota Napalm) and Portland, Oregon's Fire on the Mountain (signature sauce: Raspberry Habanero). Buffalo and New York State are well represented and even Charlie the Butcher's beef on weck and Bocce Club pizza join the wing crew. There are chicken wing Christmas ornaments, day-glo orange wing hats, and even a mechanical bull in the shape of a chicken wing. TV personality and Itunes podcaster Mark DeCarlo has a booth and chefs Marco and Armand trade poultry recipes backstage. The night, however, belongs to the buffalo chicken wing fans who in the twelve years of the Buffalo Wing Festival have consumed 3.8 million wings weighing 212 tons…and that doesn't even count the blue cheese.

George Shea, Major League Eating's founder and MC of the Buffalo Festival every year of its existence takes the mike and shouts that he is a proponent of poultry warfare. He claims that the scorecard of the war on the bird stands at 1.7 billion chickens killed, humans zero. He implores the crowd not to rest on its eating laurels that they should, "Push forward, eat more, and continue onto wing consumption glory." As a sidebar he announces that Joey Chestnut is a scratch due to a strained esophagus from a rib eating contest in Reno a few days before.

Through the crowd, lead by The Wing King Drew Cerza, holding the chicken scepter is Sonya "The Black Widow" Thomas, a five time champion of this discipline. Already on stage is Michelle "Cardboard Shell" Lesco whom I've written regarding her dominance in Corn Indian Tacos. Also on stage is a new comer to the sport, the blond haired, tanned golden girl Miki Sudo. No competitor, male or female, has risen so quickly to the top as Miki. She is the Niagara Falls of competitive eating, or more specifically, the Horseshoe Falls of the stomach - a human digestive system akin to a crestline of 2500 feet with the power of 675,000 gallons of water a second. She is the Maiden of the Mist, and like Horseshoe Falls, her halo is a permanent rainbow with a pot of competitive eating prize money gold at its end. The day before she bested Joey and the rest of the field in a medley of Buffalo bar bites - 5 pounds in four minutes and seventeen seconds. Eating a pound a minute is like running a four minute mile and despite the fact that twelve minutes of chicken wing eating is a marathon, she in her shiny sparkly shoes and demure smile, seems ready to go the distance. The chickens don't stand a chance.

Gloria Steinem never endorsed competitive eating. We have no way of knowing if Billie Jean King ate more for lunch than Bobby Riggs, but the 2013 Buffalo Wing Festival made one thing clear: The ladies who lunch are no joke, but champions of the chomp. Eschewing title 9 regulations, golf tees that are closer to the green, and smaller basketballs, Sonya Thomas, Michelle Lesco, and Miki Sudo said (with their mouths full), "Anything a man can eat, a woman can eat better!"
And eat they did. Former champ Sonya Thomas claimed third with 141 wings. Michelle Lesco, with her wiry frame from doing 100 push-ups and 100 sit-ups a day, would eat 158 wings. Miki Sudo, The Vegas Queen of Cuisine, would emerge champion with 178. Yasir "Doggy Bag" Salem, a triathlete and

the only pro-eater to work for The Economist (and a male) would finish a distance fourth. The rest of the male field and myself included were all bridesmaids as well, but I was witness and even if Chuck Norris and John Wayne and Rick Springfield ate, they too would have lost to these three amazing women.

Sonya, Michelle, and Miki all weigh less than 115 pounds each. Combined their weight is is still less than several of the male competitors on stage. The three women could be beauty pageant contestants, but instead have aimed their X chromosomes at the male dominated world of competitive eating. At college campus cafeterias, sorority girls are cutting the line ahead of fat bloated frat boys. It is a new world food order, first in competitive eating, but soon in casual dining...one where the girl on a first date orders a prime rib and the boy a salad. Be warned America a female revolution is coming and school girls are putting down their Barbies and picking up the BBQ; Dreaming not of prom dates and wedding dresses, but of becoming the next Sonya (8 pounds 2 ounces of chili cheese fries in ten minutes), Michelle (142 gyoza in eight minutes), or Miki (8.5 pounds of kimchi in six minutes)...I am woman, hear my stomach roar!

ABOUT LAST NIGHT'S KIMCHI
(August 13th, 2013)

I thought I knew everything I needed to know about Chicago from the movies "About Last Night," and "Running Scared," but I was wrong. My weekend in The Windy City included gourmet hot dogs, ComiCon, a Kimchi Eating Contest, Superhero Strippers and a 8 to 10 pound weight fluctuation each day.

My hosts were Pat "Deepdish" Bertoletti and Tim "Gravy" Brown, who own and operate a food truck and lifestyle brand named, "Glutton Force Five." Deepdish, a Kendall Culinary School grad and chef creates the food (cheeseburger nachos and Elvis bread pudding with bacon frosting) and Gravy, a marketing director for both HVAC and The Admiral Theater (a former Vaudevillian Theater turned into a modern day nudie palace) creates the buzz. Both left Major League Eating to pursue other options involving the food truck, Hollywood, and the internet. The remaining Glutton Force are mascots Party Bot, a pink unicorn, and Mr. Snugglesworth, a loveable bulldog who eschews physical fitness. Glutton Force Five are more than an animatronics Rock-fire Explosion band come to life. They are more than sex, food, drugs, and rock-and-roll stars. They are true American Food Outlaws where "excess" is just another word for lunch.

These are the highlights of my weekend in Chicago, or least the ones that can be printed without an ensuing criminal investigation:

Pat and I drink tall boys while we wait our turn at Hot Dougs, a venerable hot dog mecca open a scant five hours a day. The line is long, but the payoff is amazing. While a New York dog is about about the meat and bun (and maybe a little sandy salt air at Coney Island), Chicago dogs are all about the toppings - the traditional includes: yellow mustard, onions, dayglo relish, tomato slices, a whole pickle spear and celery salt. Voltaire must have coined cultivating one's garden while digging into a Chicago style hot dog - it's common ground for carnivores and vegetarians and it makes a hot dog into a sandwich. Hot Doug's also has a host of gourmet dogs and as Pat makes small talk with Doug, we order eight. My favorite is an escargot hot dog with brie cheese and parsley butter, but every dog was like a Michelan star restaurant in a bun.

The next day we go Mexican in Pat's neighborhood, eating first at El Milagro where the char grilled steak is covered in cabbage and salsa. One taco is the size of a burrito and the burritos are the size of hubcabs. For the truck, Pat has been experimenting with a duck skin taco with green avocado jalapeño salsa. In his spare time working at a huge catering plant, he fried 60 ducks and saved the skin for the food truck. He made only 15 orders of tacos out of all that skin, giving the food folks a taco orgy of the mouth. Pat and I then head to Don Pedro's on West 18th street. On the counter as you walk in are chicharrones (fried pork skin) as big as a bodybuilder's arm. In the back, a door opens, and out of the smokey haze, two men carry a coffin sized stretcher of carnitas. It looks like something out of a "Hostel" movie. Pat and I split a pound and half of carnitas tacos and our waitress comps us two deep fried brain tacos for dessert.

Gravy is working Chicago's ComiCon to advertise for his self-created originally programmed "Comic Strip" at the Admiral, where strippers dress in latex superhero outfits and fight each other until, well, the latex comes off. ComiCon is packed and in a genius move of counter program, the World History of Money convention is in the same building, thus giving the comic book nerds someone to pick on. One hasn't lived until they have seen a fat shirtless kid dressed as Hawkman, make fun of another kid carrying his replica buffalo nickel collection. ComiCon has celebs of all sizes from Verne Troyer to Lou Ferrigno. Why Andrew McCarthy was there seemed strange…is there a big John Hughes/Swamp Thing connection I don't know about? I spotted a fleeing Brandon Routh, not in a cape, but clearly no one wanted to tell him that a new Superman movie has come out. ComiCon fans are unnaturally nice and perhaps the best part was watching fans interact with the comic artists and buy original sketches and idling doodles for reasonable prices. There is plenty on sale, by the time we found Gravy Brown at his booth with the latex laden strippers, he had already picked up a Freddy Krueger basement diorama with working incense boiler and a five foot prop statue of Greta, the bikini clad female Gremlin from part two of the movie. Later that night, Mr. Snugglesworth would howl at Greta, showing his bulldog allegiance to Mogwai everywhere.

We finally made it to the The Admiral, where a sold out crowd of fanboys watched strippers dressed as catwoman, Harley Quinn, and Bat Girl do battle. The show was great, Gravy - a modern day "Boobs" Fosse had choreographed the numbers to be heavy on movement and nip slips. By the time the topless storm troopers appeared, there wasn't a dry boxer brief in the house. I could write more, but I don't want to objectify super heroes.

The 18th annual Korean festival hosted the six minute kimchi contest. When I arrived a combination "They Shoot Horses, Don't They" marathon dance contest and K-Pop B-Boy breakdance competition was in it's fourth hour. I scanned the Major League Eaters assembled and realized I was about to be beaten by three women (Sonya Thomas, Miki Sudo and Michelle Lesco). The dungeon parlors of NYC may be awash in this kind of beating, but it was new to me on the MLE circuit and shows that the meek may inherit ComiCon, but the ladies are taking over competitive eating. Indeed, all the women ate more than me - Miki Sudo won by tripling my 3 pounds and eating 9 pounds of kimchi. As if the sponsors' pink belly bearing shirt wasn't emasculating enough, I clearly didn't have the testosterone to place in the prize money.

Perhaps this is too much information but kimchi is a lot more spicy coming out of the human body than going in. Jed "The Jalapeno King" Donahue once said that a spicy competitive eating contest would turn one's colon into the seventh circle of hell, and I finally realized why one should put toilet paper in the freezer before such a contest. The Korean Festival was amazing, the fans stayed through a rainstorm to watch a fermented cabbage storm and I felt pretty good about eating all that kimchi — I can't say if my flight mates on the plane ride home felt as good about my consumption and digestion as I did, but The Windy City didn't break me, I broke it.

IS COMPETITIVE EATING TOO SEXY FOR THE 4TH OF JULY?
(July 5th, 2013)

Someone who can fit sixty-eight wieners in his mouth must be confident in his sexuality, however, Joey "Jaws" Chestnut, in a July 4th burst, irrevocably changed the innuendo, forever linking his mouth with the number, "69" by eating that world record number of hot dogs in just ten minutes. Oh, he also ate the buns. Freud said, "Sometimes a cigar is just a cigar." Groucho Marx countered (upon meeting a mother of 10 children), "that he enjoys his cigar, but sometimes takes it out of his mouth."

Am I the only one who found the Nathan's International Hot Dog Eating Contest closer to pornography than peristalsis? Did you notice the grunting, sweating, writhing, the stuffing and bun lubing (in water, fruit punch, or lemonade)…the agony and ecstasy on each competitor's face. It was an orgiastic celebration harkening back to the Roman's Vomitoriums (minus the purging due to disqualification), it was an emetophiliac's wet dream (adding the rule, "you heave you leave"), it was a sabermetric nightmare leading to a near 1000 hdbs consumed across all competitors. It was more food porn than on the Food Network; it was a pork sword orgy on ESPN! Or perhaps it was just a lot of people eating quickly in order to beat the holiday traffic.

Joey's 69 hdbs was the grand spectacle, but if you were not one of the 40,000 folks at the corner of Stillwell and Surf, then you missed the small stuff. Celebrity counting judge Chef Morimorto receiving Tim "Eater X" Janus' recipe for hot dog ceviche. Matt "Megatoad" Stonie, pound-for-pound the toughest pro-eater on the planet, becoming only the fifth human to eat 50 or more hdbs in ten minutes. Sonya "The Black Widow" Thomas making a Danica Patrick-like burst in the last 7 seconds to win the female championship. Jeff Butler proving that excellent posture and pro-eating can be copacetic. Badlands Booker, backed by the Brooklyn Community Choir, rapping, "Frankster's Paradise." So many more memories…so much antacid.

At Ruby's on the boardwalk, many of the competitors gathered to swap stories and drink digestive beer. In the distance, the AstroLand Rocket was a shell of its former self, but Coney Island, the City of Fire, has always been a phoenix rising from its ashes. For the first time since 2001, I was in the crowd as the spectator, not on the competitors' side of the table. Would my eating career take the path of Coney Island and arise again, stronger and better, or like the Steeplechase Ride, would it be a stagnant distant reminder of the joyful screams that fill the July 4th Coney Island sky? It was the first July 4th that I didn't eat a hot dog, not a single one. I was tempted, but due to not qualifying for the big dance, I felt I didn't deserve the garlickly goodness of a Nathan's dog. On Saturday, my mind was still on the contest. I sat at Gallagher's 2000, a peeler joint in Long Island City.

The ESPN rebroadcast of the contest was on TV and I was explaining the nuances to a Hungarian stripper named Lucy. She was an avid watcher, not of the grand moments, but of the little ones. She asked many questions regarding why on our country's day of independence we would celebrate it with a "Kolbasz" Eating Contest? Then, as Joey Chestnut was wrapped in the American Flag, she noticed he respectfully, delicately, wiped his mouth with the flag. Lucy asked if that was common? I simply answered that some American's salute with their hands others perhaps prefer to kiss the flag as what could be more American than the stars, stripes, and a little mustard?

THE LONELINESS OF THE LONG DISTANCE EATER
(November 12, 2017)

In Alan Sillitoe's, "The Loneliness of the Long Distance Runner," the narrator, sent away to Bristol's Boy's Reformatory, finds he can only really think, while alone on a long run - not to escape the prison but to escape the drudgery of a life predicted. I've always enjoyed Sillitoe's, "Saturday Night, Sunday Morning" as a mediation on the night one is away from the factory and drinks to excess before the reality of Sunday's mundane world arrives, head-splitting and aching (the main character is also sleeping with his co-worker's wife, so he's probably got more worries than just the hangover.)

Revisiting "Loneliness," makes me realize that Sillitoe has written a fine analogy for competitive eating - granted we love a Saturday night after-party - but it's the long runs, on foot for runners, but with hot dogs and buns for pro-eaters, that provide the journey into oneself and the realizations that occur when we (or the HDBs) arrive at the other side.

Indeed, speed-eating is a talent, and the number one Gustatory Gladiator on the planet, Joey "Jaws" Chestnut recently told the number two eater, Carmen "Cutthroat" Cincotti that he should always demand a fee for his talent. Currently, I am ranked #29th and pretty much agree to every freebie appearance or gig I am asked. Recently, I judged a meatball cooking contest (The East Village's Boulton and Watt's hand-ground lamb ball with whipped feta and pesto lost to Trademark's traditional sauced ball with secret ingredient ricotta cheese.) I also had 3 hours of my competitive eating stories put to a reasonable one-hour improv by the talented Bridge and Tunnel troupe. One sketch, based on when Eater X and I had banked over 1000 Nathan's hot dogs in deep frozen storage, presumed hot dogs as currency and set at a strip club the improv troupe, "Made it rain hot dogs," leaving the stage strewn with 60 wieners, of which, only one was mashed, like the career of many failed gurgitators. I felt for the smooshed dog, once again realizing the power of communing with one's meal (or contest food.)

To aim towards taking the chomping talent to paying my too-damn-high rent in the East Village, I contributed to a burgeoning YouTube video channel run by Major League Eating (in addition to a fee, they reimburse food and EMT costs.) I recreated Willy Wonka's magic chewing gum, famously eaten by Violet Beauregarde, by blending in a powerful Nutribullet, tomato soup, roast beef, baked potato with butter and sour cream, and blueberry pie ala mode. It formed a brown sludge that tasted like, well, brown sludge. I also tackled other eating myths in the hopes that the MLE channel will go viral, much like #3 eater Matt "Megatoad" Stonie's own channel where he gorges himself (on 100 slices or bread or 12 pints of ice cream) to the tune of $300K a year.

I launched via my fashion label, Big Nate Apparel ("Nonactive Wear for the Nonactive" ©), a clothing line of my visage. After all, my Grizzly Adams meets Salvador Dali mug is one billboard famous in Coney Island. The line, found at here and there features artwork by Richie Miller - wonderful negative space ready for serious food spillage (as a pairing I recommend the fuchsia sweatshirt with roasted beets.) As a seventeen year competitive eater, I've not sung for my supper, but suppered for my rent. I've mouth-slammed a crave case as entertainment at a Bar Mitzvah (I ate against an older brother because in Judaism you become a man on that day, but in Major League Eating, one has to be eighteen to pro-eat.) I've been a video game avatar, eaten against puppets, and in a real life Wolfing of Wall Street, entertained on the trading floor by showing off hot dog technique while Eater X demolished the last of sub-prime tubesteaks. I do believe my competitive eating is a talent, but to turn charred brown into plump green has been a struggle. My mind and stomach is open to ideas - as if a giant neon sign blinks, reading "Will eat food for food or other basic sundries."

My next contest is the venerable St. Elmo's Steakhouse shrimp cocktail eating contest at the Meijer Tailgate on Georgia Street in Indianapolis as part of the Big Ten Football pregame celebration. I was there it's inaugural year in the outdoor contest, as 20 degree weather caused the spicy horseradish and succulent shrimp to form a seafood snowball. Even the great Joey Chestnut (current record holder with 15 pounds in ten minutes) had to look into his frozen hand to see how many shrimp he was holding before it disappeared into his cold belly. Like the a Sillitoe narrator says, "Every run like this is a life - a little life, I know - but a life of misery and happiness and things happening as you can ever get really around yourself." Each Major League Eating contest is the same - it's a marathon not only of mastication, but of contemplation - filled with agony and victory and satiety - each bite, chew, and swallow bring us closer to the finish line and closer to understanding ourselves.

THE WING BOWL STORY

Wing Bowl is a radio station event that has served as a consolation pep rally for Philadelphia Eagles fans the Friday before the Super Bowl. It consists of tailgating and then packing the Wachovia Center with 20,000 inebriated Philly meatheads. At 7 am a pageantry filled processional parade files into the pit. The parade features twenty-five amateur chicken wing eaters, their entourages, crudely constructed floats, and Wingettes - local strip club strippers and morally casual women. The 32 minute three round eating contest (the winner gets a car) takes a back-seat to the bacchanalia of drinking, tit-flashing, and fist-fighting. Pseudo celebrities, porn stars, and El Wingador all make appearances however, the success of Wing Bowl by the radio station and its sponsor is simply if no one dies. I have attended for the past five years each year, I pray I never have to return.

Thursday, February 4th 3:33 PM
I am the beverage manager of two NYC high end strip clubs but I work during the day when the clubs are closed. Like Tantalus everything seems like it is within reach but during my dayshift, the only topless women are the 1970s Penthouse photos that plaster the walls. I am at Scores NY putting the finishing work towards a Super Bowl party. Mostly, I am wondering where the promised 42 inch screen TV giveaway from Manhattan Beer is? I track it down to a delivery van and feel that my work is done. Until, I hear that the Super Bowl party may move to the Penthouse Executive Club because the projection

screen TV looks better at that location. No offense to upper management, but I would guess that most patrons will be focused on the tint and contrast of the seventy-five half-naked entertainers, not the TV quality.

4:33 PM
Where is Badlands? I am on the frigid corner of 34th and 8th about to board the Bolt Bus to Philly. The breeze is blowing up my shorts and the bus is about to pull out without my traveling companion, Eric Badlands Booker. Booker is a fellow competitive eater and at over 400 pounds cuts an impressive swath. Despite his man mountain status he is the nicest guy I know and shows love for everyone. He is sweet on the world, like the universe's largest Hershey kiss. His tragic flaw, however, is that he is notoriously late sometimes by three days. As the bus is about to depart, Badlands boards huffing and puffing. I have saved him a row of seats to which he responds, "It's all good!"

5:33 PM
On the bus everyone is on technological devices. I have a typewriter at home and don't own a cellphone. Badlands has a laptop, a cellphone, a blackberry, an mp3 player, a flip cam. The woman seated behind us is explaining how exciting the Wi-Fi on the bus is. I ask her if my library book will still work? She puts her headphones on. I have brought sandwiches for Badlands and I from Salumeria Biellese, a French and Italian Charcuterie that is actually affordable. Its a hole in the wall place on 29th and 8th that acts like a

meat beacon to my stomach. I have brought a spicy sopresetta with provolone and a capicola with mozzarella. I also have a dried fennel boar sausage as a gift for Pat "Deepdish" Bertoletti, another competitive eater and aspiring celebrity chef. Badlands and I split the sandwiches and discuss Jay Zs new album, movies, and the upcoming Catfish Eating World Championship. It is a pleasant ride.

6:33 PM
We are dropped off along the highway of the Cherry Hill Mall. We await a pick-up from US Male, the crawfish eating champ of the world. He is also a NJ mail carrier, but chooses to spell his nickname referring to his Y chromosome and not his job. Despite his single entendre name, he is a swell dude who bleeds Eagles green and lives for Wing Bowl.

7:33 PM Where is US Male? Badlands and I take shelter across the highway at the Red Lobster. I have three Yuengling beers and call the manager over to discuss their Ameripure Oysters. He states that the pasteurization process allows them to serve the oysters safely. I state that it is a jingoistic practice pitting our American insecurities against the welcoming Gulf mollusk. Our voices raise above the family dinner din until a table of women recognizes Badlands from his Wife Swap appearance and then we all take photos together. US Male arrives during our Red Lobster lovefest. I refuse to waver on my anti-Ameripure stance, however, so we leave.

8:33 PM - 11:33 PM
The Trappe Tavern, near Rick the Managers house. The Trap, as it is known to the locals, is the booze hole gathering spot for Rick the Managers entourage. Since Wing Bowl no longer allows professional eaters, Rick Russo a prominent landscaper, has moved latterly from a manager of wingettes (chicken wing cheerleaders) to actually consuming the wings in competition. The fifteen person team is assembled at a table off the main bar. Joey "Jaws" Chestnut three time Wing Bowl champ and his Hooters manager friend, have flown in from California, Deep Dish Bertoletti, the Key Lime Pie eating champ of the world, has flown in from Chicago. Everyone else is relatively local Wing Kong, Steakbellie, Yellowcake, and Jeff "The Natural" Olsen. Rick the Manager has several relatives and morally casual women join the group. The Trappe crowd treats us as hometown heroes, although girls at the bar keep mixing up Deep Dish and the Natural due to their similar Mohawks.

The Trappe Tavern is a diverse crowd that wouldn't been seen in an NYC establishment. The backwoods of Pennsylvania have brought together old rummies, Sex in the City girls, soccer Moms, Frat kids, and one Goth chick. The ten competitive eaters seem to blend in well with the crowd. Deep Dish has a two beer syringe that causes him to go from sober to drooling drunk in fourteen minutes. The waitress is beset with more food orders than drink orders. Instead of side dishes, everyone simply says, "and another order of wings." I have three orders myself before switching to cheesesteaks. Yellowcake's cheesesteak arrives and when he turns to the bar for a drink, Steakbellie and Deep Dish eat the two halves to the nub and then return the scraps to the plate. Yellowcake turns back around with that, You guys look. This joke never gets old and repeats itself through two dozen cheesesteaks.

12:33 AM We head to Pumptown, the only strip club within miles. No one seems to know the origins of the dubious name. The peeler joint is inside an oversized construction trailer. Oddly enough, the DJ looks exactly like Notorious B.O.B, the chili spaghetti eating champ. When Notorious B.O.B arrives we try to get a photo of the two doppelgangers by the 1985 television set, but despite allowing smoking, full nudity, and couch dances, Pumptown's no photo policy is strictly enforced. I switch to High Life beer and enjoy a pole dance routine by a raven haired beauty that rivals anything I've watched at the Olympics. We applaud and the crowd showers her with crumpled up dollar bills as if she was a wastebasket. Respect and degradation go hand-and-hand at Pumptown.

2:33 AM We are at Rick The Managers house to pick-up his float. Like, the float in "Animal House" this one is constructed from car parts including a police light and siren. This one has a lot of glitter and a vague jailhouse theme. The temperature is dropping outside. I switch to warm coffee and espresso vodka. Everyone moves inside and congregates in two rooms. In the kitchen a giant tomato pie and a six foot sub is served. The food is gone in twenty minutes. In the living room, Rick puts on an independent movie that he and his wife, Sherri star in. Most people pass out on the carpet. Facedown and asleep, Deep Dish has a piece of tomato pie stuck to his cheek. I notice that the end credit crawl lists the pickle eating champ, Beautiful Brian Seiken, yet he did not appear in the movie. In my overfed drunken state, I decide to move outside and mediate on this inconsistency. The sky is dark. I close my eyes. Rick shakes me awake with my team t-shirt emblazed with the logo "Eat every meal like its your last." Apropos as, again, if no one dies, Wing Bowl is deemed a success.

3:33 AM We depart with the float trailer hitched to someones car. I have lost track of logistics at this point. Badlands has lost his jacket. I ride with Yellowcake and a plump wingette who is wearing five inch stilettos, fishnet stockings, and legwarmers and not much else. We head to downtown Philly.

4:33 AM We are walking in through the loading dock at the Wachovia Center. Its drafty and dark outside, but the vinyl maroon jackets of the many security guards gleam brightly in the fluorescent hallways of the giant sports stadium. The lighting really brings out the cellulite in a drunken teetering wingette, dressed in black booty shorts. She is part of Damaging Doug's group. I nod a greeting to Doug, who looks like a cross between Jabba the Hut and the Comic Book Guy on the Simpsons. He wears voluminous elastic pants. He and I usually have pleasant conversations regarding his competitive eating techniques, but Steakbellie moves me along as several security guards are scrutinizing the case of water in my hands. The case of 24 water plastic water bottles under shrink wrap contains no water at all. Instead, I have substituted the water with every varietal of clear alcohol except moonshine (which I couldn't find on short notice). On the bottom of each bottle is a sharpie pen code. V-pin for instance, stands for Pineapple Vodka. Although beer is sold at the concession stands at 6 am, backstage drinking is frowned upon and booze is always confiscated. However, like Kobayashi in The Usual Suspects, I am hiding in plain sight. The water bottles clear the security station.

Rick the Manager is a popular guy at this years Wing Bowl and we are slated to enter the arena second to last, just before defending champ Jonathan "Super" Squibb. Squibb is a mild-mannered accountant who as an unknown won last years contest with too many chicken wings to remember in the 32 minutes. His float is pretty lame, simply a bunch of rubber chickens with a boxing backdrop. One of Squibbs crew says "Super" is off, getting into the zone. His wingettes are ample bootied black girls and the Wachovia clean-up staff is snapping cellphone cam photos of their derrieres. Our spot is conveniently located next to a soda vending machine and the mens room. Without mixers for our 26 bottles of booze (I have two plastic bottles in my jacket pockets: Laphroig for Steakbellie and Absinthe for me. Everyone hits the vending machine. Notorious B.O.B sharpies his initials on the top of the collapsed backboard, hoping that the overhead cam at the next Sixers game will reveal his initials. Badlands is a loud drunk. Joey is a drooling drunk, but is showing off his two wing bowl rings from previous years. He couldn't find the third ring but the gaudy Super Bowl like rings are valued at $9000 each by the Wing Bowl jewelry sponsor. Joey wanders off wanting to speak to someone in charge. Jeff The Natural and I decide to take a quick lap of the backstage area.

5:33 - 6:33 AM Everywhere you look are bleary-eyed strippers, drunken fat guys assembling floats with power tools, and roving bands of entourage folks in costumes ranging from hillbilly gear to James Bond tuxes. Steakbellie sees his old wrestling team dressed as Jersey Shore characters with orange facepaint, fake plastic chests, and gelled hair. I see head wingette Katie Morgan heading to the locker rooms. I break my cardinal rule of only getting VHS tapes signed and I have her autograph my "Zach and Miri Make a Porno" DVD which I've brought in case I bump into the humorous cute porn star. Another porn star, Mary Carrey heads into the hallways. She is wearing what looks like a tightly wrapped beige carpet. I compliment her on her performance in "Pervert." She loved making the film. Joey Chestnut reappears and wants to know where to meet her later. The Gold Club she says. I ask her if she or Gary Coleman received more votes in the California Governor Election. She did. I have mixed feeling about this, but we all pose for a photo. I make it back to our station. Ricks wingettes have changed into their policewomen outfits. Nip slips abound. Someone in our group has an upside Eagles outfit on their legs. A fake head in a helmet hangs from the crotch. We help him put white sweatpants with eye holes cut out over his arms and head. He put cleats on his hands and runs around looking like a falling Eagles player. It all looks surreal and everyone cant stop laughing at the upside Eagle guy. I have been drinking cherry soda spiked with an entire plastic bottle of coconut rum. I feel pretty good.

Bill "El Wingador" Simmons approaches. The five time Wing Bowl champion has bleached blond hair and the body that looks like a truck. Since he was a South NJ truck company owner before becoming the most famous chicken wing eater in history it makes sense to me that he resembles the machines of his trade. He is an actual Transformer, changing from truck driver to wing champion, like a sauce-stained Optimus Prime. He and I chat about how much more fun it is to not have the pressure to eat. I ask him how his signature line of hot sauce is selling he gives me the thumbs up and I wish him and his family well. He encourages me to keep drinking.

7:33 AM Trying to get out float to the entrance, Badlands trips over a dividing two-by-four and the whole rig crashes into the wall. We charge ahead blindly despite our float coordinator, Gentleman Jerry trying to wrangle some sense of order. Yellowcake has a football, The Natural has the rubber 8 ft hands, and no one can find the upside down guy. Some skit is supposed to happen, but Joey wont go along. Joey had given his pass to someone else, gotten relegated to the stands behind the Plexiglas (Steakbellie got a great photo), banged on the glass with his Wing

Bowl rings until they let him backstage again, and then somehow either got tossed from the Wachovia Center or made it onstage and dropped an F bomb on the radio broadcast. He may have done both, but we can barely understand his yelling.

We are inside the Rick the Manager float and I can hear the 20,000 crowd yelling and whooping and throwing stuff. I've switched to apple rum at this point but my buzz is waning. I point out to everyone that once we ditch the float we will be in the center area for the duration of the contest. Deep Dish has to piss so I encourage him to urinate on the inside of the float or the Wachovia ground. When else does someone get a chance to tinkle with 20,000 people cheering their bladder? Nothing seems to go right during our entrance, but perhaps that is the point. The crowd is riled up, pressing against the Plexiglas, shouting profanity. The few women in the stands are encouraged to flash but the camera crews aren't allowed to show exposed breasts on the Jumbotron. A cat-and-mouse peek-a-boo begins between strippers on stage, and the crowd reacting to the Jumbotron. Fist fights break out at random sections of the stadium. Perhaps my buzz is not waning because everything is a blur. I'm in the pit and the contest starts. I try to focus on something, anything but I give up. I realize this is as close to the Apocalypse as one can get without actually experiencing the Apocalypse. At some point Snookie from Jersey Shore is introduced and gets on a mechanical bull in the pit. The boos shake the rafters, beers are thrown, the radio host announces that it was not the reaction he was expecting. It seems despite assembling a stadium of DNA impaired drunken dolts, he is surprised that the crowd has taste. The crowd wants Snookie dead or at least injured. As Snookie flips the crowd the bird, I wonder if the Plexiglas will hold. The crowd is pacified with Jumbotron images of past glory pukes (the Sloth puke from Wing Bowl 15 is shown nine times). No one follows the action on stage; Super Squibb simply decimates the competition. The crowd grows listless, but an occasional puker brings them back. Obi Wing, a mutton chopped Wing Bowl regular tries to bring the energy back by spitting up a handful of wing meat, stripping off his shirt and diving under the table. Rick the Manager appears in the pit and we decide to exit.

8:33 AM The bright morning sun feels good. I light a cigar and watch someones limo roll by. Obi Wing wanders by me, barefoot, shirtless and clutching a homemade light saber. Steakbellie appears with two trays of the leftover Wing Bowl wings. We open them up and steam erupts they are still warm. Granted they are the color of jaundice. The giant steaming trays each hold hundreds of wings. We hand one to B.O.B who has donned sunglasses and sits in the back of Rick the Managers car. B.O.B. says nothing but begins eating the wings and flinging the bones out the window. The rest of us attack the other tray like vultures. The wings taste like they were made from chicken that died instead of chicken killed for the purpose, but we don't slow until the tray is gone. The asphalt ground looks like a Santeria ritual has taken place. The radio hosts wander past our scene.

One of them asks me, Did Joey Chestnut really piss on the Wachovia floor? I say, Absolutely not. That was Deep Dish Bertoletti.

9:33 AM Club Risque. Wing Bowl is the largest strip club day in Philly. All the clubs open at 8 am for afterparties featuring, "Legs and Eggs" strippers and a free breakfast buffet. US Male and I wander past Rick the Managers parked car. B.O.B's tray of leftover wings is 1/8 full and sits on the sidewalk. We head into the club. It's four deep at the bar, there are two offering of scrambled eggs (one has flecks of something in it, perhaps vegetables), and it's really dark. No one can move anywhere, it's impossible to get a drink, and the only light provided via neon is headache inducing. It's like being trapped in psychedelic elevator. At least the bacon taste good. Nothing changes for three hours. When I exit the club, I am blinded by sunlight again. Seagulls have carried off the discarded chicken wings except for one pile of four or five wings that looks like dog shit.

12:33 PM Tony Lukes. We find ourselves needing another round of cheesesteaks.
I like a mushroom steak wit, provolone and hot peppers, but the hot peppers are overpowering my sandwich. Each is four or five inches long. I can't handle the hot. Badlands has passed out in the corner and looks like Buddha granted a Buddha with cheese whiz running down his shirt. I decide we need to head back to NYC. There is nothing more we can learn from Wing Bowl.

2:33 PM We Greyhound bus it back. I fall asleep standing in line. I wake up at Port Authority.

5:33 - 7:33 PM I walk to the Penthouse Executive Club and work for an hour. I walk down to Scores NY and learn that the Super Bowl party has been moved to Penthouse. I am ambivalent about it all because I have been to Wing Bowl and survived. I've reached my lifetime quota of Super Bowl tie-in strip club parties, even one that is required by my job.

8:33 - 10:33 PM Back Forty. I surprise my girlfriend by arriving back in NYC around twelve hours ahead of schedule. She expects me to be fall down drunk and covered in sauce, glitter, and grime. Partially true, but I am coherent enough to attend her birthday dinner thrown by her yoga friends. Her birthday is a week away, but the yoga studio she manages set-up a dinner party at a neighborhood trendy joint, Back Forty. It's the new kind of restaurant in Alphabet City with big windows and wooden tables, candles and expensive cocktails. Our group of ten is seated at a the prime table with a street view either because this is a group of all attractive yoga hardbodies or because one of the yogis has brought her 1 year old kid and the restaurant wants to keep a Gossip Girl setting in the rest of the place.

I start off with a rum and beer cocktail simply because rum had been so very good to me at 7 am this morning. I switch to stout beer with dinner and since Ive been on a 24 hour meat bender, I switch to steak tartare. My dietary habits have become primal and savage so I also order fried chicharron (pork skin) which arrives like Chinese shrimp chips, lightly fried with air pockets filled with flavorful grease. I have donuts for dessert, which though I prefer in the morning, seem to be the perfect cap to a day of gluttonous food, beverage, and inhalant choices. The yogis are hip chicks and though they don't finish their desserts (I do) they pop outside for a smoke. I split bourbon with my girlfriends friend, Joelle. We decide on Elijah Craig, as his name sounds religious, austere, and strong. The bourbon is at least two of the three and it warms us as we head into the airy night.

11:33 Lakeside Lounge. My girlfriends philosophy grad school friends are no where to be found. I take a pass on another drink, but the remaining ladies split a beer and we chat about dirty photos in the photo booth. The girls continue the party and head to the West Village. I head home and am prone moments after removing my contact lenses and socks. My pillow is a sniper and I feel nothing, not even my eyes closing.

Saturday, 10:33 AM

My girlfriend is from New Orleans so our coffee of choice is Nola's Community Coffee (packed with chicory). I have ordered a King Cake for her birthday, but the swanky restaurant wouldn't let us bring in the night before. King Cake is actually a perfect morning accompaniment as it resembles coffee cake swirled with cinnamon (sometimes filled with cheese or fruit). Instead of the coffee crumb top, three colored icing covered the wreath shaped cake purple, gold, and green its Mardi Gras made of sugar. The Nola King Cake tradition is that a plastic baby is placed in the cake and whoever gets the slice with the baby buys the following years cake. When I go to the cake on the counter I see a note from my roommate, Tim Eater X Janus. Janus is a sugar fiend, often rising in the middle of the night to quaff soda, snack on pixie sticks, and gobble gummi products. In his attempt to avoid the baby slice (he is also very frugal and King Cakes run about fifty bucks) he took the smallest piece possible to taste the cake. Amazingly, the plastic baby was curled into a tight fetal position in his sliver. I find the cake doughy and nice, but a little too sweet for eating a ton. The next contest on the Major League Eating circuit is King Cake at the Mardi Gras Casino in Atlantic City. Tim will be eating, but I will be out of town. Eater X and I are only allowed to discuss competitive eating in the kitchen as it annoys my girlfriend. Knowing the contest is ten minutes, non-dunking, Tim and I have a brief discussion of beverage accompaniment for his contest. Washing the King Cake down with a warmer substance will be key. I head back into the living room and my girlfriend and I Netflix Roku a couple Brazilian films, "Moro No Brazil" about the many blends of music, and "Bye Bye Brazil" an odd film about a traveling gypsy caravan.

2:33 PM The local Laundromat. A man who is the equivalent of a human troll doll stares at the change machine and screams, Ha Ha Ha you scumbag! He makes me realize why folks like having home washer and dryers great convenience and less wackos.

4:33 PM I have soup for lunch. Soup is the gateway food for me back towards healthier consumption. My girlfriend and I Roku "Manouche" which as best I can figure is the Brazilian "Dark Crystal." She presents me with an anti-Valentines day gift - an amazing homemade knit hat with a pointy top and a red star in the brown wool. It is a combination of a Russian Army hat (it even has Russian buttons on it) and the ones worn by the scary flying monkeys in the Wizard of Oz. I give her a Snuggie in return, thinking of her studying philosophy in our cold apartment. She is not pleased. Note to self: Nothing with an "As seen on TV!" sticker on the box is romantic.

7:33- 10:33 PM Our planned date night has a surprise that I don't reveal to my girlfriend. She doesn't enjoy subway travel and grills me on our destination on the D train ride. I have procured two tickets to the New York City ballet. Not even Vince Vaughns character in "The Break-Up" would go to the ballet to win back Jennifer Anistons' character. I figure I'll receive major boyfriend brownie points. I make two missteps. My girlfriend points out that one is suppose to dress up for the ballet. I told her to dress comfortably and she is in jeans and a sweater. I am wearing shorts, a Hogs and Heifers jacket, and my new evil monkey Russian hat I figured if I was the most underdressed person at Lincoln Center then standing next to me, her attire would look semi formal. It's the Thornton Melon school of thought: if one wants to look thinner, hang around fatter people. Also, our seats are so nosebleed that we might as well watch the ballet from the Barnes and Noble across the street. The ballet is Sleeping Beauty with a storyline that even a dolt like me can follow. My girlfriend is a ballerina turned modern dancer, so she gives me the background on Balanchine and the New York Ballet School versus A.B.T., I enjoy the first act. She feels their arabesques are too open. The costumes are lavish, the shoes are pointy, there are tons of little kids on stage isn't it past their bedtime? The second act drags for me although Little Red Riding Hood and a bunch of non Sleeping Beauty characters make appearances. Is it just for merchandising?

11:33 PM We head to a late dinner at Ramen Setagaya on 1st ave and 9th street. Since seeing "Tampopo" years ago, I have been a ramen addict. My girlfriend shares my passion, but she prefers the broth at Ippudo on 4th ave. She is right of course, but Setagaya has a salted egg appetizer that makes me want to go "Cool Hand Luke" on the place. The warm bowls of noodle soup fog the cold front window. We slurp happily.

Sunday, 8:33 AM
Its bitterly cold, but I brave the elements both to walk my girlfriend to the subway for her yoga managing shift and then to jog. The wind upshorts me and even blows through my running shoes. I take it as a challenge as I lumber across the Williamsburg Bridge. It's slow going and my mind wanders to breakfast. I finish the jog on Houston street and head to Whole Foods where I buy granola and Greek

yogurt. Also, enough sundries to make a massive amount of guacamole for later in the day.

10:33 AM I have returned to my normal non-Wing Bowl diet for breakfast. I do yogurt, flaxseed, and grape nuts or granola. I read The Post.

11:33 AM - 12:33 PM I decide that the Brazilian film I most need to watch is the 1984's "Blame it on Rio" with a pre-boob job Demi Moore. I own it on VHS but due to hooking up the Roku I am a couple cables short of getting modern technology to accommodate my favorite movie format. Today is a day of action so I consult manuals, diagram the connections, and head to Best Buy. I end up at Radio Shack, but I have everything I need to get the VHS back to its fuzzy picture finest.

1:33 PM - 2:33 PM I now have a toggle box that switches me from the DVD player (I use Judd Apatow's "Funny People" as the test DVD) to Michael Caines booming voice in "Blame it on Rio." I make guacamole while enjoying the film. I find that the secret to good guac is a Serrano pepper, a mango, and Cajun seasoning. I store the guac with pits in it (to avoid browning) for later consumption. My girlfriend returns from yoga teaching and I have quinoa cakes and hummus waiting.

2:33 PM - 4:33 PM Celtics vs. Orlando on TV. I bleed Celtics green. Sadly, my blood and yelling encouragement are not enough to help the Celtics hold onto a first half lead, rebound from a third quarter deficit, or win the game in the close 4th quarter finish. I remove my green headband, take off my Dennis Johnson jersey and I put my Kevin Garnett sneakers back in the closet.

5:33 PM "Pull My Daisy" at the film anthology archives. Despite the biggest jock day in sports, I decide to appeal to my arty side. I have been waiting years to see this film, a 29 minute black-and-white 1959 film. Instead of writing an original screenplay Jack Kerouac submitted an unstaged play and then narrated the filmed result. When people ask why I became I competitive eater, the true answer is that I consider myself honoring the long tradition of Jack Kerouac and The Beats and Ken Kesey and the Merry Pranksters This is my chance to see the country, one bite at a time. Chris Kenneally, co-director of "Crazy Legs Conti: Zen and the Art of Competitive Eating" has called me an Eatnik instead of being On the Road, I'm on the plate. The Film Anthology shows films most people have never heard of and many people have no interest in, but for some, like myself the place is a cinematic preserve of oddities and treasures. I usually sit in the back row of the small theater where there is a giant wooden bench. You can usually lie down and watch the film (or video) and it seems like one has a really big living room. "Pull my Daisy" doesn't disappoint and I am enthused as I walk out of the theater. I am struck by Kerouac's line, "Some of them are doing something and some of them are saying goodbye." I don't know why

7:33 - 10:33 PM Superbowl and a trough of guacamole. Who dat won? Nola did with guac leftovers. My girlfriend is texting her New Orleans friends and family. New Orleans is a city close to my heart and stomach my adopted hometown. I am filled with joy and way too much guacamole.

It was a stellar Super Bowl weekend, the way life is suppose to be.

I HAVE ACHIEVED HOT DOG ENLIGHTENMENT, TIME TRAVEL, AND AM ONE WITH EVERYTHING (HOLD THE MUSTARD)
(July 4th, 2016)

On July 4th, 2016 on stage at the Nathan's Famous International Hot Dog Eating Contest's 100th anniversary, I achieved enlightenment by eating the singular perfect garlicky natural-casing wiener nestled in a spongy bun. This Holy Grail of hot dogs was a century in the making and the totem that tore a rip in the time/space continuum and opened my gateway to Nirvana. Around me my fellow Major League Eaters ate astronomical amounts of HDBs (hot dogs and buns) in ten minutes, pushing the physiological limits of human consumption while I ate but one. That one, however, turned my stomach into a flux capacitor and allowed my enteric brain (neurons that governs the function of the gastrointestinal system - the cerebral gut) to journey to a mystical destination: Nirvana. I am one with everything and used no condiments. On the back of each eaters' jersey is their personal best in HDBs but my jersey's number reformed into the infinity symbol. As an added bonus to achieving enlightenment, unlike previous July 4th contests, I still have room for apple pie. I've been a Major League Eater for fifteen years and unbeknownst to the ranked eat-letes and voracious fans of the pro-eating circuit, I have been preparing for this journey throughout my speed-eating career.

In secret, I have spent time in each city that I travel to for consumption contests studying with shamans, spiritual guides, Zen masters, Butoh instructors, yogis, and once at a Hooters Chicken Wing Eating contest I had an ill-advised meeting with a Santeria consultant (we had differing opinions on what to do with poultry.) A brief history of my stomach can be gleaned through the hundreds of MLE contests I have participated in - I've competitively eaten from A (Asparagus - 4 pounds in ten minutes) to W (Watermelon 3 whole, six minutes). Sadly Xiaolongbao, Yogurt and Zucchini have yet to be sanctioned.

A brief history of humans' attempts to either time travel or achieve enlightenment is still too long for this writing, but let me mention a few highlights:

In Christianity, many believe "Revelation" is an allegory of the spiritual path and the ongoing struggle between good and evil. Today MLE's George Shea, signature hawker boater hat upon head preached 20 feet in the air on a riser above 35,000 fans at Stillwell and Surf Avenue at Coney Island and screamed, "They say that competitive eating is the battleground upon which God and Lucifer wage war for men's souls and they are right."

In mysticism, eschatology refers metaphorically to the end of ordinary reality and reunion with the Divine. Again, I quote George Shea introducing me:

"He was first seen standing at edge the shore between the ancient marks of the high and low tide, a place that is neither land nor sea. And as the blue light of morning filtered through the blackness it revealed a man who hails from the far corners of the globe where the dark arts are still practiced. This is a man who has been to the beyond, he was buried alive under 60 cubic feet of popcorn he fought his way out for survival, he is known as David Blaine of the Bowel, The Evil Knievel of the Alimentary Canal, the Houdini of Cusini...Crazy Legs Conti"

Last week, my food stuntman abilities were tested as I climbed atop a Wonder Wheel car and ate 12 Nathan's HDBs while it revolved. I cheated death by not falling and also avoided getting squashed or knocked off by the swinging cars. I survived the stunt and gained a new respect for Coney Island and the thrills it gives and provides. Unlike Icarus on wax wings, my SkySuit got me to terra firma with only some hot dog detritus and Tang stains (Tang was good enough for space so it's good enough for bun-dunking in the clouds.) The view was incredible, the ride exhilarating and life-affirming, and the 13th dog eaten safety on the ground and a few beers at Ruby's on the Boardwalk delicious. However, I knew I had one shot at elusive enlightenment and it would involve a "Altered States" meets "Back to the Future" effort -

Step 1. locate the perfect hot dog in 2016, on stage at July 4th while celebrating the birthright of America through competitive eating.

Step 2. Morph into that hot dog and travel back via the cerebrum of the gut, my enteric brain to 1916 when Ida and Nathan Handwerker created the first Nathan's (not yet famous) hot dog that lead to the juggernaut that is the Major League Eating hot dog contest. Sort of Kafka's "Metamorphosis" but with less buzzing around and more sizzling and grease.

Step 3. Quickly ingest the perfect dog at the buzzer of the contest, in essence, eating myself from the past and achieving in the present, in the words of philosopher Karl Spackler, "total consciousness. Which is nice."

Some of my preliminary research lead me to Albert Einstein, who perhaps after a large lunch, posited that if space-time is sufficiently twisted, a time traveler can, while traveling toward the future all the time, circle back and visit an event in his own past. I wasn't around 100 years ago so I had to abandon Einstein. Theoretical physicists Kip Thorne and Sung-Won Kim identified a universal physical mechanism (the explosive growth of vacuum polarization of quantum fields), that may always prevent spacetime from developing closed time-like curves. I understand about .33% of what they discovered but thought I had found the answer by cribbing their studies of the existence of "wormholes" and could synchronize the consumption of myself (transformed into a once-in-a-century HDB) that would rip open "the wiener hole" in the space/time continuum. I worried that the scientific community might not take my ripped wiener hole theory seriously so I had to look much further back in history to Aristotle, who wrote: "What is eternal is circular and what is circular is eternal." I used this as my mantra and my guide. Granted a hot dog is more of an oblong, but I believe the concept holds.

As it happened at the buzzer of this years' contest, my journey was two-fold (similar to the pro-eating technique separating the dog from the bun manually while orally reuniting them in the mouth for their journey to the stomach) - I travelled backward and forward in time the same moment, I closed my eyes and transformed as the last century of frankfurter chomping ended and the next began. It was glorious; almost indescribable but I will try to give you a view into the beyond. My stomach expanded as if all the Macy's July 4th Fireworks went off all at once while Katy Perry (also in my stomach) sang, "Firework." My enteric brain became a Möbius strip assembly line of hot dogs. I entered an M. C. Escher drawing and left though an Alejandro Jodorowsky film. Every meal I ever ate flashed on the inside of my closed eyelids and then I felt a warmth, like a hug from humanity, and I opened my eyes to the new world before me.

The Bunette behind me quizzically turned her flip card to "1." On my left a Nathan's rep, holding four plates, looked dejectedly at the 20 uneaten HDBs. On my right, in the maelstrom of meat, the bejeweled yellow mustard belt held aloft, dazzled in the sun. The American flag was shoulder-wrapped around the victor; The confetti guns fired. The confetti filled the air.

Some will question my dedication to competitive eating - - if I've tanked my Major League Eating ranking by consuming just one hot dog and bun while the elite eaters around me consumed record number HDBs at the 100th running of the dogs. Naysayers and internet haters may doubt if I truly went to the beyond and back. Religious scholars, luminous academics, hard-wired scientists may doubt my arrival at Nirvana coupled with time travel achieved by eating a hot dog, but I feel beatific - It's July 4th and I've just eaten the American Dream. My stomach may be untraditionally unfilled but my mind is satiated and most importantly, my soul, like a belch, emanates from deep within and dissipates in the Coney Island air, heading upwards to the ether and back to the beyond.

Crazy Legs Conti was born in Boston, played high school basketball for Belmont High School, and then sat the bench for three sports at Johns Hopkins University (He excelled at the pre-game meals.) He also majored in Writing Seminars and minored in Film Studies. He moved to New York City and worked in the independent film industry for The Shooting Gallery, working with directors like Billy Bob Thornton, Al Pacino, and Morgan Spurlock. He left film producing to focus on his creative endeavors in writing, TV, and film. He has written numerous screenplays, TV scripts, and blogged for The Huffington Post.

In addition to writing, Crazy Legs is a top-ranked eater with Major League Eating. He holds world records in buffet food, French cut string beans, and Lumber Jack Breakfast (pancakes and bacon.) He has eaten his way out of an eight-foot box of popcorn, The Popcorn Sarcophagus, earning him the moniker the Houdini of Cuisini. He rode on top of a Wonder Wheel car, while wearing a Sky Suit, and ate Nathan's hot dogs and avoided death. He has eaten 459 oysters on David Letterman (Letterman ate three), quaffed hot sauce on Emeril, and consumed cannoli on "The Sopranos." He is the subject of the popular documentary, "Crazy Legs Conti: Zen and the Art of Competitive Eating," (co-directed by Chris Kenneally and Danielle Franco).
He has been to Guantanamo Bay to eat hot dogs with the sailor-soldiers and Alaska to conquer fifty pound cabbages and reindeer sausage.

Much of this writing appeared on The Huffington Post or www.crazylegsconti.com. Crazy Legs is grateful that you've taken the time to digest it. He currently lives in New York City but eats everywhere.

Cover Photo by Brenda "B-Money" Backus

Crazy Legs Conti © 2019
Revised with slightly less typos 2020

Made in United States
North Haven, CT
12 June 2024

53542310R00189